SAFE
STRATEGIES
for
FINANCIAL
FREEDOM

VAN K. THARP, D. R. BARTON, Jr.,
AND STEVE SJUGGERUD

McGraw·Hill

New York Chicago San Francisco Lisbon London Madrid Mexico City
Milan New Delhi San Juan Seoul Singapore Sydney Toronto

The *McGraw·Hill* Companies

Library of Congress Cataloging-in-Publication Data

Tharp, Van K.
  Safe strategies for financial freedom / by Van K. Tharp, D. R. Barton, Jr., and Steve
  Sjuggerud.
      p.   cm.
  Includes index.
  ISBN 0-07-142147-5 (cloth : alk. paper)
    1. Finance, Personal.   2. Stocks.   3. Saving and investment.   I. Barton, D. R.
  (Doyle Rayburn), 1960–   .   II. Sjuggerud, Steve.   III. Title.

  HG179.T4518   2004
  332.024—dc22   2003024384

2 3 4 5 6 7 8 9 0   AGM/AGM   3 2 1 0 9 8 7 6 5 4

ISBN 0-07-142147-5

McGraw-Hill books are available at special quantity discounts to use as premiums and sales
promotions, or for use in corporate training programs. For more information, please write to
the Director of Special Sales, Professional Publishing, McGraw-Hill, Two Penn Plaza, New York,
NY 10121-2298. Or contact your local bookstore.

This book is printed on acid-free paper.

CONTENTS

ACKNOWLEDGMENTS

When I wrote my first two books with *financial freedom* in the title, the question always came up of how exactly does someone achieve financial freedom through trading? What is financial freedom and how many people achieve it? When financial freedom is defined by some really large amount of money, like a billion dollars, it becomes a rarity, but when it is defined as never having to work again, it's possible for almost anyone. Thus, I'd like to dedicate this book to the many people who have inspired me by quitting their jobs and attaining financial freedom through investing and doing what they love.

When I talked to McGraw-Hill about writing this book, I wasn't very excited about it. It was envisioned as a simplified version of my earlier book, *Trade Your Way to Financial Freedom*. However, my good friend D. R. Barton, Jr., agreed to write some of the sections. Without his inspiration, this book wouldn't have been possible.

Later, we needed some models to help people decide when to use what strategy and under what circumstances. Steve Sjuggerud has always been great with those sorts of models, so I invited him to join us and his contributions have been terrific.

One of the real geniuses of real estate is John Burley. John and I have attended each others workshops and we are co-presenters of the audiotape program *Infinite Wealth*. I love his concepts, and John is someone who walks his talk. Most people believe that high rates of returns are impossible, but John never does a deal unless his return is at least 40%

cash on cash, and he has done over 1,000 such deals. Thus, I was thrilled when he agreed to write a chapter for this book.

I met Justin Ford through my good friend Bob Meier. I was very excited to learn that Justin was teaching parents how to make their children financially free shortly after they finish college. His chapter can make a significant difference in how our children think about money. Thank you, Justin, and I hope all the children of the world learn to become financially free as a result of what you are doing.

Kathleen Peddicord contributed the international real estate portion of this book and, she offers some excellent opportunities for people to think outside of the box. We are very grateful for her contribution.

Bruce Du Ve, Ken Long, and John Mauldin wrote full-length chapters to this book that could not be included because of size limitations. We are very grateful for the contributions you made and are offering your material as free supplements to this book. All three are great friends, and I appreciate everything you did for the book as well as your friendship.

I'd especially like to acknowledge the many people who read the first edition of this book, which was full of typos and other mistakes. John Martin read one of the very first editions. As a result of his comments much of that original material was scrapped and a new book took shape. Ron Ishibashi and Sara Rich did an amazing job going over the first draft of the final version of this book. I'd also like to thank Balraj and Meena Aggarwal for their comments on the manuscript and their help in making it more readable.

Mike Palmer made particularly significant contributions to this manuscript. Mike is a professional writer who excels at writing exciting copy that everyone wants to read. He did an amazing job of going over the initial manuscript, pointing out what was confusing and giving suggestions for making it easier to read. Your help was really terrific. Thank you, Mike.

I would like to thank the staff at IITM. Without you it would have been impossible to write this. You do a great job of giving me the time to do what I do best and love to do—write. Melita Hunt and Ana Walle have both been a great inspiration for what could be accomplished, and they pushed hard. Melita is a great writer and had some excellent suggestions for the book. Cathy Hasty, Tamika Williams, Doreen De'Block, and Kristy Barbour all looked at the manuscript and made useful suggestions.

Greg Godek helped develop a plan for this book so that you'd be excited about reading it. We're very greatful to Greg for his assistance and to everyone who contributed to the successful sales of this book.

I'd also like to thank our editors at McGraw-Hill for their wonderful help. These include Steven Isaacs for getting the book going and Julia Anderson Bauer for her helpful suggestions and contributions in editing the final manuscript.

Finally, I'd like to thank the people whose stories are contained in the book. We have changed your names to protect your privacy, but you know who you are, and I hope your stories inspire many people to reach similar successes.

My deepest thanks go to all of you and to the many people who also contributed but were too numerous to mention.

—Van K. Tharp

Over the years that I have known Van Tharp, I have enjoyed growing our relationship from client to acquaintances to good friends. Without Van's vision, this book would be a shadow of what it has grown to be.

Brian Arundel gave selflessly of his time and talents to provide us some truly appreciated editorial input. Brian is a true professional who helped us with form and function as well as helping to solidify the message of the book. Thanks for your timely help, Brian.

I, too, would like to thank John Martin for the time and energy he expended in helping me out of a writing rut. A top-level thinker and a caring friend, John has earned my deep respect. It's an honor to call him a friend.

John Riddle has helped me understand the publishing world and has given me the benefit of his skills and experience. I really enjoy working with a good friend whose uses his gifts so well.

—D. R. Barton, Jr.

All of the authors would like to thank Antoinette and Jared Kuritz and Veronica Burnside for their help in promoting the book.

PREFACE
HOW YOU CAN QUIT
WORKING—FOREVER!

"Enough is never enough!"

—FERENGI RULE OF ACQUISITION #97

Financial freedom is possible. And when you achieve it, a world of possibilities opens up for you. You can quit working. You won't be dependent on a job for income. You won't have to take orders from a boss you might dislike. You'll be free from those long commutes to and from work. Most important, you can start doing whatever you like. There will be more time to be with your family and friends. Hopefully you'll use some of your newfound time to help others and give of yourself. Perhaps this book will inspire you to spend some of your free time looking for interesting investment opportunities.

Financial freedom is within your grasp if you are reading this book. It doesn't matter whether you are a minimum wage worker who is struggling to make ends meet or someone who is earning a great salary and enjoys working. Either way, you'll learn how to attain financial freedom within a few years. In fact, financial freedom is often easier to attain for those who have learned to maintain their lifestyle on less money. This book will show you exactly how to do it without clipping coupons or pinching pennies. Financial freedom means that you can maintain your current lifestyle—perhaps even have a better one—and not have to work. If you want to keep working, you can use the extra money to raise your standard of living even higher or to help others. It's your choice.

In this book, you will learn a simple strategy that will free you forever. You can live wherever you please and do whatever you want. All you have to do is complete a few simple exercises in Part I of this book; adopt some of the strategies in Parts II and III; and practice the risk control methods given in Part IV. Once you start, you'll see yourself moving closer and closer to financial freedom every month. We'll even show you how to monitor your progress.

When I first learned these concepts, it took me six months to put them into practice and become financially free. I then taught these principles in a seminar we called the Infinite Wealth workshop. There were 30 people in that workshop, and by the time it concluded, 5 of them discovered that they were already financially free. They had been struggling with money or they wouldn't have come to the workshop. Yet all they had to do was change their thinking and do a few simple things to become financially free. The other 25 people in the class estimated that it would take them anywhere from six months to five years to attain their financial freedom. And I'm now hearing success stories all the time from people I've introduced to this idea. You'll hear from a few of them later in this book.

Financial freedom is a realistic objective for you if you are reading this book. Financial freedom doesn't mean that you have all the money in the world. It doesn't mean that you are so fabulously wealthy that, no matter how foolish you are with money, you still would never have to work again. Financial freedom simply requires that you change your thinking and have money work for you instead of you working for money. And you can achieve it quickly—within six months to seven years depending on your current financial status and your personal psychology. You do it by having passive income, income that comes in whether you work or not. When your passive income is greater than your expenses, you no longer have to work.

Financial freedom is not about how much money you have or how many toys you have. Instead, it comes from a concept developed by R. Buckminster Fuller, one of the real creative geniuses of the twentieth century. Bucky, as he was called, said, "If you stopped working today and continued to live at your current standard of living, how long would you last? If you could last a month, then you are one month wealthy. If you could last five years, then you are five years wealthy. And if you could last forever, then you are infinitely wealthy." Many people interpret this to mean, "If I need $4,000 per month to live on and I have $400,000 saved up, then I am 100 months wealthy."

However, there is a much better way to look at this concept. What if your $400,000 produced passive income, income you received without having to work? For example, what if you made 12% in passive income from investing in certain stocks with your $400,000? Twelve percent of $400,000 is $48,000, so your $400,000 could give you $48,000 in income. When you divide that yearly income by 12 months, it amounts to $4,000 per month. You could live off that income indefinitely and be financially free. You would never have to work again.

Of course, there are a number of issues with this idea. You might think that stocks paying dividends of 12% or giving those rates of capital appreciation are unrealistic. Not true! You simply have to know where to look. There are stocks that give returns of 15% or more in today's market. For example, Steve Sjuggerud (whom you'll hear from later) recently found several stocks that he called "virtual banks." One stock, Anworth, had a dividend payout amounting to 43% interest over two years when he first recommended it in August of 2002. Another virtual bank, Annaly Mortgage, which Steve recommended in March of 2002 paid similar dividends. Both still pay good returns as of this writing, and both have appreciated considerably since Steve recommended them. There are always opportunities like this available to you. But this isn't a book about which stocks to buy. Instead, my goal is to show you how to find such opportunities. In fact, I'll do even better than that! I'll show you strategies in many different investment arenas that pay even higher rates of return.

You might wonder if the $4,000 per month that person needed for financial freedom included taxes. It should, but if you meant $4,000 per month after taxes, then you either have to minimize your taxes or include them in your monthly number. The good news is that you'll pay much less in taxes on passive income than you will on earned income. When your money works for you, the returns don't get taxed by nearly the amount that your income gets taxed when you work for money.

What if the price of a stock goes down? What if it starts to pay less in dividends? These are valid concerns about risk control, a topic that is covered in Part IV of this book. Consider generating diverse streams of passive income so that if one area is weak at any given time you have others to support you. When your passive income is greater than your expenses, you don't have to work. You are infinitely wealthy and have attained financial freedom.

The other part of the financial freedom equation is your expenses. I went through an acquisition period in my life that lasted over two years. I acquired every toy I could possibly want as soon as it attracted my attention. For me, the joy of getting each toy was the most fun. Once I obtained them, however, those same toys tended to own me. I had to maintain them. I had to clean them. I had to keep track of them. And, often, I could not sell them for nearly the price at which I had bought them. Those items all owned me.

We live in a consumer society. We are told that if we want to feel good about ourselves, we need this or that luxury—a bigger house, a better car, more toys. "He who has the most toys wins" seems to be a rule that many people live by. This mind-set demands instant gratification, and that often requires spending more than we have, which leads to borrowing money. And to help us along, as soon as we get into college, we are given the opportunity to get credit cards. (My niece, a Malaysian citizen in her third year of college in the United States, has never worked in this country but gets two to three credit card applications each week.) People run up huge debts and pay 18% to 21% interest per year on them. And even though interest rates have been going down, most credit card interest rates don't go down at all.

Most people enter the job market with a load of credit card debt. If they do manage to save enough for a down payment on a home, they quickly take out a home equity loan to consolidate their debts. That encourages them to run up more credit card debt, which could cause them to lose their house. The average American family has more than $7,000 in credit card debt, which means that they are paying about $100 each month just to service that debt. That $100 in debt payment is probably a lot more than they are saving, and this situation keeps most people a long way from being financially free.

USA Today (August 12, 2003) reported that the average college senior has more than $3,000 in credit card debt and that 28% of college seniors have more than $7,000 in credit card debt. This is on top of their college loans. Debt has become a chronic problem. We'll help you deal with it in Chapter 3.

Most people get their financial education through friends and family. The most common advice in these ad hoc schools of life is, "Get a good education so you can get a good job. When you've done that, you can buy a nice home, a new car, and a big-screen television. After all, the house is only $1,200 per month, the car is only $400 per month, and the television is only $120 per month. You can afford it." Unfortunately, this philosophy doesn't prepare anyone to be financially free. Instead, it conditions people to work at a job to pay for items that continue to cost money—sometimes for as long as they own them. Your banker may even allow you to list some of these items as assets if you approach him for a loan.

I want to offer you a better definition of *assets*. Assets produce positive cash flow that comes to you on a regular basis. So anything in your life that pays you because you own it is an asset. Anything you pay to own, on the other hand, is a liability.

Under this definition, the home you live in is probably a liability, even if the mortgage is paid off, because you still have to pay insurance, taxes, and repairs to live in it. And chances are your home doesn't produce one penny of cash flow for you each month. (Some might argue that if your home goes up in value it is an income-producing asset, but you don't receive that income until you sell it.) Even though you would have to pay money to live somewhere else and you are not spending money on housing, that simply means your home is a lesser liability, but it's not an asset under this definition. In order for something to qualify as a real asset, it must be producing a positive cash flow—money coming in to you on a scheduled basis.

As I began to discover how much my possessions were starting to own me, Bucky Fuller's concept of infinite wealth reshaped my thinking. And once I began thinking in terms of passive income and infinite wealth, I started to actively reduce my financial freedom number. As a result, I became financially free within six months. It doesn't take super intelligence to do it. It just requires some simple changes in your thinking and some action. Anyone can do it.

My goal in writing this book is to help you reshape your thinking in the same way and take some simple steps. The key to financial freedom is to know your financial freedom number so well that if anyone were to ask you, you could immediately say something like, "I'm $2,400 per month away from financial freedom." Financial freedom is about reducing that number, and this book is designed to teach you how.

Safe Strategies for Financial Freedom has five parts. Part I describes the steps needed to attain financial freedom. It includes four chapters that form the basis for developing a personal plan to achieve financial freedom. When you finish, you'll understand that financial freedom is easily within your reach.

Part II is about the stock market. We'll show you stock market strategies that will help you achieve returns of 20% per year or better. Chapter 5 assesses the long-term condition of the stock market and includes a simple 1-2-3 model so that you can continually update yourself on the market conditions. There is a possibility that stock prices could go down or stay flat, so most people will lose money in the market over the next 10 years. But if you follow the sound investing principles we've outlined and use the model to determine what the market is doing, you can make returns of 20% or more—often much more.

In Chapter 6 we show you the danger of simply buying stocks and then holding them. Ken Long, however, has developed a strategy that allows you to switch between mutual funds so that you can outperform the market. We'll tell you how to get the latest version of Ken's strategy, and we'll show those who qualify how to get information about hedge funds, which are designed to give you absolute returns.

In Chapter 7 you'll learn some strategies that perform well when the market is going down. One bear market mutual fund strategy, had you employed it in 2001 and 2002, would have returned you 25% or more both years. In Chapter 8, you'll learn some stock market strategies that work particularly well in today's market. All you need to do is select what is right for you.

Part III describes other kinds of investment strategies. You'll learn how to monitor inflation and deflation. If inflation comes roaring back, you'll be able to make huge returns by investing in the types of assets described in Chapter 9. You will learn what kinds of assets work best in various economic climates. Chapter 10 describes the potential for a major fall in the U.S. dollar and presents interest rate strategies you can profit from. One such strategy can keep you safe from fluctuations in the dollar and requires only one decision each year. Had you employed that strategy, which works best when the dollar goes down in value, an investment of $10,000 in 1970 would have grown to $323,000 today.

You'll get an introduction to the factors that influence the real estate market in Chapter 11 and then learn some top-notch real estate strategies in Chapter 12. John Burley, who wrote Chapter 12, won't touch a real estate deal unless he can make at least a 40% annual return from it. John has done over 1,000 such deals in the last 10 years and every one of them pays him a monthly income. And what John does, you can do as well.

Part IV is about risk control This is the most complex part of the book, but also one of the most important. The techniques given in Part IV will help you turn the great strategies that we present in Parts II and III into safe strategies. What good does it do to make 25% or 50% on your money if you have the potential to lose it all? Part IV gives you information to keep that from happening.

Chapter 13 presents six fundamental concepts to keep your strategies safe. One such concept is knowing how and when to get out of a strategy. Chapter 14 covers position sizing. This is the most critical concept in this book. No strategy is safe without proper position sizing, yet many professional money managers have never heard of it. And once you understand position sizing, you'll have a huge advantage over those professionals in meeting your objectives. Be sure that you thoroughly understand the material in this chapter.

Chapter 15 explains how to know your strategy inside out. It shows you how to keep up with macroeconomic conditions affecting the market and how to plug the risk-reward distributions you expect from your strategy into a simulator so that you can understand what to expect in the future.

Part V of this book is about the future. In Chapter 16 you'll learn how to fix mistakes. You'll discover that the most important quality you can have as an investor is personal responsibility. If you have this trait, you can shape your own destiny by correcting your mistakes. If you don't have it, you'll simply repeat your mistakes over and over again.

Chapter 17 shows you how to protect your future by educating your kids. Justin Ford presents a simple strategy that your children (and grandchildren) will love. You can get them started, and by the time they graduate from college they could easily be financially free. Don't miss this great chapter.

Finally, Chapter 18 presents a four-step plan to make sure you get started now. Those steps include assessing the economy so that you know what strategies will work; selecting strategies that are right for you and for current economic conditions; applying risk control techniques to make sure your strategies are safe; and, probably the most important step, continually working on yourself. You are the most important factor in your financial freedom.

Safe Strategies for Financial Freedom may well be the most important book you'll ever read. So let's get started now.

PART I

DEVELOPING YOUR PLAN TO QUIT WORK NOW

Financial freedom is the ability to quit your job so that you never have to work again. It's saying good-bye to your boss, to working overtime on something you don't want to do, and to those long, crowded commutes on the freeway. It's also saying hello to doing whatever you want, living wherever you want, helping whomever you want, and eliminating most of the restrictions on your life. Does that sound appealing? You don't have to give up anything to do so except the way you think about money.

If you are tired of work, or even if you like working and want more of a choice, then this book is for you. You'll learn a simple formula for changing your thinking that most people can use to become financially free within five years. When we teach these concepts to people, most of them estimate that they can be financially free within three months to two years. And they come back to tell us their success stories.

Take the case of Fred, who first attended one of our Peak Performance courses about four years ago. He didn't have a lot of money. In fact, he was considering taking a huge step that could eat away most of his financial resources—going back to school. Despite going back to school as a full-time student, Fred also started on a journey to become financially free. He and his wife applied the Peak Performance concepts together after the seminar. Once they recognized what each of them valued independently, they jointly determined the direction they wanted to go. This direction was not just financial but incorporated other values as well.

They then developed a multitier financial freedom strategy that hinged on investing in low-risk yet high-yield opportunities in the stock market and real estate and on the acceleration of their home mortgage. He found a Dow dividend yield strategy that was right for him and adapted it to his personality. He then began trading the strategy tax free through Roth individual retirement accounts he and his wife opened.

The real estate strategy involves getting strong cash flow by purchasing residential properties and then leasing them out with an option to buy or with owner financing to achieve tax-free profits. He estimated that he needed only five really good properties in terms of cash flow and solid equity to achieve financial freedom once he and his wife were debt free. Within two years, he had 40 properties, all generating positive cash flow with a partner who managed the business while he focused on the demands of the degree. At that point, his professors insisted that he drop his real estate projects to finish his degree, so he and his business partner split up.

Fred still has five properties. He and his wife have paid off their automobiles, and they have enough money in the stock market to pay off their home if they want to (they do not need to do so because the accelerated payments will retire the mortgage in a few more years). Thus, in four years they have become debt free just from their stock holdings and the acceleration of the mortgage on their home. His wife has completed the real estate broker course and looks forward to working with Fred. He should have his degree by the time you read this, and he'll probably obtain his financial freedom within three to six months of his graduation. He confided that the unification of intent he and his wife developed from the Peak Performance course is the driving force behind their investment strategies.

Fred now knows that financial freedom can be manifested by knowing yourself, identifying low-risk yet high-yield strategies that are right for your personality, tailoring a plan accordingly, and then fulfilling the plan with a laser focus. Most important, he has achieved balance in his life by focusing on all of his top values, not just on money. He now focuses on enjoying each day instead of satisfying his ego by grasping with a constant unsatisfied craving for more money. He says he has found many other unexpected riches on the peak performance path to financial freedom, including a stronger marriage, less dependency on the approval of others, a balanced diet that moderates alcohol consumption and promotes physical fitness, and the development of healthier relationships with individuals who engender the personal traits he wants more of in his life.

If Fred can do it, so can you. Here's our promise: Do the exercises in the first part of this book and you'll learn how to achieve financial freedom in one to seven years, depending upon your situation. These exercises will help you develop a plan for financial freedom. Once you have that plan, you'll be well on your way.

Later in the book you'll learn strategies to obtain rates of return that most people only dream about. You'll learn how to read market conditions so you'll know what works in the current economy—whatever it might be—and how to select strategies that are right for you. Above all, you'll learn how to turn profitable strategies into safe strategies. None of these steps is difficult. You just have to do each one. That's all there is to it.

Part I of this book will help you develop a specific and thorough plan for developing financial freedom. Chapter 1 gives you step-by-step techniques for determining your financial freedom number. Then you can transform your future by concentrating on reducing that number to zero or better. But you must take action.

Chapter 2 deals with a fundamental concept in financial freedom— paying yourself first. If you don't pay yourself first, no one else will, so you need to start immediately. We will give you some techniques to get started.

Chapter 3 presents some immediate actions you can take to reduce your financial freedom number. We are not talking about altering your lifestyle here, just taking some simple steps to reduce your expenses.

Chapter 4 focuses on the other side of the financial freedom number—your assets. In this chapter you'll list all your assets and determine how much passive income they bring in. With this information, you'll be able to determine if you can safely redeploy those assets to earn higher rates of return. We will show you how to safely get higher rates of return in today's market later in the book. Your first step is to appraise your current situation realistically.

We'll also introduce you to the concept of a paradigm shift—a change in your thinking. You may only need to make a simple paradigm shift and take one or two action steps to become financially free immediately. When that happens, you can quit working forever.

CHAPTER 1

WHAT IT TAKES FOR YOU TO NEVER HAVE TO WORK AGAIN!

"There is a strong correlation between investment planning and wealth accumulation."

— Thomas Stanley and William Danko

Imagine that you never have to work again in your life. If you do choose to work, all the extra money that comes in is used to improve your lifestyle and help those you care about. You take two month-long vacations each year. You even have a list of places you want to visit — exotic places around the world that most people will never get to see.

You are now free to spend most of your time doing the things you love to do. You spend at least 30 hours per week on your hobbies. In fact, you have a new interest—finding deals and investigating investment opportunities. The amazing part is that your new hobby will bring you much more money than you ever made while you were working 50 hours per week at a job.

You also have plenty of time to exercise, to eat right, and to be happy. Now that you are financially free, that's just what you do. All it took for this to happen was a small shift in the way you thought about money. It took you about 18 months to achieve this financial freedom and it started with a simple step—determining your *financial freedom number*.

Discovering Your Personal Financial Freedom Number

People have been brainwashed to think that they need millions of dollars to be financially free. This is not true. Financial freedom is not just a goal for the rich, and you don't have to be a genius to achieve it. All you need to do is look at how much money you require to live comfortably every month. Then find ways to bring in that money each month from investments that work for you rather than from you working for money. When you have this passive income every month, you are financially free.

Let's start with the first step—determining your financial freedom number. Your financial freedom number represents the difference between your passive income and your expenses. If your passive income is greater than your expenses each month, then you are financially free. It's that simple.

Let's go through the exercise of determining your financial freedom number right now. It will only take you about 15 minutes. And isn't it worth a few minutes of your time to figure out what it takes to get rid of your boss, your job, and your money worries?

Step 1: Calculate Your Monthly Expenses

If you currently keep track of your personal and household expenses, this step will be simple. If you don't have such records handy, don't despair. We'll first make a rough estimate of all your expenses. If you can easily look up a helpful piece of information, go ahead and do it. However, it's very important that you take no more than *one minute* on any expense category. The reason for this time limitation is simple. When starting a distasteful task, one of our coping mechanisms is to procrastinate. It would be easy to convince yourself that you'll do this exercise as soon as you get all your records together. If you allow yourself to wait, it may take a day, a week, or a year to compile those records. You can't wait that long to get moving on an important task. And chances are good that your best estimates will be very close to actual numbers. So get started! Keep in mind that your figures should be based on what you actually spend. Use the worksheet provided in Figure 1.1.

Start with your monthly income and write that down here. Monthly income is _____. If you are a U.S. taxpayer, you can take the informations from line 22 of your 1040 tax return. If you take this number from your tax return, remember to divide it by 12 to get your monthly income. (If you are not from the United States, take the total income figure from the tax return that you do file.)

For example, determine how much you spend per month in category one, charitable expenses. If you give $300 to charity each month, enter that amount. You might then determine that you spend $670 on taxes, which is the second expense category. Fill in all of the expense items in each category. If you discover that you spend more than you make (i.e., your expenses seem to be more than your combined income), then determine what's wrong. Either you made an error in your computations or you are spending too much (meaning that you're using your savings or borrowing money each month to pay expenses). But don't worry; you will learn how to fix the problem later.

When you finish, do a reality check to make sure that your number makes sense. For example, if you make $4,000 per month and typically run out of money by the end of the month, then total monthly expenses of $3,500 before savings do not make sense. If you run out of money by the end of the month, how can you have only $3,500 in expenses? You've obviously missed some expenses, and you need to find them. If your numbers suggest that you are saving $500 each month, be certain that $500 is what you are actually putting away. Be honest with yourself and determine where your money is going.

This exercise was intended to give you a good estimate of your expenses. If you do only what was asked and the numbers add up, you will probably get 90% of the intended results. If you want to dig deeper for more accuracy, take whatever time you need to gather the records to verify or correct your original estimates.

Now you know what it currently costs you to maintain your standard of living. This is your base number and, for many of you, it is also your financial freedom number.

Figure 1.1 Monthly Expense Categories

Divide any annual expenses by 12.

Expense Category	Monthly $$
1. Charitable giving	_____
2. Taxes	
a. Federal income tax	_____
b. State income tax	_____
c. Social Security	_____
d. Medicare tax	_____
e. Real estate taxes	_____
f. Sales tax	_____
g. Personal property tax	_____
h. Other taxes	_____
3. Housing	
a. Mortgage or rent	_____
b. Utilities	_____
c. Insurance	_____
d. Maintenance	_____
4. Food	
a. Groceries	_____
b. Eating out	_____
c. Junk food/snacks	_____
5. Automobile (automobile payments are in category 7)	
a. Gas	_____
b. Maintenance	_____
c. Insurance	_____
6. Personal insurance	
a. Life	_____
b. Health	_____
c. Other	_____
7. Debt repayment (not covered above)	
a. Credit cards	_____
b. Automobile	_____
c. Furniture	_____
d. Appliances	_____
e. Investment debt	_____
f. Student loans	_____
g. Other	_____
8. Recreation and entertainment	
a. Vacations	_____
b. Other trips	_____
c. Evenings out, concerts, movies, etc.	_____
d. Other (videos, CDs, etc.)	_____
9. Clothing	_____

Expense Category	Monthly $$
10. Medical expenses	
a. Nonreimbursed medical	_____
b. Nonreimbursed drugs and prescriptions	_____
c. Medical insurance	_____
11. Personal expenses	
a. Hair and beauty care	_____
b. Laundry and dry cleaning	_____
c. Alcohol	_____
d. Tobacco	_____
e. Other	_____
12. Educational expenses	_____
13. Miscellaneous	_____
Subtotal Monthly Expenses	_____
14. Capital depreciation (i.e., stock market losses)	_____
15. Savings	_____
Total Monthly Expenses	_____

If you have high miscellaneous expenses or determine that you "don't know where it all goes," it may be a good idea for you and your family to track your true daily expenses over a two-week period. You'd be surprised at how easy it is to spend on unnecessary items. Learn where your money goes.

Step 2: Determine Your Passive Income

To find out how close you are to being financially free, you'll also need to determine how much passive income you make on average each month. For most people, the list of passive income sources is much shorter than their list of expenses. Passive income represents the cash flow produced when money (or an asset purchased with money) works for you. This cash flow may come from an investment in real estate, in a business, in stocks, in bonds, or in other financial instruments. Although the cash flows from a passive source, it is generated by having an asset work for you rather than by directly trading your time for money. With that said, passive income still requires management and oversight. And in the start-up phases it may require even more time and energy than traditional jobs. But the end result is an asset that produces cash flow (or passive income) without directly trading an hour of work for an hour of pay.

A valid example of passive income would be the cash amount that you receive from a rental property after all expenses (i.e., principal, interest, taxes, advertising, maintenance, property management, vacancy, insurance, etc.) have been paid each month. If the property costs you money after you have deducted all expenses, then it is a negative cash flow property and needs to be recorded as such until the rent increases or the costs go down and the property is making money.

If the rental property is providing you with cash every month after the expenses have all been paid, then it is a positive cash flow property. Sure, you may have to put some time into maintaining the property and collecting the payments, but you are not directly trading an hour of work time for an hour of income. Your property (asset) is generating cash flow for you. And this cash flow is what we are calling passive income.

Note that the value (or appreciation) of the property is not included in this calculation. Values go up and down and cannot truly be determined until you actually sell the property. In addition, changes in property value do not generate cash flow, just changes in value on paper. What we are referring to as passive income is the actual income that you receive as cash on a monthly, quarterly, or yearly basis.

Another example of an income stream that is not passive would be a side job that pays additional income, such as an engineer who gets paid to do surveying work on weekends or a factory worker who gets paid for overtime. Both of these examples involve trading time for income, so they are not passive income.

Figure 1.2 shows several types of passive income. As you fill out the worksheet, remember that you need to use monthly numbers. Don't worry if you don't have any sources of passive income yet. That's what you're reading this book for. Just be honest with yourself so you can accurately determine what you need to do to create your financial freedom.

Figure 1.2 Passive Income Worksheet

Complete this form to the best of your ability. Do not get bogged down on exact figures. Spend a maximum of one minute on each category. Err on the conservative side rather than fooling yourself that you are receiving more than you actually are. You can amend this worksheet later and may get a pleasant surprise if you find your passive income is higher when you check your records.

Passive Income Item	Monthly $$
1. Rental property income (after all expenses)	_____
2. Stock or other dividends (not reinvested)	_____
3. Limited partnership income (listed on your tax return)	_____
4. Managed money that returns regular income (e.g., a mutual fund or hedge fund; if you are losing money, this should be negative. This is normally part of partnership income so don't include it twice.)	_____
5. Income from a business you own but do not primarily operate (others run it for you or it self-generates cash)	_____
6. Royalties for books, music, etc.	_____
7. Income from investing that requires no more than an hour per week of your time	_____
8. Patent income	_____
9. Trust income	_____
10. Alimony/child support	_____
11. Other	_____
My Total Passive Income Is	$_____

Step 3: Determine Your Financial Freedom Number

You now have the two numbers you need to make your financial freedom calculation: your passive income number and your total monthly expenses. Subtract your total monthly expenses from your passive income. If this number is zero or greater (meaning that your monthly passive income is greater than your monthly expenses), then congratulations! You are financially free. You just need to manage your finances and investments so that you keep that freedom.

If your number isn't greater than zero, then your job is to drive it toward zero or better. The other steps in this plan are designed to help you do just that. From this point on you can take a two-pronged approach to achieving financial freedom: driving your monthly expenses down while simultaneously raising the amount of your monthly passive income.

Let's look at how to calculate your number. Let's say your monthly expenses total $3,700 and your monthly passive income is $400. Your financial freedom number is the difference between them, or −$3,300. If you could figure out how to reduce your expenses by $3,300, how to increase your passive income by $3,300, or some combination of the two, you would be financially free. And you could do that fairly quickly.

Continue to use the worksheets in this chapter to help you compute your financial freedom number. Consider keeping an expense ledger and calculate your number monthly. You can also contact IITM for more worksheets, guidance, or assistance with this—we *want* you to be financially free.

What Your Financial Freedom Number Means

In the remainder of this book you are going to learn ways to reduce your financial freedom number. These include reducing expenses you don't need to keep your standard of living; reducing your taxes and your debt—neither of which have anything to do with your standard of living; redeploying your assets so that they earn more passive income; and developing new assets that bring in passive income.

Your overall objective is to make sure your passive income is greater than your expenses, and your financial freedom number is your measuring stick. The closer your number is to zero, the closer you are to financial freedom. If your financial freedom number is −$1,500, it will require much less time and effort to reach zero than it will if your number is −$9,000. Thus, some people who might have considered themselves to be poor will find that they are actually close to financial freedom. Others might find that their journey to financial freedom is longer than they thought it would be because they have a bigger number. But no matter what your number is, financial freedom is within your reach within five years if you simply change your thinking. Yes, really!

KEY IDEAS

➤ You don't have to have millions to be financially free.

➤ You will achieve financial freedom when your passive income equals your living expenses.

ACTION STEPS

➤ Calculate your current monthly expenses.

➤ Determine your current level of passive income.

➤ Subtract your monthly expenses from your current level of passive income to determine your financial freedom number. Fill in your financial freedom number here _____.

➤ Request a free report, *Seven Ideas on Reducing Your Financial Freedom Number*, by calling 919-852-3994 or 800-385-4486; or visit our website at iitm.com.

CHAPTER 2

SAVING FOR YOUR FINANCIAL FREEDOM

"The secret is to spend what you have left after saving, instead of saving what you have left after spending."
—FRANK AND MURIEL NEWMAN

Jim Jackson is a simple guy. He has a degree from the local state college and owns a small engineering consulting service with about 20 employees. He works about 50 hours a week, but he could sell his business tomorrow and never have to work again. His house, a simple four-bedroom ranch house in a modest neighborhood, is paid off, and so is his car. He's accumulated $650,000 in savings, and he's putting that money in investments that return him about $50,000 per year in income—more than enough to pay for his lifestyle, to finance his charitable contributions, and to allow him to travel wherever he wants to go. Jim is debt free, and it all began with saving.

People may know about saving, but Americans don't save well. The U.S. savings rate dipped to 0.3% of income in October of 2001—the lowest level since the Great Depression. You can end up like the vast majority of Americans, who have next to nothing in savings and who will be working forever. Or you can change and end up like Jim Jackson. The choice is obvious. It's time to change your savings habits to fuel your journey to financial freedom.

Paying Yourself First: Automatic Investment Plans

The government knows that getting paid first is important if you want to collect your money. That's why income taxes are taken out of your paycheck before you even see it.[1] You need to set up the same practice. Planning to save some of the money that you take home doesn't work, so arrange to have the money taken from your paycheck before you bring it home.

One of the simplest ways to begin paying yourself first is to start an automatic investment plan. Most banks and mutual fund companies have services that will move money into a segregated account automatically for you each month. Since most people end up spending whatever they have in the bank every month, the secret is to divert about 10% of your income each month into another account before you can spend it. Chances are you won't even miss that money. You can then rest assured that your investment capital is building monthly.

Saving a portion of your income every month is a timeless practice that will lay the foundation for your financial freedom. How you put these monthly savings to work is explained in Parts II and III of this book. This part encourages you to make a commitment to change your psychology. You have to think like a financially free person before you can become one. Your goal is to start (or continue) saving to build your asset base.

Using the Power of Compounding

Max Walker is 35 years old, making $2,000 per month. He commits to saving 10%, or $200 per month. Let's look at what would happen to that money if Max put it into a tax-free source earning 5% to 25% per year. Table 2.1 shows what would happen to that money over time if it were compounded annually at various rates of return. These values are based on tax-free returns, which a 35-year-old investor could obtain in a Roth IRA.

Notice that at 20% Max would become a millionaire by the time he reached 57, and at 15% he becomes a millionaire at 63. However, this

Table 2.1 Saving $200 per Month at Various Rates of Compound Interest

Time	5% Return	10% Return	15% Return	20% Return	25% Return
5 years	$13,601	$15,487	$17,715	$20,352	$23,480
10 years	$31,056	$40,969	$55,043	$75,219	$104,386
15 years	$53,458	$82,894	$133,701	$233,140	$383,174
20 years	$82,207	$151,874	$299,448	$621,930	$1,343,823
25 years	$119,102	$265,367	$648,706	$1,697,057	$4,654,029
30 years	$166,452	$452,098	$1,384,656	$4,595,568	$16,060,352

book is about financial freedom, not becoming a millionaire, so let's look at Table 2.2, which shows the monthly passive income being produced on the amount accumulated at various rates of return. In this case, Max just needs $2,000 per month to live on to replace his current income. This assumes that he is satisfied with his current lifestyle and that inflation doesn't increase his needs dramatically.

Notice that Max becomes financially free (without following any of the other steps) within 24 years at 10% return. At 25% return, he becomes financially free in about 10 years.

You might believe that such high returns are unrealistic, but they are not. Some of the simplest strategies in this book have the potential to return a lot more than that. For example, the bear market mutual fund strategy, discussed in Chapter 7, has averaged 25% per year or more in down markets based on weekly decisions. The max yield strategy, pre-

Table 2.2 Passive Income Produced by Saving $200 per Month at Various Rates of Compound Interest

Time	5% Return	10% Return	15% Return	20% Return	25% Return
5 years	$56.64	$129.06	$221.44	$339.19	$489.16
10 years	$129.40	$341.41	$688.04	$1,253.65	$2,174.71
15 years	$222.74	$690.78	$1,671.27	$3,719.00	$7,982.80
20 years	$342.53	$1,265.61	$3,743.10	$10,365.51	$27,996.31
25 years	$496.26	$2,211.39	$8,108.82	$28,284.29	$96,958.95
30 years	$693.55	$3,767.48	$17,308.20	$76,592.79	$334,590.67

sented in Chapter 10, turned $10,000 into over $323,000 based upon making one decision each year.

What if Max makes and needs $5,000 per month to live on instead of just $2,000? In that case, he would commit to saving 10% of his monthly income, just as he did when his income was lower. If he saves 10% of his new income, the numbers and timing work out roughly the same. Thus, as long as he's putting 10% away in savings, he'll still be able to be financially free in the same amount of time.

Saving for financial freedom is just the tip of the iceberg. People can execute ideas overnight that will add $5,000 or more to their monthly cash flow. Once you become familiar with the concepts and start thinking about reducing your financial freedom number, the ideas will come. In fact, if you start helping your children save when they are young, they could easily be financially free within a few years of graduating from college. Justin Ford will show you how to help your children accomplish this in Chapter 17.

Tip: How to Cut Thousands Off Your Financial Freedom Number

Jill had learned several techniques for putting together huge deals that netted very large cash flows. She had very little of her own money, but she felt that if she could find a great enough return, people would be happy to put up money just to share the returns with her.

Within three months Jill pulled off one such deal. She showed an investor how he could secure a $5 million property for only a small down payment. She also found a tenant for the property, which gave her investor a positive cash flow of $140,000 per year. The investor was delighted, but to make the transaction happen he had to work around an option Jill had on the property. The net result was that Jill got half the cash flow, or $70,000 per year. Jill increased her monthly passive income by $5,833 in just three months.

Learning How to Save

There are two keys to saving for financial freedom.

First, you must overcome the impulse to "have it right now" through a credit card purchase or other borrowing. This type of spending puts you deeper in debt, making compound interest work against you instead of for you. Debt dramatically increases your financial freedom number. If you are already heavily in debt, then you need to pay particular attention to the next chapter of this book, which involves debt reduction.

Second, you must become conscious of your financial freedom number. If you know your number and financial freedom is important to you, then you will always be looking for ways to reduce your number. You'll think about the impact your purchases have on your number and you'll come up with new ideas to help you play the financial freedom game more effectively. You won't be worried about how to get more money and more possessions. Instead, you'll be thinking about how to reduce your number.

Once you become financially free, any additional income you earn can be used to increase your assets, which will in turn produce more passive income. The net result is that you will be able to quickly raise the standard of living at which you are financially free and help others as well. If you were making $3,000 a month in passive income and you raise it to $5,000 per month, you have just raised your standard of living by $2,000 per month.

ACTION STEP

Pick up the phone today and call one of the following numbers:

➤ Charles Schwab: 800-435-8000
➤ T.D. Waterhouse: 800-934-4448, option 4
➤ Rydex Funds: 800-820-0888
➤ Profunds: 888-776-3637

The financial freedom game is totally different from the old "how can I get more" game. It's much more fun, much more attainable, and much more personally satisfying. Now let's take one more step in our planning.

When you make the call, ask for an account application and an application for an automatic investment plan. If you don't have one already, ask for an application for a Roth IRA.[2] This will allow you to contribute approximately $3,000 per year and receive all of your gains tax free. (You can check the amount by searching for "Roth IRA" on google.com.)

These are just suggestions. We receive no compensation from these companies. We selected them because they are either discount brokerages that allow wide mutual fund investing or mutual fund families that specialize in index funds (including inverse index funds, covered in Chapter 7). Initially when you only have a limited amount of money, it's a good idea to invest in an index mutual fund. Once you have $10,000 or more, you can move to more sophisticated strategies.

KEY IDEAS

➤ Paying yourself first is a simple concept, yet it is ignored by most Americans.

➤ Automatic investment plans are an effortless way to pay yourself first.

➤ You must conquer the mind-set that demands immediate gratification. To obtain financial freedom you must delay gratification until you can pay for what you want.

ACTION STEP

My automatic investment plan was started on _____ (fill in the date).

Notes
1. With many types of passive income, taxes are not taken out first.
2. There are limits on opening a Roth IRA. Check with an accountant before you take this step to determine if you qualify. Contribution limits are going up to $5,000 or more, so stay on top of this area.

CHAPTER 3

GETTING OUT OF DEBT IN JUST A FEW YEARS

"The Noah Principle: Predicting rain doesn't count; building arks does."

—ROBERT CAMPBELL

You probably don't realize it, but it's likely that you are throwing away thousands of dollars each year. Fortunately, keeping that money is an easy way of getting closer to financial freedom. So let's get to it.

Look at each expense category on the worksheet (Figure 1.2) you completed in Chapter 1 and determine if any category (or an item within a category) can be reduced or eliminated without altering your lifestyle. Note, for example, the subcategories for alcohol, tobacco, and junk food meals. If you are addicted to any of these, you might be amazed at how much you spend on them monthly. Eliminating any one of them could improve your lifestyle by making you healthier.

Suppose you spend $250 per month on cigarettes—not an unreasonable amount for someone who is addicted. If your financial freedom number is $5,000, then eliminating that one expense would improve your health and bring you 5% closer to financial freedom. That's equivalent to putting $30,000 into a passive income investment that pays you 10%, or $250 per month.

Let's look at a few other suggestions. You can buy automobiles wholesale at auctions or on eBay. In addition, quality cars depreciate more slowly than other vehicles. For example, you can purchase a Lexus with about 100,000 miles on it for less than $10,000. You can drive it 50,000 miles and still sell it for close to what you paid for it.[1]

Many people are making car payments of around $350 per month. If you are $5,000 away from financial freedom and can save that $350 per month—or even part of it—you could reduce your number by another 7%. That plus the 5% you could save on cigarettes would bring you 12% closer to financial freedom.

How to Cut Expenses Without Much Effort

You could reduce your total expenses by as much as 20% just by following these commonsense suggestions.

Cut Up Your Credit Cards

Don't buy anything unless you have enough money in the bank to write a check for it. This is especially important if you have credit card debt. Wait until you can afford it.

Never Buy on the Spur of the Moment

Wait a day and see if you still want it. If you do, then buy it. Chances are, however, that you won't. Look at the countless things you've bought that are now obsolete. How many of them cost over $1,000? If every one of them were now passive income to you of $10 per month, you'd be a lot closer to financial freedom.

Calculate How a Major Purchase Will Affect Your Financial Freedom Number

Remember that you could probably invest that money at 12% interest or better (see Parts II and III of this book) and return 1% of that amount in monthly passive income. Thus, if you are making a $1,000 purchase, you are giving up $10 per month in passive income (i.e., you could use that money to reduce your financial freedom number by $10).

ANITA'S STORY

Anita attended a financial freedom class once a week for 12 weeks. Her initial financial freedom number was $3,700. She had declared bankruptcy, and this number included $2,000 a month that she was required to pay toward her house. And because of missed payments she was about to lose her house to foreclosure. She was distraught. Reducing her financial freedom number was the furthest thing from her mind—she just wanted to save her house. She couldn't understand how she had created these exorbitant costs, and she was too busy trying to dig herself out to think of creative solutions.

The class helped Anita see that there was a way out. Within a week she managed to secure investors to pay off the house on a short-term basis with a bonus payable for their assistance, while another friend secured a home loan and effectively rented the property back to Anita on a rent-to-buy basis. Anita's debt to the bank was gone; she now paid $900 a month toward the house (a reduction of $1,100), which effectively reduced her financial freedom number to $2,600. The investors were happy, the bank was happy, and Anita was happy. It was a winning situation all around.

Anita's lessons were:

1. Stopping for a moment to look at her true financial position, being honest with herself and others, and not sugarcoating her situation.
2. Being responsible for the financial position that she created to ensure that the same mistakes would not be repeated.
3. Asking for help.
4. Being open to the possibility of something new. She's still living in her house and she reduced her financial freedom number by $1,100.
5. Learning about passive income. She had a major insight about working for money versus having money work for you, and she is now continually on the lookout for opportunities to create additional passive income.

Suppose you purchase a Sony PC120 camera for $1,150 at an electronics store while you are on vacation in Singapore. As soon as you buy it new, it drops in value by at least $300 as it becomes a used camera. And when this model is discontinued, the loss will be more like $500. If you invested that money at 12%, you could use it to reduce your financial freedom number by $11 per month for life. In fact, you probably can do a lot better than 12%. Would you be willing to give up an income of $11 per month for the rest of your life for that camera? Although these amounts may seem small or insignificant, they add up to provide financial freedom for you and your family. You don't have to miss out on the camera or family photos; just be open to looking for alternatives.

Consider Buying Through the Internet

Most new products are sold much cheaper over the Internet than they are through stores, so determine the Internet price before you buy. Go to google.com or to eBay.com and look up the item. However, check the feedback rating of anyone you might buy from on eBay, and don't be afraid to ask them questions if anything concerns you.

For example, let's say I decide that I must have that PC120 Sony camera. I see it selling for $1,499 at a local Circuit City store. When I search for the same camera through google.com, I find it for $1,095 at a New York camera store—cheaper than the Singapore price. Both carry the same guarantees, including a three-year extended warranty for $399. Where would you buy the camera?

If You Buy at a Retail Shop, Get the Best Price You Can

The store owner might say they never discount, but ask for it anyway. And if they offer 10%, ask for 20%. You will be surprised at what you can get. In fact, if an item costs $200, tell the store manager that you can get it for $150 through the Internet but that you'd rather buy it at his store and get it now. Perhaps the manager will match that price or at least come close. You lose nothing by asking.

When You Ask for a Discount, Say You Are on a Budget

Tell the store manager that your boss or your spouse won't let you spend more than a certain amount for that item and see what happens. Sometimes it works.

Before You Buy Anything, Think How You Could Generate That Much Passive Income

If you want a new computer that will cost you $70 per month, ask yourself if you can make some sort of investment that will create the $70 per month that you need to pay for it. That's the way someone who wants financial freedom needs to start thinking.

Taxes May Be Your Biggest Expense

You'll want to spend a significant portion of your expense reduction time in the area of taxes. We should all pay our fair share of taxes, but there is no ethical mandate to pay one penny more than is legally required.

DID YOU KNOW? THE HISTORY OF U.S. TAXES

The federal government was not allowed to tax your income until the Sixteenth Amendment to the Constitution was passed in 1913. That amendment was ratified by two-thirds of the states only because the government promised the final states that personal income taxes would never exceed 7% and that most people would be exempt. In fact, until World War II, personal income tax never exceeded 2% of the gross domestic product (GDP), but that all changed when the government needed money.

Tax-Cutting Strategies

You might be surprised to realize that your tax rate could be 50% to 55%. Look at the taxes you listed on the worksheet (Figure 1.1) in Chapter 1. What percentage of your total expenses are taxes? If you receive a salary, you can add on about 10% because your employer by law is required to pay half of your Social Security taxes, your unemployment taxes, and worker's compensation (really another tax for you). And since your employer pays those taxes for you, he or she will count that toward your salary even though you never get to see that money.

As you convert from earned income (income earned through wages) to passive income (income earned through investments), taxes like Social Security, Medicare and Medicaid, unemployment, and worker's compensation will cease to be issues for you. Thus, if you need $3,500 per month to live on, you probably pay about $750 per month in taxes, or about 21%. If that $3,500 were passive income, your taxes would drop by about $260 per month or more because that income is no longer subject to wage-based taxes. This means you'd have at least $260 per month extra to spend or invest, and that your financial freedom number is really only $3,240—about 7% less than you thought.

Another good way to reduce taxes is to own a C corporation. The first $50,000 of income earned by a C corporation is taxed at only 15%, depending upon the nature of your business. In addition, many of the expenses that you now incur after taxes as an employee could become

---

ACTION STEP

Determine at least five expense reductions you can make this month and enter them in the spaces below.

_____

_____

_____

_____

_____

Did You Know? About Consumer Debt

Consumer debt per capita was an astonishing 18 times higher in 2001 than it was in 1961.[2] This is one area where most people can make significant strides in reducing their monthly expenses.

When you get a credit card, you are encouraged to make very small monthly payments. Often the payment just covers the interest, and sometimes it doesn't even pay it fully. It's a trap! For example, suppose you buy a new high-definition television on sale for $2,500. You have no interest charges for three months, so it sounds like a good deal. However, when the interest rate does kick in, it is 18%. Your minimum monthly payment is $40, so you've just raised your financial freedom number by $40 per month. If you just make the minimum monthly payment, it will take you nearly 18 years to pay for that television set. And the television will be obsolete long before the 18 years are over. But that's not the worst of it. The worst part is that you have compound interest working against you. By the time you finish paying for it, you will have paid a total of $8,280—for an obsolete $2,500 television.

before-tax expenses in a C corporation. In fact, there are 229 special sections of the Internal Revenue Code that allow C corporations to deduct expenses that other entities (including S corporations) do not enjoy.

One expense you should not reduce is your charitable giving. *Wealthy people understand that abundance comes from enriching others.* We all know that the more you give, the more you receive. However, do not give for that reason; give for the sake of giving to others. It is rewarding in more ways than you can ever imagine. In fact, the authors plan to give 13% of the royalties of this book to charity.

The topic of how to legally reduce your taxes is beyond the scope of this book. The authors are not tax experts and tax laws change yearly, so consult a professional for specific advice.

Now, put all of the above into practice and monitor your results monthly.

With your living expenses on the way down, especially taxes (if possible), we can look at one other key area of expense reduction before we move to the income side of the financial freedom equation. That key area is debt reduction.

Making Your Debts Disappear with the Payoff Priority Technique

John Burley was a financial planner who was able to retire at the age of 32. He shares his secrets in a marvelous manual called *Automatic Wealth*.[3] In it he outlines a procedure for wiping out all debt—including a home mortgage—in 5 to 10 years with just a 10% increase in the current payment. Sound interesting? Here's how it works:

The first step to getting out of debt is to make sure you never use a credit card unless you plan to pay off the entire balance each month. If you owe money on any card, cut it up and throw it away. We made this point earlier, so do it now if you haven't already done so.

Step two is to make a record of all of your debt, along with the balance owed and the minimum monthly payment. Then divide the balance owed by the minimum monthly payment to determine how many months it will take you to pay off the debt and to determine a payoff priority: home mortgage, auto loan, appliance loan, and three credit cards are typical kinds of debt.

The payoff priority shown in Table 3.1 has nothing to do with interest rates or the size of your balance. It is determined by dividing the balance owed by the minimum payment due. The highest priority goes to the lowest ranked number, the second highest priority goes to the second lowest number, and so on. These priorities are shown in the last column. The appliances had a ratio of 9.24 months and became your highest priority because you can pay that bill off the fastest and get it out of the way. Your MasterCard bill becomes the second priority because you can pay it off the second fastest, and so on.

Your final step is to commit to applying an extra 10% of the total amount you are now paying on your debts toward debt reduction. The monthly debt repayments in Table 3.1 total $3,000. The debt reduction

Table 3.1 Sample Debt Repayment Calculation

Debt Source	Balance Owed	Minimum	Months to Pay Off (Column 2 ÷ Column 3)	Payoff Priority
Home	$257,000	$1,775	144.80	6
Car	$18,475	$395	46.77	4
Appliances	$3,945	$427	9.24	1
Visa #1	$7,245	$195	37.15	3
MasterCard	$2,391	$183	13.07	2
Visa #2	$1,475	$25	59.00	5
Total		$3,000		

will be accelerated by applying the extra 10%, or $300, to the first priority debt, the appliance debt. Add $300 to the current minimum payment of $427 and you will immediately start making payments of $727 per month on the appliance debt. The extra $300 per month helps you pay off this debt in just six months. Meanwhile, you continue to make the minimum monthly payment for your remaining debts.

Now that debt one is paid off, take the $727 and spoil yourself for one month—spend the $727 for one month only—and the following month take the money you were paying toward appliances and add it to the payment on your second priority, the MasterCard bill. This balance should now be about $1,700 because you've been making minimum payments for seven months and haven't incurred any new charges. When you add $727 to the $183 you were paying, your payment on this bill jumps to $910. Thus, it takes only three more months to pay this one off. Spoil yourself again, this time with $910. The beauty of this procedure is that you get to see your debts disappear rapidly. In just 11 months you've paid off two full debts and have congratulated yourself by spoiling yourself and your family.

Now take the $910 and apply it to priority number three, your first Visa card. That boosts your Visa payments to $1,105 per month. In seven more months that bill will be gone. Then have fun for a month with the $1,105 and then be sensible and reapply it to your debts.

DID YOU KNOW? ABOUT MORTGAGE DEBT

Many financial advisors argue that you should have a 30-year mortgage on your house. This is good debt. It gives you an appreciating asset and the interest is tax deductible. Your mortgage makes sense when you have real estate that is appreciating faster than the interest rate you are paying on your mortgage—that's it. But when real estate goes down, which does happen, mortgage debt makes no sense.

Statistics suggest that the average person owns a home for about six years. Many refinance every three or four years. Each time they do, they begin a new 30-year loan and pay 1% to 3% of the value of the loan just for the privilege of doing so. Let's say you stay in your home about six years and then move. On a $100,000 loan at 7.5%, you will have made nearly $50,000 in payments after six years, yet you will have paid off only a few thousand dollars of that loan. It's a good deal only if your house has appreciated in value to well over $150,000.

Your fourth priority is your car payment. In approximately 19 months you have taken your car debt down to $14,775, maybe even lower depending on interest rates. You now add the $1,105 to the monthly payment of $395 and you get a new payment of $1,500 per month. You'll have your car paid off in 11 months.

Thus, in about two and a half years, you will have paid off four major debts, you have an extra $1,500 per month, and you've spoiled yourself every couple of months. Just think, all of this achieved with 10% or $300 extra put toward debts, which would have probably just disappeared otherwise in day-to-day expenditure. If your financial freedom number was $5,000, you will have reduced it by 30% in two years. But we are not finished yet.

Your number five priority was your second Visa bill, which hasn't gone down much in two years because most of your payments were being applied to interest charges. It's now at $1,355. With the added money, you can pay it off in one month. Thus, you will have paid off everything but your house.

You now have an extra $1,525 to apply to your house payment. It has shrunk by about $7,000 to $249,500. You are now making house payments of $3,500 per month, with more than half of that going toward the principal. As a result, you can pay off your house in about 8 years and be totally out of debt in about 10 years. All you did was add an additional $300 per month to your payments. It's that easy, and you might be able to accomplish it in as little as five years, depending upon your situation.

It's time to do your own calculations. Complete Table 3.2 within the next two hours and put the additional 10% toward your number one payoff priority this month. Gather all your debt payments together: your mortgage, student loans, credit card bills, consumer debts (e.g., car payments, payments for appliances, furniture, or electronics), and any other loans you must repay. Record the debt source in column 1 of Table 3.2. Record the balance owed in column 2 and the minimum monthly payment in column 3. Then complete the calculations for column 4 by dividing the balance by the minimum monthly payment. Rank them in column 5 to determine your payoff priorities.

Table 3.2 My Debt Repayment Calculation

Debt Source	Balance Owed	Minimum	Months to Pay Off (Column 2 ÷ Column 3)	Payoff Priority
Mortgage	_____	_____	_____	_____
Car	_____	_____	_____	_____
_____	_____	_____	_____	_____
_____	_____	_____	_____	_____
_____	_____	_____	_____	_____
_____	_____	_____	_____	_____
_____	_____	_____	_____	_____
_____	_____	_____	_____	_____
_____	_____	_____	_____	_____
_____	_____	_____	_____	_____
Total		_____ 10% = _____		

Hopefully, you don't have enough debts to fill in the entire table. But if you do, the procedure will still work. Remember to add 10% of the total minimum monthly payments to determine your extra contribution toward debt reduction. What if you've already been paying more than the minimum monthly payment? That's great! In that case, add an extra 10% to the amount you've already been paying—and consider it your commitment to financial freedom. The reward of paying off long-standing debt will make this small extra investment seem trivial when you look back on this exercise several years from now.

Additional Considerations for Debt Reduction

Consider renegotiating your debt. Lenders would rather be paid even a small amount than have you default. As a result, you can probably negotiate your debt in several ways. One strategy is to call your lender and say you need help paying your debt. You just might get it. You'll never know unless you ask.

Another approach is to work with a company that helps consumers manage their debts. Find one that provides its service for a fee. Those

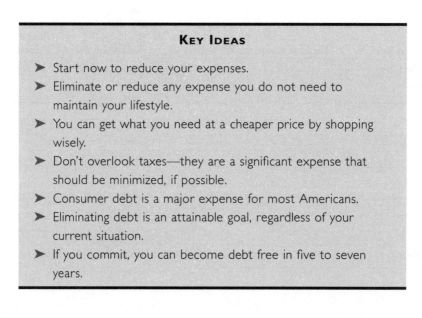

KEY IDEAS

➤ Start now to reduce your expenses.
➤ Eliminate or reduce any expense you do not need to maintain your lifestyle.
➤ You can get what you need at a cheaper price by shopping wisely.
➤ Don't overlook taxes—they are a significant expense that should be minimized, if possible.
➤ Consumer debt is a major expense for most Americans.
➤ Eliminating debt is an attainable goal, regardless of your current situation.
➤ If you commit, you can become debt free in five to seven years.

that have no fee often make tremendous profits through hidden charges, so be careful. Sometimes these companies help you consolidate your debt at a lower interest rate. If you can do this without taking out a loan on your house or paying high charges to the debt consolidation company, then do so. Sometimes these companies can actually get your debt reduced.

ACTION STEPS

➤ Destroy credit cards that have balances you cannot immediately pay off in full.
➤ Complete Table 3.2.
➤ Make your first accelerated payment toward the debt you calculate as your first priority for payoff.

Notes

1. The most important factor in this type of strategy is the research. What are the retail and wholesale prices of the vehicle you are buying? Check the vehicle's background through CarFax on the Internet. If you buy through eBay, check the dealer's feedback rating and talk to him or her on the phone.
2. Data from the Philadelphia Federal Reserve, www.phil.frb.org.
3. John R. Burley, *Automatic Wealth: A 30-Day, Step-by-Step System for Unlimited Riches (Without Having to Make More Money)* (Glendale, Ariz.: Burley & Associates, 1998). Available through iitm.com, or call 919-852-3994 or 800-385-4486. Burley also has a helpful book titled *Powerful Changes*. Call 800-561-8246 or visit johnburley.com to order.

CHAPTER 4

MAXIMIZING WHAT YOU ALREADY HAVE

"When you stop working, assets feed you and liabilities eat you."
—ROBERT KIYOSAKI

L et's take some active steps now to increase the money flow in your life. Chapters 1 through 3 concentrated on the defensive side of your plan. You determined your financial freedom number and learned how to reduce it by being a little wiser in the way you live. This chapter continues your financial freedom plan, but we now focus on offensive strategies. Here you'll concentrate on increasing your passive income. Let's begin by analyzing your current assets.

Taking Stock: Your Assets and What They're Doing for You

Most people have major assets that they are not deploying effectively. It's a little like an army with millions of troops all over the world but only 50,000 concentrated where the fighting is. You need to determine what all your assets are doing for you, not just the few that are working the hardest.

First you need to understand what an asset really is. When you do a traditional balance sheet, anything you own that has value is put in the asset column. This means that your house, even though you owe $223,455 on it and make payments of $1,764 per month to the bank, is still an asset. It is appraised at $350,000, so you have an asset that is worth $126,545. However, that asset is not bringing you any money. Instead, it costs you money. In the financial freedom game, you are only allowed to consider assets that are bringing in passive income. The assets that are costing you money are really liabilities in this game because they add to your financial freedom number (which must be decreased to give you financial freedom).

The purpose of this step is to determine which of your assets could be deployed more productively. You also want to look at the returns you are making on productive assets. For example, suppose you have $10,000 in a checking account earning 0.2% interest. That checking account counts as an asset because it brings in $20 each year. In other words, it reduces your financial freedom number by $1.67 per month ($20 divided by 12 months). However, you could put that money to use more productively.

Begin by listing all of your assets that are bringing in passive income and the annual rate of return for each one. Your list might look something like Table 4.1, which lists the assets of Jeff, a millionaire who is not financially free. Also, Jeff has monthly expenses of $16,000.

Table 4.1 Assets Producing Passive Income

Name	Cost	Net Monthly Income	Net Annual Income	Yearly Return	Current Value
Checking account	$120,000	$20	$240	0.2%	$120,000
Rental property	$17,000	$375	$4,500	26.47%	$175,000
Royalties	0	$200	$2,400	?	?
Limited partnership	$30,000	$300	$3,600	12%	$30,000
Fast-food franchise[a]	$750,000	$4,200	$50,400	6.72%	$750,000
Totals		**$5,095**	**$61,140**	**5.69%**	**$1,075,000**

[a]A franchise run by a manager can count as passive income to you because you are not putting in the time to run it. A restaurant in which you are the owner and manager would not count because you are probably putting in 14 hours a day to run it. Being a restaurant manager would be your job, and if you stopped working, the income would probably stop.

Jeff has over a million dollars in assets, but they provide him with only about a third of the passive income he needs to be financially free. His assets are actually a lot more challenging to redeploy than the assets of the average person. We need to find nearly $11,000 per month in passive income for him to become financially free.

In this table, the cost of the asset is the amount of cash Jeff put into it. It does not include any appreciation. The rental property, for example, was purchased with $17,000 in cash, as recorded in column 2. Monthly income, entered in column 3, is income after expenses. Jeff has rental income of $1,250, but he has payments of $875 going out, so his net monthly income is only $375. The annual return is simply the yearly income (after expenses) divided by the value of the asset. Anything over 15% is good. The last column indicates how much cash the asset would generate if it were sold today. Notice that Jeff has $1,075,000 in assets, but those assets bring in only $5,095 in passive income each month. This amounts to a yearly return of about 5.7%.

Now it's your turn. Fill in Table 4.2 for your current income-producing assets.

Table 4.2 My Assets Producing Passive Income

Name	Cost	Net Monthly Income	Net Annual Income	Yearly Return	Current Value
Checking account		_____	_____	_____	_____
_____	_____	_____	_____	_____	_____
_____	_____	_____	_____	_____	_____
_____	_____	_____	_____	_____	_____
_____	_____	_____	_____	_____	_____
_____	_____	_____	_____	_____	_____
_____	_____	_____	_____	_____	_____
_____	_____	_____	_____	_____	_____
_____	_____	_____	_____	_____	_____
_____	_____	_____	_____	_____	_____
Totals	_____	_____	_____	_____	_____

Now let's look at your traditional assets, those things that have value but don't bring you income. We're going to call these your nonproductive assets. They are important because you could sell them and turn the cash into productive assets.

Table 4.3 shows a hypothetical list of nonproductive assets. This is what the list of a typical baby boomer in her fifties might look like. We'll say that this list belongs to Mary, and that Mary has no real income-earning assets, just these nonproductive ones. She will provide a good example for most of you. The liquidation value is the net value you might get if you were to sell an asset within the next three months. If you deduct anything you owe on the item plus the cost of selling it, the remainder is its liquidation value, computed in column 3 of Table 4.3.

Think about things you own that would have value if they were sold. Look around your house at furniture and other items. Also consider what you have in your strong box in the attic or your safe-deposit box at the bank. List everything. Then decide upon the 10 most valuable items you could sell and list them in Table 4.4. Check the liquidation values by comparing your item with similar items that have sold on eBay recently.

DID YOU KNOW? HOW TO FIND AN ASSET'S LIQUIDATION VALUE ON EBAY

1. Go to eBay.com. When you get there, you'll see a Search box on the top line.
2. Click on the Search box and you'll see a Basic Search box. The second box from the left on top of that says Advanced Search.
3. Click on that box. Then plug in what you want to search for and click on Completed Auctions. This will give you a search of all of eBay's completed auctions for the last 90 days.
4. If you are getting too many irrelevant items, go back to the Advanced Search area and narrow your search to a specific category. If you are not getting anything, you might also click on Search Item Descriptions.
5. Note: eBay's search procedures change frequently, so if this doesn't work, go to the Help menu.

Table 4.3 Typical List of Nonproductive Assets

Asset	Cost	Liquidation Value
Home	$315,000	$145,000
Boat	$25,000	$5,000
Stamp collection	$2,500	$7,500
Jewelry	$12,000	$3,000
CD collection	$7,000	$1,200
Art	$3,000	$500
Husband's car	$35,000	$17,000
Wife's car	$27,000	$12,000
Silver coin bag	$8,000	$4,000
Totals	**$434,500**	**$195,200**

Redeploying Your Assets to Maximize Returns

Your job now is to sell or redeploy your assets so that you can increase
your passive income. This step will determine what you are made of
psychologically. Let's use Table 4.1, which shows the hypothetical assets
of a millionaire named Jeff, as an example. Jeff is a good illustration
because he has a lot of assets to redeploy.

Table 4.4 My List of Nonproductive Assets

Asset	Cost	Liquidation Value
Totals		

ACTION STEPS

➤ Fill out Table 4.2, listing your passive income assets and the return you are getting from that source.
➤ Make a list of your other valuables.
➤ Fill out Table 4.4, listing your most valuable nonproductive assets.
➤ Look over both completed tables and think about how your assets are performing.

Jeff might be a millionaire, but he is not financially free. In fact, his financial freedom number is probably a lot higher than yours. He has $5,095 per month in passive income, but that is just about equal to the payments on his personal residence. Jeff needs $16,000 per month to be financially free, so his financial freedom number is $10,905. But look at the value of his passive income assets. They are worth more than a million dollars. *If Jeff could get an 18% return instead of 5.69%, he'd be financially free.* And, as you will learn in Parts II and III, there are lots of ways to earn 18% or more on your assets if you develop good financial intelligence.

Jeff has $120,000 in his checking account because a financial planner told him he should have six months' worth of cash available if he needed it. What if Jeff invested this money in some of the investments available today that yield 15%? He could select one that is fairly liquid, such as the max yield strategy in Chapter 10, applied when the dollar is going down. Instead of a $20 return per month, he'd have a $1,500 return per month. He'd be 15% closer to financial freedom, and he could do it within 24 hours.

Notice that his rental property has a net value of $175,000. He could probably take out an equity loan for $150,000 at 7% and redeploy those assets into something with a huge return. But to be conservative, let's say that Jeff decided on an investment returning 15%. If he did that, he would make a net return of 8% on his $150,000. This would give him an additional $1,000 per month in passive income, and the entire pro-

---

DID YOU KNOW? ABOUT VIRTUAL BANKS

What if you could borrow money at 3% and lend it out as a 6% mortgage with the money guaranteed by the government? Well, there are companies that Steve Sjuggerud calls virtual banks that do just that. They make the difference between the 3% interest they pay and the 6% interest they charge on their mortgages, and they do so with about 10 times leverage. Furthermore, they must pay 90% of their income out as dividends. Two of these companies, NLY and ANS, as of this writing are paying about 14% dividends with the potential for huge capital gains as well.

---

cess might be completed in 30 days. Thus, within a month, Jeff would have increased his passive income by 50%, or $2,500, and moved 23% closer to financial freedom.

The last item on Jeff's list that he might do something with is his franchise. He could consider selling it. If his net profit after the sale was $700,000, he would lose $50,000 in value and $4,200 in passive income. But what if he invested that money in a fairly conservative investment yielding 10%? He'd now have $70,000 extra passive income per year, or $5,833 per month. He'd increase his passive income by $1,633 per month and move 19.4% closer to financial freedom.

If Jeff did a little more research and found a 20% investment for his $700,000, then he would have an extra $140,000 in extra passive income.[1] He would have increased his passive income from $4,200 to $11,667, for a net gain of $7,467. After this move, he would be only $938 away from financial freedom. He would probably save more than $938 in taxes by moving $10,000 from earned income (i.e., he'd stop working) to passive income, and he could probably do so in about six months. Remember what's been done, because it might apply to you as well.

In our example, Jeff, with a financial freedom number of $10,905, could become financially free within six months by simply redeploying his assets. It would take no adjustment at all in his expenses even though he probably could reduce his number significantly by also doing that.

Did You Know? Tax Lien Certificates Yield 16% or More

Many states sell tax lien certificates (or tax deed certificates) when people don't pay the taxes on their real estate. Every state is different, but some pay as much as 50%. And you can get them today, secured by real estate. For more information on this topic see *The 16% Solution* by Joel Moskowitz (Andrews McMeel Publishing, 1994).

You may not have the kind of assets Jeff has, but you probably have some assets that could be redeployed. And if you do, chances are you could reduce your financial freedom number by anywhere from 10% to 100%.

Look at your passive assets from Table 4.2. How can you redeploy them to reduce your number? You might want to revisit this exercise after you've finished Part II and Part III of this book. Write down at least three possibilities in the space below:

How I Can Redeploy My Current Passive Income Assets?
1.
2.
3.

Now let's look at what you can do with nonproductive assets, using Mary's assets in Table 4.3 as an example. All of Mary's assets are unproductive. She just collected things because that's what people in our culture do. Fortunately, she doesn't have far to go to reach financial freedom. Her number is $2,741, so she's much closer to financial freedom than Jeff is with his lavish lifestyle.

First, Mary has about $145,000 worth of equity in her house. She's currently paying 8% on her mortgage, but she could refinance her house on a 15-year mortgage at just over 5%. She has about 17 years remaining on her existing mortgage, so it would actually be paid off a little earlier by refinancing. And because of the reduction in interest, even though she will pull out about $85,000, her payments will remain the same.

Suppose she redeploys her assets in an investment earning about 14% per year. (Yes, we'll show you how—keep reading.) This will give her an extra $992 per month. She's moved 36% closer to financial freedom in just two months.

Second, Mary has a number of other assets that could be sold. If she sold her two cars and used the car strategy explained in Chapter 3, she could eliminate $700 per month in payments. She would also have an

---

SUZANNA'S STORY

When Suzanna first heard stories about people doing deals that made 80% to 100% returns per year, she thought it was all hype. Nevertheless, she decided to do some research. She attended a workshop that taught some of the techniques and made 20 real estate offers during that course. None were accepted because she offered only about 60 cents on the dollar. However, her understanding was that only about 2% to 5% of such offers are accepted anyway. All of her offers were sight unseen, so she inserted a clause that gave her a way out. It said "pending inspection and approval of my partner."

Suzanna decided to keep at it, making about 20 offers every weekend. To her surprise, she had two offers accepted within the first month. She followed through and closed on her first property in a month. She bought it for $55,000 and it cost her only $6,000 to close the deal.

She then applied other things she'd learned. She advertised a fixer-upper house with a very low down payment and easy qualifying. Thirty people responded to the ad, and she sold the house for $77,000. The new owner put down $3,500 and was paying 9% interest on the balance. When the deal was complete, Suzanna had only $2,500 of her own cash in the deal, and she was getting a positive cash flow of $279 per month after making payments on the house (she still had the primary mortgage).

Suzanna has done 15 of these deals in nine months and she's already become financially free.

---

additional $9,000 in cash (after buying two used cars at $10,000 each), which she could redeploy to make an additional $90 per month. If she did that, she would be only $959 away from financial freedom. However, she thinks that doing so will affect her lifestyle, so she won't.

She also won't touch her jewelry (especially at a 75% loss), her art, or her CD collection. However, the family seldom uses the boat. She doesn't even look at the stamp collection or the silver coins that she bought as a hedge against inflation. Thus, she's willing to liquidate all three. Selling the boat, stamps, and coins will net $26,500.

Mary decides to try real estate wraps. She figures she can do four of them with that money. Real estate wraps are strategies in which you sell a property you own, but the buyer makes payments to you as if you were the bank. You collect interest on the loan, and if the buyer defaults on the payments you get the house back and can resell it. John Burley describes this strategy in more detail in Chapter 12.

Mary buys a course on doing wraps and studies it.[2] It takes her about six months to do four wraps, and her net return on them is about 70%. This bring her closer to financial freedom by $1,545.83. As a result, she is now financially free. She did it in about eight months, mostly by redeploying her assets.

Okay, now it's your turn. In Table 4.5 list up to 10 nonproductive assets that you would be willing to liquidate. Also note what you are not willing to liquidate and why. This reveals a little about the things that you might want, more than financial freedom, so think about it. Doing so may identify a tendency toward self-sabotage, if you feel deep down that you don't deserve financial freedom, or the belief that financial freedom is not possible. The topic of psychological blocks to financial freedom could fill an entire book, but that's beyond the scope of this book.

Adding Strategies That Significantly Increase Your Passive Income

Parts II and III of this book cover some strategies you might use to increase your passive income. If any of them appeal to you, you'll need to do more research and become a specialist in those areas. You need

Table 4.5 Nonproductive Assets I'm Willing to Redeploy to Achieve Financial Freedom

Asset I Will Redeploy	Liquidation Value
Example: Old collection (stamps, records, books) that I no longer pay attention to	$2,000

to both deploy your assets and protect them. The investment fundamentals given in Part IV are critical to protecting your assets, so be sure that you understand them before you invest.

There are several critical points we want to make in this next section.

First, *you don't need money to make money*. What you need is research and the ability to network with people who have money. For example, suppose you do some research and come up with a deal that will return 50%. Let's say the deal will cost $500,000 and will return $20,833 per

---

ACTION STEPS

➤ Determine what steps you can take to make your income-producing assets even more productive.

➤ Determine how to redeploy your nonproductive assets to make them more productive.

➤ Put this into action. Set goals—what you intend to do by when—and do them!

month. That type of return is outstanding (and it is possible). If you can convince an investor to put up all the money for half the return, you'll make over $10,000 per month without needing any of your own money. Would you put up money for a 25% return if it was a sound and safe deal? Most people would, so it's not that hard to find investors. You just need to find the right deal. If you find a good enough deal, you can use other people's money to make money. We live in a world of abundance, which may be another area where you need to shift your thinking.

A second key point is that *passive income is taxed at a lower rate than earned income, and it might not be taxable at all.* Thus, if you need $5,000 per month for financial freedom, and that includes $1,700 per month in taxes, you might be able to save $500 or more just by switching from

---

DID YOU KNOW? USING OTHER PEOPLE'S MONEY

One of the difficulties of doing high-yield real estate deals is that they rely on your personal credit. You can only do so many wraps and then the bank or mortgage company suddenly says, "You have too much debt," and stops giving you loans. You might have borrowed $500,000 to buy 10 low-priced houses but used only about $50,000 of your own money to complete them. You might be making a 50% return on your money, which should qualify you for a lot more such deals. However, the banks don't see it that way and they tend to limit how many deals you can do.

How do you overcome this problem? Find other investors! One of the authors of this book has done just that. He found someone who was an expert at doing such deals. The expert did all the work, while one of us put up the money. The expert and the investor split the cash flow. The expert gets an infinite cash flow (but he has to do the work), and the investor gets about a 30% yearly cash flow. Would you do such a deal if you didn't have to do any work and could get about 30% on your money for the next 30 years? Of course, you would if you thought it was safe. And if you are the person doing the deals using other people's money, then your return is infinite. That's the power of using other people's money.

earned income to passive income. Thus, your financial freedom number would be really only $4,500.

Some real estate deals are not taxable at all. For example, you can depreciate your real estate assets each year. That depreciation doesn't cost you anything, but it can be used to offset the passive income you receive from that real estate for tax purposes. Thus, your real estate income might not be taxable at all.

When you sell your real estate, you can do what is called a 1031 exchange. In a 1031 exchange you simply exchange your real estate for another piece of real estate that is of equal or greater value and you postpone your taxes on the sale.

For example, suppose you own a duplex that you bought for $250,000. You've depreciated it over 15 years and it is now on your books at a value of $125,000. You decide that it is time to sell it so you can get a bigger depreciation. You sell your building for $600,000, which would normally give you a tax bill on your $475,000 of profit (profit is the amount received, less your basis adjusted for depreciation). However, you do a 1031 exchange for a $750,000 building. On the new building you get bigger rentals and much bigger depreciation. You also get to postpone taxes on the sale. This is given as an example; always consult a professional tax advisor.

When you start to think about your financial freedom number instead of how much you can accumulate, time is no longer a key factor in achieving financial freedom. Time is important when you think about saving $200 per month to build up an asset. However, you've learned a lot of ideas that don't involve time, including reducing your

---

ACTION STEPS

➤ Think about finding great deals where you could use other people's money, giving you an infinite rate of return. One such idea could make you financially free overnight.

➤ Revisit this section of the book when you are more familiar with the strategies described in Parts II and III.

➤ Commit to studying and researching more about great deals.

expenses, redeploying your assets, turning nonproductive assets into productive ones, and using other people's money with the idea of making great returns. Time is not a significant factor in these suggestions.

Making Paradigm Shifts: Financial Freedom Is Closer Than You Think

One of the keys to financial freedom is to start thinking outside of your normal frame of reference. Don't let your thinking be restricted by what everyone else says can and cannot be done. When you get rid of these limitations, the ideas you come up with are called paradigm shifts. In the Infinite Wealth workshop, presenters Van Tharp and John Burley encourage people to make major paradigm shifts.[3] What can you do that's totally different from anything you've ever done before? What can you do that's totally different from how you normally think? Such paradigm shifts can have a major impact on your becoming financially free.

Let's look at six examples of paradigm shifts, some of which we have already talked about.

Six Paradigm Shifts That You Can Make Now

1. *Start thinking in terms of your financial freedom number rather than how much you are worth.* At this point you should know your number and be thinking about how to reduce it. This is a major change from concentrating on how much you are worth and how you can get it all now.

2. *Taxes are a major part of your financial freedom number, and it is legal to work within the system to reduce your taxes.* Just shifting from earned income to passive income could reduce your financial freedom number by 10% or more. However, if you choose entities that allow you to deduct your expenses before you are taxed, you can probably reduce that number by as much as 30%. This will take some work and careful planning.

3. *Your accountant should work for you.* You may have to go through some accountants or financial planners who will tell you, no matter

How to Use a Paradigm Shift to Become Financially Free

Pete only needed $2,600 per month to become financially free. He had a mortgage on his house of $325,000 at 8.5% interest. His monthly payments were $4,537, so his mortgage accounted for all of his financial freedom number and more.

Pete found a good deal on a condo that could generate a positive cash flow and had a lot of potential for appreciation.

If Pete financed the condo, he'd have to take out a business real estate loan at about 8%. It would be very difficult to get a positive cash flow paying that much interest. He went to a mortgage broker who suggested a creative strategy. Pete's house was worth about $550,000 and the condo was worth about $150,000. He could get a loan for both for about $670,000. With that loan he would get $40,000 in cash, 100% financing on his personal residence, and the financing he needed on the condo.

That might not sound great, but the loan was based upon the short term LIBOR rate and the starting interest rate was just 3%. Pete's initial payment was only $1,832. In addition, he got a positive cash flow of $470 per month from renting the condo, reducing his out-of-pocket costs to just $1,362 per month. In addition, Pete invested the $40,000 in a high-yield bond fund paying $300 per month. Thus, his net outflow per month was now only $1,062.

By using creative financing, Pete moved $3,475 toward financial freedom. And since he only needed $2,600, he was now financially free, with excess money to enjoy or invest in more assets.

what you suggest, that "you can't do that." Find one who will give you productive suggestions. Tell your accountant what you want to do and ask him or her to help you find a way to do it.

4. *Financial freedom can be obtained within months by reducing expenses, redeploying assets, and using other people's money on good ideas.* All you have to do is change your thinking. Ask yourself, "How can I reduce my number to zero within six months to a year?" If you think that way instead of thinking, "This will take

years," then you will come up with ways to accomplish that. This book is designed to help you with that objective.

5. ***People who don't work for money tend to think in terms of systems to make them money.*** A system is something that a person of average intelligence can do very easily because it is somewhat automatic. For example, a fast-food chain has many systems working within each franchise. It has systems for greeting customers, systems for preparing the food, systems for cleanup, systems for food delivery, and many others. The franchise works because it has a lot of systems.

   Business owners typically think in terms of systems to improve the efficiency and profitability of their business. The average person doesn't think in terms of systems. People ask, "What's the stock market going to do?" or "What should I buy?" Instead, they should ask, "How can I develop a simple system that will control risk and make me money?" We'll give you a framework for doing that in this book, but you must start thinking in terms of simple systems instead of "what should I do now?"

6. ***For things to change, you must change first.*** This is a revolutionary idea for most people, yet the assumption behind it is very simple: you produce the results that you get. We discuss this concept in Chapter 16 on how to fix mistakes. Essentially, if you are not producing the results you want, you must look to yourself for the reason. Ask yourself, "What can I do differently? What are the issues which might be blocking my success?" You might have had to face some of these same issues when you undertook the redeployment of your assets. What stopped you from converting all your nonproductive assets to passive income–producing assets? If you had even one that you were not willing to convert, take a look at the reasons why. They will provide a great window into what's going on for you. Once you are aware of these issues, you are well on your way to overcoming them.

Most people in our Infinite Wealth Workshops come up with 10 to 20 paradigm shifts. You should maintain your own list as you complete this book.

KEY IDEAS

➤ You could become financially free just by redeploying your assets more effectively.

➤ Nonproductive assets (which really are not assets) can be turned into productive assets.

➤ It's possible to jump right to financial freedom by using other people's money and helping them become financially free in the process.

➤ Consider making a paradigm shift. How can you change your thinking to become financially free? One thought plus the appropriate action might do it.

ACTION STEPS

➤ Start a financial freedom notebook and record your number and ideas as they come to you.

➤ In your financial freedom notebook, also keep a list of paradigm shifts you could make in order to achieve financial freedom.

➤ Think about psychological issues that keep you from taking important steps toward financial freedom.

➤ The December 1999 issue of *Market Mastery* contains an article titled "Paradigm Shifts for Wealth and Trading Success," which was inspired by people at our Infinite Wealth Workshops. Call IITM at 919-852-3994 or 800-385-4486 for further information.

Notes

1. We are illustrating the principle of redeployment here. The safety of your money is another issue, which we'll discuss later in this book.
2. Joe Arlt, *Real Estate Wraps*. Course on Tape. Available through the International Institute of Trading Mastery, Inc. (IITM), 919-852-3994 or 800-385-4486.
3. For more information on IITM's Infinite Wealth Workshop, call 919-852-3994 or go to iitm.com. The workshop is available annually as a three-day workshop or in a home-study version.

PART II

PROFITABLE STOCK MARKET STRATEGIES FOR GOOD TIMES AND BAD TIMES

In Part I you developed a plan for financial freedom. Now it's time to cover some simple strategies that will help you use the stock market to reduce your financial freedom number.

Chapter 5 will give you a general background on the economic factors influencing the stock market. The market probably entered a major bear market cycle in 2000 that could last at least another 15 years. However, the news is not all bad because you'll learn techniques that will allow you to profit no matter what the market does. You will be profiting while others are losing money. And even if we're wrong about the market, we present a simple model that will tell you in less than a minute when to expect a strong up market, such as the 2003 market, and when to expect a dangerous down market.

Chapter 6 helps you understand mutual funds. If the market is heading down for a long time, then most mutual funds are a very dangerous place to be. Many of them might not survive the next 10 years. However, it's possible to outperform the market averages through mutual funds every year. You'll learn how here. In addition, for some of you, hedge fund investing may be the best strategy. You'll learn how to get the appropriate information in Chapter 6.

Chapter 7 presents strategies that could help you profit handsomely when the market is going down. You'll learn how to invest in bear market funds and how to spot highly overvalued stocks and ride them down for big profits.

Chapter 8 presents more key stock market strategies. You'll learn how to follow the recommendations of a newsletter and how to determine when a newsletter is good. You'll also learn how to screen for and buy stocks that are very efficient—a technique that has worked very well during market recoveries. Most important, you'll learn how to buy stocks at a discount to their liquidation value. If we are right about the market conditions, you can use this technique to purchase a portfolio of undervalued stocks that could be the top performers when the market turns around. And we'll show you how to do it almost risk free.

CHAPTER 5

TIMES WILL BE VERY TOUGH FOR STOCKS, BUT NOT FOR YOU

"It is not natural for us to learn from history. Children will cease to touch a burning stove only when they are themselves burned; no possible warning by others can lead to developing the smallest form of cautiousness."

—NICHOLAS TALEB

By the year 2015, we could see the S&P 500 as low as 186 and the Dow Jones Industrials as low as 2700. If that happens, you will still be able to make good profits and become financially free by following the strategies recommended in the next few chapters.

"Buy stocks and hold them" was the conventional wisdom for much of the 1990s. You didn't need an investment strategy, and you didn't think about getting out. The folly of the conventional wisdom has been exposed. Folks who bought and held tech stocks saw their portfolios crumble by 75% or more from 2000 through 2002. Many retirement nest eggs went up in smoke. And elderly people who never expected to work again are now bagging groceries at the supermarket or working for minimum wage at fast-food restaurants.

What went wrong with the conventional wisdom? The simple answer is that stocks are not always a good buy. For much of history, stocks have been a reasonably attractive investment proposition. A few times in history they have been extraordinary bargains. But there are also times when stocks are a bad investment. Unfortunately, now appears to be one of those times.

DID YOU KNOW? MARKET INDEXES CHANGE

This may be especially interesting to die-hard buy-and-hold traders and investors. Did you know that there is only 1 stock remaining of the original 30 in the Dow Jones Industrials? That stock is General Electric.

All indexes (Nasdaq, Dow, S&P 500, etc.) discard companies and stocks that are not performing and replace them with performing ones. Is it any wonder that the figures that we rely on so heavily for our trading decisions should be monitored carefully?

Our purpose is not to predict markets, but to give you a framework to guide your thinking about when you should be in stocks, instead of just blindly buying and holding. You'll learn a relatively simple model that will tell you if you should be investing heavily in stocks, if you should cautiously buy stocks, or if you should avoid them.

In the rest of this chapter, you're going to learn about long-term megacycles in the market and what causes them. As we write this in early 2004, the long-term direction of the stock market is down. If you want to know why the markets are headed down, you'll need to read this section carefully.

You will also learn how to tell when the long-term cycle of the market is ready to change. The signs will be obvious. Prices will be very undervalued because nobody will want to buy stocks anymore. People will be fearful. Stocks will be a tremendous bargain at that point in time. You'll learn exactly what to look for and how to know when it is happening.

Finally, you will learn the 1-2-3 model, which will tell you about the current condition of the market. There are three major factors that affect the market, and the 1-2-3 model gives you signals so that you'll know what to do for each condition. The market will have sharp rallies (up trends) during the next 10 to 15 years, as it did in 2003, and you could profit handsomely from them if you know how to read the signals. As this is being written, the market has been going up against the major trend, and the 1-2-3 model gave that signal in April 2003. You'll learn how to update the model once each week in less than a minute.

Once you understand the long-term bias of the market and what the market is currently doing, you'll know exactly which of the stock strategies presented in the next few chapters will be most profitable for you.

So let's look at why the market may be headed down over the long haul.

Debunking Conventional Wisdom: The 18-Year Megacycles of the Market

History shows us that stocks move in long-term cycles. Stock markets go up over long periods, and then they go down. On occasion they go way up. After that happens, they often go way down. As we write, we've completed the greatest up move in history, which ended in early 2000.

There are three types of markets: bull markets that go up and make long-term investors happy; flat markets that do nothing; and bear markets that go down and make investors unhappy. The most profitable bull market of the century occurred between 1982 and 2000. Had you invested $10,000 in a basket of major stocks back in 1982, it would have turned into $150,000 by 2000. And if you were aggressive and invested in tech stocks (the Nasdaq Composite Index, for example), $10,000 would have become $300,000. It was quite a ride. Many people made a lot of money.

Bull markets tend to end when everyone is in the market and convinced that it will go up forever. When people are so excited about the market that they are fully invested, there is no one left to buy and the bull market is essentially over. This occurred in early 2000.

The 1982–2000 bull market might be called a primary bull market because it lasted so long. In fact, it was the greatest bull market of the twentieth century. It had short-term corrections in 1987 and 1990 that might be called secondary bear markets, but the overall move from the 1982 lows to the highs of 2000 was a primary bull market.

According to market historian Michael Alexander, we have had many such markets, although not as extreme, during the last 200 years.[1]

Table 5.1 Primary Bull Markets

Bull Market	Approximate Dates	Real Yearly Returns[a]
Good feelings	1815–1835	9.6%
Railroad boom	1843–1853	12.5%
Civil War and beyond	1861–1881	11.5%
Pre–World War I	1896–1906	11.5%
Roaring Twenties	1921–1929	24.8%
Post–World War II boom	1949–1966	14.1%
High-tech period	1982–2000	14.8%

[a]These figures represent the change in value on the New York Stock Exchange (NYSE), not the Nasdaq, which is where the greatest gain was in the high-tech period.

Table 5.1 lists primary bull markets dating back to 1815. On average, these bull markets lasted about 15 years and earned investors about 13.2% per year. We were in bull markets for 103 years during the period from 1815 to 2000.

Unfortunately for people who believe in buying and holding stocks, primary bull markets tend to be followed by primary bear markets. These are major shakeouts, which tend to correct the excesses of the bull market. The United States is now in such a primary bear market, which began in early 2000.[2] Table 5.2 lists primary bear markets.

Table 5.2 Primary Bear Markets

Bear Market	Approximate Dates	Real Yearly Returns
Pre–War of 1812	1802–1815	2.8%
First Great Depression	1835–1843	−1.1%
Pre–Civil War era	1853–1861	−2.8%
Banking crisis era #1	1881–1896	3.7%
Banking crisis era #2	1906–1921	−1.9%
Second Great Depression	1929–1949	1.2%
Inflation era	1966–1982	−1.5%
War on terrorism	2000–present	?

DID YOU KNOW? ARE STOCKS REALLY SOUND?

As late as May 2002, the Nasdaq was already down about 70% from its lofty top. At that time, the total debt of all Nasdaq stocks (based upon data published by Nasdaq) was $2.3 trillion. If you take out the biggest companies (i.e., Microsoft and Intel), you have only $2 trillion worth of stocks with a debt of $2.3 trillion. That's a lot like buying a $20,000 car with a $23,000 loan. This is certainly an ugly picture for the rest of the market. It's no wonder that the Nasdaq stopped publishing this debt data in May 2002. Perhaps now you can understand why we're in a primary bear market. And, as of early 2004, we suspect that the valuations are much worse.

The average primary bear market lasts 18 years and shows a real return of 0.3% per year.[3] Thus, stocks may be facing a long period of decline ahead.

You might ask, "Will the market continue going down? What's going on?" The largest decline in the United States so far has been in the Nasdaq Composite Index (basically technology stocks), which went down more than 75% in the first three years of this bear market. During the boom years, from April 1994 through June 2000, all of the Nasdaq companies together earned $159.8 billion. From July 1, 2000, through September 31, 2001, those same companies lost $161 billion. In other words, seven years of profits were given up in just 15 months.[4]

How Far Down Will the Market Go?

Generally, the market will tell us when it has corrected sufficiently because it will go down to normal values (or below). And those normal values will be your guide to when to go back into the market to buy stocks for the long term. We can judge these normal values by two factors—the price-to-earnings ratio of stocks and the dividends that stocks pay.

Using Price-Earnings Ratios to Determine the Bottom

Many investors judge the value of a stock by the ratio of its price to its earnings. This is called the price-earnings (P/E) ratio. For example, a company that earns $1 per share and sells at $15 per share would have a price-to-earnings ratio of 15.

If you're not sure what the P/E ratio tells you, the best analogy is a house. If the *price* of a house you're considering is $100,000 and you're confident you can *earn* $10,000 a year in rent after expenses, that house is selling at a P/E ratio of 10 (10 × $10,000 = $100,000). If you could earn $10,000 a year on a $50,000 house, it would probably be a good deal because the house would be paid for in five years, and all the earnings after that would be gravy. A house with a $50,000 price that earns $10,000 a year in rent is at a P/E ratio of 5.

Clearly, paying 5 times earnings is better than paying 10. However, paying a million dollars or more for this house, which would mean you're paying over 100 times earnings, would not be a good deal.

Over the last century, the average price-earnings ratio of stocks was about 14.5, while over the last 50 years that ratio has been about 16.[5] At the peak of the bull market, the price-earnings ratio of stocks was in the mid-40s, nearly three times the average. This suggested that at least a 50% correction was warranted just to get to normal levels. But bear markets do not correct to normal levels. Instead, they correct to extremes.

Where will the market be one year from now? It could be up 50% to 100% from current levels or it could be down. It's much easier to answer where the market will be in 2010. The optimistic answer is that it won't be much higher than it is today.

Before this bear market is over, you will see rallies that will be sharp enough to bring people back in and then major collapses that will take away their wealth (if they don't follow the sound risk control principles described in Part IV of this book). The last years of the bear market will be the collapse stage. This is when people give up. Exhausted stockholders will dump their shares for whatever the market may bring.

Stocks in this phase will sink to the point where prices are of great value. The price-earnings ratio of top blue-chip companies will be way below the historical average, perhaps 6 to 10 times earnings. However, psychologically no one will want to buy, so everything will be a bargain. At the bottom of the 1974 market, the S&P 500 stocks sold at seven times earnings. At the bottom of the 1982 bear market, the S&P 500 stocks sold at eight times earnings.[6]

Bear markets usually drop to the point at which blue-chip stocks are a great value. For example, assuming that corporate earnings stop falling (a big assumption in a primary bear market), the Dow Jones Industrials would have to drop to 2700 and the S&P 500 would have to drop to 186 to reach a price earning ratio of 7, which would historically be an area of great value.[7]

Using Dividends to Determine the Bottom

Let's look at another measure of the value of stocks—dividends. Dividends really amount to the passive income you get when you own stocks. In the early days of the stock market, corporations had few restrictions on how they reported their earnings. As a result, the only believable earnings data were the dividends paid by the company. If a stock paid dividends every year and generally increased the amount of payout each year, investors could be certain that the earnings reported were real. Thus, high dividend payouts became a sign of a great company.

In the earnings growth era of the last bull market, few companies paid dividends. Even after three years of bear market correction, the Dow Jones Industrials only paid an average dividend of 2.36%. Based on historical data, the companies in that average will be at bargain prices when they pay a 5% to 6% dividend. This would suggest that the Dow Jones Industrial Average should correct to someplace between 3774 and 4543 before this bear market is over. Let's also look at the S&P 500, which currently pays a dividend yield of 1.77%. For that average to pay a 5% to 6% dividend, it would have to drop to a range between 262 to 315 before this bear market is over.

Using Market Psychology to Determine the Bottom

Major bear markets end when everyone is fearful, and we've seen no sign of that yet. When that occurs, the best stocks will be paying dividends of 5% to 6% because no one will want to own them. Pension

---

DID YOU KNOW? MARKET PSYCHOLOGY AT STOCK MARKET TOPS

By early 1999, the stock market had become a hot conversation topic at parties. Everyone was talking about investing. By the fall of 1999, even the bartenders at the hotel where we hold most of our seminars were becoming market experts. When one of them suggested that they try to get into a session, the other bartender responded, "We don't need that. I could teach that workshop." And a waiter at a posh local restaurant claimed that waiting on tables was something he did part-time. He had already made $176,000 in the stock market and was going to retire soon. (Ironically, if he really understood financial freedom, he probably could have retired already.)

Everyone was a stock expert because all you had to do to make money was buy technology stocks or technology mutual funds. Almost any technology stock would do. Magazines were full of advice from fund managers, especially those who had performed well. And the advice the average person got was: "Buy good stocks and mutual funds and never sell them. Have a long-term horizon, stay invested, and you'll get rich."

A primary bull market like the one that ended in 2000 drove prices to insane levels. By the time it reached the top, most people were participating just because of greed and excitement. They had no plan to guide them, and their decisions were generally irrational.

---

plans will tell their managers they cannot buy stocks because they are too risky. If you mention stocks to your friends, they'll think you are crazy to even think about anything so risky. You won't turn on the television and hear people saying you should buy stocks and hold on to them. And until you see this extreme fear in most people, the market bottom will be a long way off.

Pervasive fear is what will produce the extreme values seen at market bottoms. Few people will be willing to buy stocks, so stocks will pay great returns. Some stocks will even sell for much less than the current liquidation value of the company. Some will even sell for less than the cash they have on hand.

There are many ways the current bear market could play itself out. The best case for investors in such a dangerous time would be for the market to flatten out and remain that way for a long time. Gradually, corporate earnings would begin to rise until the market was strongly undervalued. Under these circumstances, the market probably would not fall as much. Perhaps the bear market would end with blue-chip price-earnings ratios in the 10 to 12 area. Perhaps something could happen to produce a dramatic shift in corporate earnings. These and numerous other events are certainly possible.

Before you become disheartened by all of this bear market talk, remember that this book is about safe strategies for investors and traders. Many of these strategies are designed specifically for bear markets and, if you use them appropriately with all of the risk control strategies given in Part IV, they will allow you to profit handsomely. So how can you determine what the market is doing right now?

Understanding What the Market Is Doing in Any Climate

Once you understand the market conditions that exist, you can find the appropriate strategies. The 1-2-3 model for stock market performance can guide your decisions in this regard. The model takes its name from the three major factors that affect the market: the valuation of the market, the interest rate climate as determined by the Federal Reserve, and the price of the market. Let's look at how these factors work together.

Green light—buy
Yellow light—hold
Red light—sell

The model tells you that if all three factors are in your favor, we're under a green light: time to buy. Under green light conditions (which have occurred 26% of the time since 1927), stocks have risen 19.5% a year.

If two out of the three factors are in your favor, it's a yellow light: hold. This has occurred 50% of the time, and stocks have returned 10.7% a year under yellow light conditions.

If two out of the three factors are against you, it's a red light: time to sell. Stocks have lost 9.7% a year under red light conditions.

If you had been armed with this knowledge, you would have known that the market was under red light conditions for the years 2000 through 2002. The stock market collapse would have come as no surprise to you.

Following are the three most important questions to answer about the stock market:

- Is the stock market too expensive?
- Are the Feds in the way?
- Is the market going up?

The answers to these questions cover nearly all of the bases that affect the markets, so let's look at each question closely.

Is the Market Too Expensive?

What's an expensive market? The clearest, time-tested measure of whether stocks are cheap or expensive is the price-earnings ratio.

Expensive is defined as the average P/E over the last 75 years. From 1927 until mid-2002, if you'd bought stocks when the P/E was above 17.0 (when stocks were expensive), you would have made only 0.3% a year. The P/E was above 17.0 about 36% of the time. However, if you'd bought when the P/E was below 17.0, which occurred 64% of the time, you would have made 12.4% a year in stocks. Right now, the P/E is significantly above 17.0—the market is expensive. This is shown in Figure 5.1.

Are the Feds in the Way?

The second factor in determining how likely stocks are to rise is the availability of money. When corporations can borrow money cheaply,

Figure 5.1 Are Stocks Expensive? Yes.

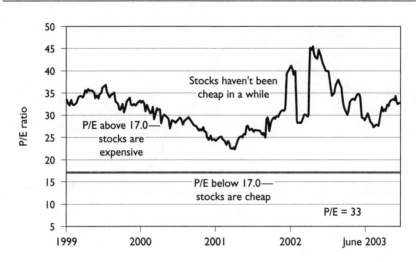

the stock market tends to rise. When money is expensive, the stock market tends to fall. And one of the best indicators of the current money situation is whether the Federal Reserve is tightening or lowering interest rates.[8] When the Federal Reserve is tightening money (i.e., raising interest rates), the stock market tends to fall. When the Federal Reserve is loosening money (i.e., lowering interest rates), the stock market tends to rise.

How do you know when the Feds are in the way? It's simple. It's the six-month period following a hike in the Fed funds rate. The Feds are out of the way either after the six-month period has ended or if the Fed cuts rates before the six-month period has ended. Figure 5.2 shows the pattern of discount rate changes over the last 5 years. And as you can see, as we write, the Feds are not in the way. Later in this chapter, we'll share how you can update these indicators.

Think about interest rates for a moment. If the bank starts paying 12% interest, what would people do? Chances are they'd move money out of the stock market and into the bank. Why take the risk of stocks when you can get great returns with much less risk? So it only makes sense that as interest rates rise, people sell stocks.

Figure 5.2 Are the Feds in the Way? No.

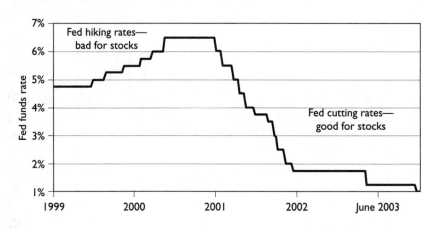

However, this is only a general rule and there are always exceptions to such rules. During much of 1999, the Federal Reserve was raising interest rates, but the market didn't start to fall until March of 2000. Similarly, when it became clear that we were in a bear market, the Federal Reserve started to lower interest rates. Since the fall of 2000 we have had 12 interest rate decreases, but the market continued to fall until the spring of 2003.

Let's take the flip side. As interest rates fall, people take their money out of the banks and bonds, to seek higher returns. Those funds usually end up in the stock market. Additionally, as interest rates fall, companies can take on projects with lower profit margins that wouldn't have been profitable under higher interest rates. This is the natural push and pull of markets.

So here is the evidence on how interest rates affect the market. Most of the time (71%), the Feds are not in the way—they're not raising rates. And when they stay out of the way, you make 10.9% a year in stocks. However, for the 29% of the time the Feds *are* in the way, it pays to be cautious. Stocks only returned 1.0% a year with the Feds in the way.

Is the Market Going Up?

No matter what the other market conditions might be, if prices are not going up, you'll have difficulty making money by buying stocks. For example, as of mid-October 2002, the Dow Jones Industrial Average had declined for seven straight months. The trend was clearly down, and people who were fighting the trend (or ignoring it by holding stocks) were losing money.

Conversely, when prices are going up, even when other conditions are terrible, you can still make money. For example, during the last six months of the great bull market from September 1999 through March 2000, market conditions were terrible. Prices were highly inflated with respect to earnings (i.e., with P/E ratios in the high 30s for blue-chip stocks), and the Federal Reserve had been increasing interest rates. Nevertheless, people were in a buying frenzy and many stocks doubled or tripled in that six-month period.

Market action is critical. The market is more complex than anyone can predict. No market model is complete without some indicator of market action. Sixty-seven percent of the time, the market is strengthening, based on our simple market action indicator. When this indicator said the market was strong, stocks returned 12.6% a year.

Thirty-three percent of the time, the market is weakening, based on this indicator. When this indicator said the market was weak, stocks lost 1.6% a year. The market momentum indicator is the 45-week average of stock prices. If the market is above its 45-week average, stock prices are strong. If the market is below its 45-week average, stock prices are weak.

As of this writing, January 2004, the market is strong. So even though the long-term cycle of the market points down, the model says stock prices are going up, and it has been correct since April 2003 when the signal was first given. The S&P 500 Index is above its 45-week average, as shown in Figure 5.3. Although we follow hundreds of indicators, all of them can basically fit into these three categories. If you know the answers to these three questions, and you use them, you will know whether to buy, sell, or hold.

Figure 5.3 Is the Stock Market Going Up? Yes.

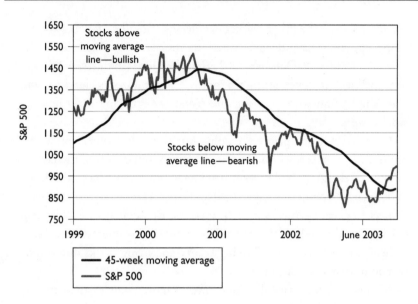

To sum up the 1-2-3 model, remember these three questions:

- Is the market too expensive?
- Are the Feds in the way?
- Is the market going up?

If you want to avoid the work of looking up the information, you can get the current status of the 1-2-3 model for free by subscribing to the

---

ACTION STEP

Determine what mode the 1-2-3 stock market model is in right now. Keep track of the information for yourself or subscribe to IITM's weekly e-mail newsletter *Tharp's Thoughts*.

Investment University e-mail at investmentu.com or Van Tharp's free e-mail at iitm.com.

Translating the Mound of Information into Profitable Strategies

Here is a summary of the critical information in this chapter.

Red Light: Sell

When the answer to two or three of the 1-2-3 model questions is yes, then stocks have returned −9.7% each year. Obviously, you need to get out of your long holdings in stocks. In addition, there are a number of things you can do to take advantage of this condition.

For example, you can use the bear market mutual fund strategy given in Chapter 7. You could also short-sell some of the highly overvalued stocks suggested in Chapter 7, but only if you understand all the risk control techniques given in Part IV of this book.

When stocks are really depressed, look for companies that fit the Graham's number criteria shown in Chapter 8. This strategy allows you to buy extremely undervalued stocks at fire sale prices. You can buy these stocks when the market has been in red light mode for at least six months and then sell off part of your holdings during the strong rallies that will inevitably occur. Using this strategy, you can probably acquire a large holding of excellent stocks for free, and we'll show you how to do that later in this book.

Finally, when the stock market is in red light mode, you should be looking at what else is going on in the markets. When the model signals red light mode, there are usually strong inflationary or deflationary pressures (see Chapter 9). With strong inflationary pressures, you might want to concentrate on gold, collectibles, or real estate (see Chapters 9 and 12). With deflationary pressures, you probably want to be headed toward cash, foreign currencies, or foreign bonds (see Chapter 10). The bottom line is to be aware of what else is going on in the market. Keep up with the other models given later in this book so you'll know where to put your money.

Yellow Light: Buy and Hold

When the answer to only one of the three questions is yes, then stocks have returned 10.7% each year. Here a rule of thumb is that you should subtract your age from 100. The resulting number is the percentage of your investment portfolio you might consider holding in stocks during yellow light mode. Thus, if you are 40 years old, you might consider holding 60% of your investment portfolio in stocks. However, we recommend that these be either highly undervalued stocks or highly efficient stocks, based on the strategies given in this book.

When the market starts to move into yellow light mode, be very cautious if stocks are still expensive. When stocks are expensive, yellow

---

KEY IDEAS

➤ We are in a primary bear market that started in 2000 and could easily last until 2018.

➤ You'll know when this bear market has played out because price-earnings ratios of the blue-chip stocks will be in the single-digit range, and dividend yields will be at least 5%. Everyone will be fearful, and no one will want to own stocks.

➤ Long-term buy-and-hold strategies will generally not work in the current climate.

➤ See Chapter 7 for bear market strategies and Chapter 8 for how to buy very undervalued stocks.

➤ The 1-2-3 model will tell you when to be aggressive in stocks, when to stick your toes into the stock market, and when to employ bear market strategies. Pay close attention to the guidelines for what to do in each of the three market conditions—red light, yellow light, and green light.

➤ Specific stock market strategies are given in the next three chapters.

light mode probably just represents a bear market rally. It could change back to red light mode very quickly or it might last six months to a year or two. This might be the time to sell some of the highly undervalued stocks that you bought selectively in red light mode, especially if you have a 70% to 100% profit. When your profit is that high, you can sell two-thirds to one-half of your stock holding, knowing that the rest of your stock can be held risk free for the long term (because you will have already gotten your money back from what you sold). See Chapter 8 for specific details on how to do this.

Green Light: Strong Buy

When the answer to all three questions of the 1-2-3 model is no, then stocks have returned +19.5% each year. At this point, you probably will have accumulated a great deal of stock through the Graham's number technique (as described in Chapter 8). You can now use the rest of your

---

ACTION STEPS

➤ Determine what mode the stock market is currently in by keeping up with the status of the 1-2-3 model provided.

➤ If we are in green light mode, read the strategies in Chapter 6 and Chapter 8. Learn the risk control methods in Part IV of this book, and then determine if you want to use any of these strategies.

➤ If we are in yellow light mode, the same advice works. Subtract your age from 100 and use the resulting number to determine the percentage of your investment portfolio that should be in stocks.

➤ If we are in red light mode, read the strategies in Chapter 7 and be sure to understand how to buy undervalued stocks based upon Graham's number technique, explained in Chapter 8. Also read about risk control in Part IV of this book and determine if you want to use any of these strategies.

funds to purchase highly efficient stocks, making sure that you follow the risk control techniques given in Part IV of this book. Stocks have returned 19.5% per year just by buying and holding. You should be able to do even better if you follow the risk control techniques we provide to guide your investing.

Notes

1. Michael Alexander, *Stock Cycles* (Lincoln, Neb.: I-universe Press, 2000).
2. The decline in the stock market during 2000–2003 was a worldwide phenomenon. As of March 2003, Japan's Nikkei Index was flirting with 20-year lows. Germany's DAX Index was down 73% since 2000 and 27% in the first three months of 2003. Most Asian countries have been in a bear market since 1997, although they have had an aggressive recovery in 2003. And even Switzerland's stock market is down 55% since 2000.
3. Real returns are adjusted for inflation. The overall real return for stocks since 1802 is 6.8%, according to Alexander. Two-thirds of that return comes from dividends.
4. This information came from Martin Weiss' book, *Crash Profits* (Hoboken, N.J.: Wiley, 2003).
5. Optimists now argue that the P/E ratio norm is 17 because that is where the trend line is currently.
6. Both of these bear markets were part of the inflation era primary bear market. The actual bottom, with prices adjusted for the loss in value of the purchasing power of the dollar, occurred in 1982.
7. Earnings are generally overstated with today's generally accepted accounting practices.
8. The Federal Reserve is the central bank of the United States. It has the power to set interest rates, print money, and control what other banks do. Contrary to popular belief, however, the Federal Reserve is *not* a government agency and is instead privately owned.

e will introduce you to a strategy that can help you make money
e of all of this.

ou haven't done so already, read the introductory quote. Let's
re the stock market industry of Charles Merrill's time with the
market industry today. The markets seem to be facing a similar
, but where are the Charles Merrills of today?

rles Merrill urged his customers to sell in the year before the
market crash of 1929. In the months before the crash he pleaded
resident Coolidge to speak out against speculation in stocks, and
same time he liquidated his firm's stock portfolio. Merrill then
rred all his brokerage clients and employees to E. A. Pierce and
nto semiretirement.

cks ran up much higher in 2000 than they ever did in 1929. But
u remember the head of a stock brokerage firm or the head of a
l fund company advising his customers to sell? No. Instead, they
ecommending that you buy and hold. In fact, analysts employed
large brokerage firms were urging customers to buy dangerously
lued stocks.

rles Merrill's advice to get out of stocks and use the proceeds to
f debts may be the right advice today. But somewhere along the
e people in charge of looking out for your money became more
ned about keeping your dollars than giving you the right advice.
interesting. If the big firms gave you the right advice, chances are
ave more wealth today, and you'd never move your money away
hem. However, with the wrong advice—where the "pros" you
told you not to sell under any circumstances—you now have less
and even less trust.

re is a serious breakdown in the business of managing your
today. The chain of accountability leads nowhere. The result for
dividual investors could be financial ruin. To show what's wrong,
nsider the case of mutual funds.

Dirty Little Secrets" About Mutual Funds

juggerud has worked in both the mutual fund industry as a vice
nt in charge of research, trading, and accounting, and in the

And
in sp
If
comp
stock
futur
Cl
stock
with
at the
trans
went
St
can y
mutu
were
by the
overv
Ch
pay o
way, t
conce
It's
you'd
from
truste
mone
Th
mone
most
let's c

THE COMING N FUND CRISIS: S OUT OF DANGI INTO PROFITS

"Now is the time to get out of debt. We do no
securities indiscriminately, but we do advis
of present high [stock] prices and put your o
order."

—CHARLES MERRILL, IN A LE

If the market does go down dramatically
mutual fund industry is in serious diffic
money in a mutual fund, it's possible that
years from now.

The purpose of this chapter is to help y
mutual fund problem so that you don't get
chapter will introduce you to the "dirty lit
funds. You'll go behind the scenes and learn
You learn about the restrictions on your fu
why it's very difficult for him or her to out
also learn why most mutual funds will lose
longed bear market decline.

Where there is a potential crisis, there is
you'll also learn about some advantages tha
portfolio manager that will help you outper

The "

Steve
presid

CHAPTER 6

THE COMING MUTUAL FUND CRISIS: STEERING OUT OF DANGER AND INTO PROFITS

> *"Now is the time to get out of debt. We do not urge that you sell securities indiscriminately, but we do advise that you take advantage of present high [stock] prices and put your own financial house in order."*
>
> —CHARLES MERRILL, IN A LETTER TO HIS CUSTOMERS
> BEFORE THE 1929 CRASH

If the market does go down dramatically over the next 15 years, the mutual fund industry is in serious difficulty. If you currently have money in a mutual fund, it's possible that your fund will not exist 15 years from now.

The purpose of this chapter is to help you understand the current mutual fund problem so that you don't get caught in a stampede. This chapter will introduce you to the "dirty little secrets" of most mutual funds. You'll go behind the scenes and learn how mutual funds operate. You learn about the restrictions on your fund's portfolio manager and why it's very difficult for him or her to outperform the market. You'll also learn why most mutual funds will lose a lot of money during a prolonged bear market decline.

Where there is a potential crisis, there is also opportunity. As a result, you'll also learn about some advantages that you have over your fund's portfolio manager that will help you outperform him or her every year.

And we will introduce you to a strategy that can help you make money in spite of all of this.

If you haven't done so already, read the introductory quote. Let's compare the stock market industry of Charles Merrill's time with the stock market industry today. The markets seem to be facing a similar future, but where are the Charles Merrills of today?

Charles Merrill urged his customers to sell in the year before the stock market crash of 1929. In the months before the crash he pleaded with President Coolidge to speak out against speculation in stocks, and at the same time he liquidated his firm's stock portfolio. Merrill then transferred all his brokerage clients and employees to E. A. Pierce and went into semiretirement.

Stocks ran up much higher in 2000 than they ever did in 1929. But can you remember the head of a stock brokerage firm or the head of a mutual fund company advising his customers to sell? No. Instead, they were recommending that you buy and hold. In fact, analysts employed by the large brokerage firms were urging customers to buy dangerously overvalued stocks.

Charles Merrill's advice to get out of stocks and use the proceeds to pay off debts may be the right advice today. But somewhere along the way, the people in charge of looking out for your money became more concerned about keeping your dollars than giving you the right advice.

It's interesting. If the big firms gave you the right advice, chances are you'd have more wealth today, and you'd never move your money away from them. However, with the wrong advice—where the "pros" you trusted told you not to sell under any circumstances—you now have less money and even less trust.

There is a serious breakdown in the business of managing your money today. The chain of accountability leads nowhere. The result for most individual investors could be financial ruin. To show what's wrong, let's consider the case of mutual funds.

The "Dirty Little Secrets" About Mutual Funds

Steve Sjuggerud has worked in both the mutual fund industry as a vice president in charge of research, trading, and accounting, and in the hedge fund industry as a fund manager. He knows how fund managers think. Van Tharp has been a coach for both portfolio managers and hedge fund managers. He also knows how they think. The secrets to which you are about to be exposed came from the background of these two authors.[1]

Beating a Benchmark

Mutual funds make great sense in theory. They take your money, combine it with other people's money, and invest it on your behalf. Even with a $2,000 investment in a mutual fund, you might own a small fraction of every S&P 500 stock. So far, so good. But instead of investing it to make you a profit, as you might expect, your fund manager has a different objective—to keep his high-paying job. You might think that his job would be to make you a profit. That way the fund can keep earning fees off your money. Actually, your mutual fund manager's job is not to make you a profit, but to beat a benchmark.

His benchmark is usually an index of stocks. Let's say that the benchmark is the Nasdaq Biotechnology Index, for example, and that the index is down 75%. If the fund manager loses only 70% of your money, he doesn't get fired. On the contrary, he gets a huge bonus because he outperformed his benchmark. Meanwhile, your nest egg has gone up in smoke.

And how does your mutual fund manager keep his high-paying job? By holding a portfolio that is almost identical to his benchmark index— so he'll never do particularly well or particularly poorly. We know this is what goes on, because we've seen it firsthand.

Your Fund Will Perform Worse Than the Benchmark— Almost Guaranteed

The objective of trying to beat a benchmark almost guarantees that your fund will not meet its objective. The more conservative your manager is, the more he will hold benchmark stocks. And the closer your fund's portfolio is to the benchmark, the less likely your fund manager is going to outperform the benchmark. You see, your mutual fund will collect fees from you whether it performs well or not. Those fees are based upon a percentage of the money under management—usually 1% to 2%. Thus, a conservative manager will probably underperform his benchmark indexes by 1% to 2%. So if the S&P 500 goes down 20% in a year, the average mutual fund will probably be down 21% to 22%. And, of course, the difference is the fees that you pay.

Most people believe that the solution to this problem is to buy an index mutual fund—one that mimics the index and charges minimal fees. Most large mutual fund families have such a fund. However, as you'll learn later in this chapter, Ken Long may have an even better solution. Please note, if you are just starting out and building your nest egg through an automatic investment plan as mentioned earlier in the book, this strategy is fine to stick with until your nest egg reaches about $5,000 to $10,000 because it is teaching you how to save.

A Vicious Downward Spiral

The net result for you in the long run is even more serious. Microsoft is a major component of all three major stock market indexes—the Dow, the S&P 500, and the Nasdaq Composite—so typical fund managers hold a lot of Microsoft shares. As of this writing, Microsoft might just be one of the worst buys in the market (trading at eight times sales).[2] But your fund manager doesn't care; he owns a lot of it because it is a huge stock in his benchmark index.

A fall in a major stock like Microsoft could lead to a vicious downward spiral in the indexes. When individual investors get tired of poor performance, they will start to sell their mutual funds. This selling will drive down shares of Microsoft even further, as funds sell the stock to meet shareholder liquidations.

This potential panic from shareholder liquidations will affect not just Microsoft, but all of the big stocks that make up the major indexes. This type of price action started to occur in the fall of 2002, but it was nowhere near a full scale panic—at least, not yet.

Your Fund Must Be Fully Invested

During much of 2002, we had the opportunity to speak to mutual fund managers throughout Asia, Europe, and North America about controlling risk and preventing losses in their portfolios. Most of them just weren't interested. They believed that if they moved to cash instead of staying fully invested they would miss the next big move up and thus fail to outperform other funds. By charter they had to stay fully invested at all times anyway, and their belief justified what they had to do. Furthermore, to stay fully invested they had to own the big stocks that made up their benchmark indexes. In essence, if the market were crashing, these fund managers would have to sit back and watch you lose your money.

How did we reach the point where the people who are supposed to be making you money sit aside and watch you lose it? If we are in a huge primary bear market, do you think these funds will survive with this philosophy? Although this is working in the current rally that started in March 2003, we want you to be aware of the alternatives, so that you can understand what is going on and make informed decisions when the market turns. Ultimately, you have to be responsible for your own investment decisions.

Using Mutual Funds to Your Advantage

You now know that mutual funds can be dangerous when the market has a downward bias. But where there is a big risk, there is also usually a big opportunity. Ken Long may have found that opportunity.

Ken is a systems developer for the U.S. Army. He has a master's degree in systems development, and he's used that skill with great success in developing ways to outfox the market.

Ken's system has a few competitive advantages over fund managers. First, mutual fund managers have to be fully invested in the market, whereas the average investor can have all of his or her funds in cash in an interest bearing account. Second, because mutual fund managers must be fully invested and they typically have large portfolios, it takes them a long time to move their money into or out of a stock without moving stock prices. The average investor doesn't have any size limitations and can go where the big boys want to go almost immediately.

Ken determines where the money is flowing, getting a jump on the fund managers, and he keeps it there until there is a better idea. Again,

Table 6.1 The Tortoise Beats the Market Every Year[a]

Year	S&P 500	Tortoise
1999	20.4%	98.1%
2000	−9.8%	26.6%
2001	−12.1%	9.9%
2002	−23.4%	−8.6%[b]
2003	22.2%	22.7%

[a]The tortoise system applied to the Strong Funds model.

[b]The Strong family doesn't have a gold fund, but fund families with a gold fund were positive for 2002.

Data from tortoiseadvisors.com

this is a huge advantage for you. Ultimately, Ken is attempting to catch a good portion of the significant upswings in the market while avoiding most of the downturns. So far, he has consistently outperformed the best-performing mutual funds and their index benchmarks. Ken's strategy is ideal for a green light or yellow light mode on the stock market model.

The mutual fund crisis will only get worse. Most funds will continue to underperform their indexes, and many will go out of business. Yet Ken Long's mutual strategy is a real bright spot. His simple system uses our advantage of being small investors to beat the big funds at their own game. The track record of Ken's system is given in Table 6.1.

Ken has prepared a special report for readers of this book that explains his fund switching strategy and how to implement it. It's available for free at iitm.com. Please read it and consider if it's right for you.

ACTION STEPS

➤ Read your quarterly statements and your monthly mutual fund returns, don't just file them. Know what your money is doing. Is it outperforming the market?

➤ Contact iitm.com and take a look at Ken Long's special report.

KEY IDEAS

➤ If the stock market goes down dramatically over the next 15 years, your mutual fund may go out of business.

➤ Your mutual fund's portfolio manager may not always be working in your favor and making money for you. His primary concern is to outperform a benchmark index to keep his job, and he has restrictions as to what he can and cannot do.

➤ Most mutual funds fail to outperform their benchmarks because (1) they typically own the index and they charge you fees to do so; (2) they must stay fully invested in down markets; and (3) they don't understand the basic risk control practices necessary for survival.

➤ If people start to liquidate their mutual funds, the major stocks in the indexes will go down the most because your fund manager will be selling those stocks.

➤ You can use mutual funds to your advantage with Ken Long's strategy. If you capture most of the major up moves in the market and avoid the major down moves, you can outperform the S&P 500 Index and most mutual funds.

Hedge Funds: A Pure Passive Investment

Where can you find a fund that averages 12% a year for 10 years with 95% positive months? Or one that has less statistical risk than long-term government bond funds and averages 10% a year? What about funds that have little or no correlation to the stock market, but just keep on making their investors smile?

These funds exist, but most people can't find them because they are private funds. They do not advertise. In fact, they cannot advertise. They limit the number of investors who can join. They have high minimum investments and often are closed to new investors. There may be risks that are not apparent in the track record. They often have lockup periods (a length of time during which you cannot withdraw your

ACTION STEPS

➤ Go to iitm.com and get the January/February 2004 interview from *Market Mastery*, "What Every Investor Needs to Know About Hedge Funds: An Interview with John Mauldin." This is available as a free e-book.

➤ If you meet the qualifications of an accredited investor, you can check out the excellent online resources for hedge funds listed below.

➤ Be sure to do your due diligence on any fund you become interested in because there is opportunity for fraud or for unanticipated risks.

Consult these sites for more information on hedge funds:

➤ hedgefund.net has information on more than 1,000 hedge funds. You have to be an accredited investor to register.

➤ Hedge Fund Association (thehfa.org) is an industry association.

➤ hedgeworld.com offers a daily newsletter on hedge funds.

➤ A good academic site with a lot of independent research papers on hedge funds is cisdm.som.umass.edu, which is the University of Massachusetts, Amherst, Center for International Securities and Derivatives Markets.

➤ The Alternative Investment Management Association has some good information but is more valuable for its links to other sites: aima.org.

➤ The contributing author to our e-book on hedge funds, John Mauldin, has a website, accreditedinvestor.ws, where you can subscribe to his free letter and analysis on hedge funds if you qualify. You can get his free weekly letter on economics and investing by going to johnmauldin.com.

funds) of one year or more. Despite these obstacles, savvy investors are flocking to these funds in an effort to keep their investment portfolios moving upward. Welcome to the world of hedge funds.

The best investors and traders tend to gravitate toward managing hedge funds. One reason is that they get paid more for their great performance. They usually charge management fees of 1% to 2% plus 20% or more of the profits they generate. But wouldn't you pay that for someone who could consistently make you 20% or more after their fees? Of course! *Business Week* (July 14, 2003) ran a piece on the compensation of the highest paid hedge fund managers. The yearly compensation of the top five ranged from $600 million for the highest paid to an average of over $225 million for numbers two through five. In addition, a sizeable chunk of the money in their respective funds probably belongs to those managers.

Another reason top traders run hedge funds as opposed to mutual funds is that hedge funds are not regulated under the Securities Act of 1933 or the Investment Companies Act of 1940. As a result, they can do many things that the government prohibits under those acts. For example, they can go short during bear market conditions, which most

---

KEY IDEAS

➤ Hedge funds are an excellent way to earn higher returns than stocks with less risk than the stock market over the long run, regardless of what happens in the markets.

➤ There are a wide variety of hedge fund styles with varying levels of risk. Make sure you do plenty of due diligence before making a hedge fund investment.

➤ Top traders and investors run hedge funds because of the high monetary rewards they receive. Even if you aren't considering a hedge fund investment in the near future, it still makes sense to understand what these traders are doing.

mutual funds cannot do. They can be mostly cash, and they can invest in what are considered high-risk speculations like options and futures. Ironically, you can do all of these things yourself. But unless you have a high net worth, you are not considered sophisticated enough to hire a professional manager to do it for you.

Because hedge funds are not as tightly regulated as mutual funds, it's possible for someone to take advantage of you through a hedge fund. However, fraud is rare. If you do your due diligence, making sure the fund is audited by an independent party and that another party holds your funds while the hedge fund trades them, then you should be fine.

As we mentioned earlier, only high-net-worth investors (also called "accredited investors") are allowed to participate in hedge funds. As of this writing, early 2004, you cannot invest in these funds unless you have a minimum net worth of a million dollars or an annual income of $200,000 ($300,000 for married couples with two incomes) for the last two years and a reasonable expectation of the same income for the current year. So even if you do not yet qualify to put money with a hedge fund, if you are a serious student of investing you should have a working knowledge of hedge funds. This subject is beyond the scope of our book, so we've made a free e-book entitled *What Every Investor Needs to Know About Hedge Funds* available to our readers. Just go to iitm.com or call 919-852-3994 for further information.

Notes

1. Also see "An Interview with Steven O'Keefe," *Market Mastery*, January 2003. O'Keefe describes his experiences as both an analyst and a portfolio manager.
2. This really means that Microsoft makes about $3.50 per share in sales and sells for more than $28 per share. If you, as a shareholder, got every penny of sales Microsoft got, it would still take you eight years to get your money back, assuming that sales didn't increase.

CHAPTER 7

STRATEGIES FOR GREAT PROFITS IN BAD TIMES

*"If you manage your money carefully, you can make similar
percentage profits in bear markets in shorter time with no more, and
perhaps even less, risk than on the upside in bull markets."*
—VIC SPERANDEO

L et's say the stock market is down heavily. Everyone you know is complaining, but you're feeling pretty good because your account is up. In fact, the more the market goes down, the more your account goes up. You feel like a genius, but your strategy is really pretty simple. Whenever the stock market barometer, our 1-2-3 model, switches to red light mode, you start using your two bear market strategies. These strategies take very little time, and they make money every week when the market is going down.

The first strategy involves investing in mutual funds that profit when the market goes down. This will require you to spend about 30 minutes each weekend looking at the market. The second strategy involves finding overvalued stocks, borrowing them from someone else (a strategy called *short selling*), and then selling them. You can expect these stocks to fall considerably during a bear market, so you should be able to buy them back when the price is much lower.

Strategy 1: Using Bear Market Mutual Funds for Profit

The bear market mutual fund strategy was developed to meet three objectives. First, it is designed to outperform the major averages during a bear market. This alone is a tall order, since most portfolio managers fail to do so. However, history has shown that the stock market has an average increase of 6.8% per year in real returns (i.e., adjusted for inflation) over the last 200 years. That number might be closer to 9% if you consider just the last 50 years, which include the huge 1982–2000 bull market. The second goal is not only to outperform the averages, but to make at least 10% per year, even in down years. Third, the strategy must generalize across instruments (such as exchange traded funds, or ETFs), but can be usable in a retirement fund.

In the last chapter, you learned about mutual funds. These are fine when the market is going up. But what about when the market is going down? We don't just want to outperform the market averages, we want to continue to make money.

According to billionaire investor Warren Buffett, "You don't have to do extraordinary things to get extraordinary results." Sometimes, simplicity works really well. With that in mind, here is a simple solution to profiting when the 1-2-3 model is in red light mode: simply invest in funds that make money when the market goes down. Since you are buying mutual funds, this strategy can be used by many retirement funds. And the strategy is based on weekly changes in the major averages.

Table 7.1 shows the average weekly changes in the major stock market averages from 1998 through 2002. It includes two very bullish years, two very bearish years, and one of the most volatile years in the history of the stock market (2000). These changes were converted to positive numbers (absolute values) and then a mean and standard deviation[1] were calculated. As you can see, the average weekly change in the Dow and S&P 500 is about 2%. In the Nasdaq, the average weekly change is just under 4%.

The bear market strategy will focus on the S&P 500—the benchmark standard of most mutual funds. If there is a long-term decline in the stock market over the next 15 years, then most mutual funds may cease to exist before the decline ends. These funds will be selling the

Table 7.1 Weekly Average Absolute Changes in the Major Indexes for 1998 Through 2002

Year	Dow 30	S&P 500	Nasdaq
1998	2.05%±1.48	2.12%±1.47	2.84%±2.14
1999	1.89%±1.58	2.04%±1.57	2.86%±2.02
2000	2.27%±1.74	2.46%±1.95	5.35%±4.52
2001	2.35%±2.34	2.27%±2.03	4.61%±3.19
2002	2.13%±1.73	2.17%±1.74	3.19%±2.07
Averages	2.14%±1.77	2.21%±1.75	3.77%±2.8

S&P 500 as people cash out, so you can expect some huge gains by going against the S&P 500 as this scenario plays out.

Both Rydex and Profunds have a set of funds that perform inversely versus the major stock indexes. That is, when the index goes down, the fund goes up in value. However, the strategy described fits only the inverse S&P 500 funds with no leverage and should not be used with the double-leveraged funds (i.e., funds that go up twice as fast as the market goes down). Table 7.2 shows the major funds for the Rydex family. You can open an account directly at Rydex for a $25,000 minimum. Contact them at rydexfunds.com or by calling 800-820-0888. You can also trade the fund through Schwab or most other discount brokers for as little as $2,500 per investment. Most fund families also allow you to open IRA accounts for $2,000.

Table 7.2 Rydex Bear Funds

Fund	Index Traded	Symbol	Price per share on 2/26/03
Arktos	Inverse of Nasdaq 100	RYAIX	$25.79
Ursa	Inverse of S&P 500	RYURX	$9.18
Juno	Inverse of 30-Year Bond	RYJUX	$20.67
Tempest	2 × Inverse of S&P 500	RYTPX	$48.44
Venture	2 × Inverse of Nasdaq 100	RYVNX	$27.45

Table 7.3 Profunds Inverse Market Funds

Fund	Index Traded	Symbol	Price per share on 2/26/03
Short OTC	Inverse of Nasdaq 100	SOPIX	$19.93
Bear	Inverse of S&P 500	BRPIX	$32.86
Rising Rates	Inverse of 30-Year Bond	RRPIX	$23.22
Short Small Cap	Inverse of Russell 2000	SHPIX	$22.49
Ultra Bear	2 × Inverse of S&P 500	URPIX	$21.60
Ultra Short	2 × Inverse of Nasdaq 100	USPIX	$18.61

Funds that have this quality include the Profunds Bear Fund (BRPIX) and the Rydex Ursa Fund (RYURX). A third possibility would be to short the Spiders (SPY), an exchange-traded fund that mimics the S&P 500.[2] However, you would not be able to do this in many retirement accounts.

The second fund family is the Profunds family. It also has a large selection of bear index funds. These are shown in Table 7.3. You can open an account with Profunds by calling 888-PRO-FNDS or going to its website at profunds.com. The minimum investment for individual investors managing their own accounts is $15,000. Once again, you can do it for much less through a discount broker, and the fund family will allow you to open an IRA account for much less. Furthermore, Profunds will allow you to exit funds several times during the day rather than just at the close.

Another possibility is to use the Prudent Bear Fund, which sells overvalued stocks, somewhat like our second strategy. This fund has averaged gains of 30% per year in bear markets (i.e., during the red light mode).

Bear Market Mutual Fund Strategy

The bear market mutual fund strategy will require that criteria be met at several stages to successfully manage such funds.

Setup Requirements

These circumstances indicate you should get ready to invest.

- The 1-2-3 model must be in the red light (sell) mode. This criterion will protect you from being in a bear market strategy when the market has an upward bias.
- The S&P 500 Index must be lower than it was five weeks previously (even if it is down only 1 point). This criterion makes you wait until the market is heading in your direction (down), even if this is only by a small amount.

Entry Rules

These circumstances indicate entering the market now. Make your entry calculations any time after Friday's closing prices are available. Note that there are three investment levels for this strategy based on your account equity: 0%, 25%, and 50%. We recommend that you allocate no more than 50% of your equity to this strategy.

- Make sure that both setup requirements from the previous section have been satisfied. If not, do nothing for a week. If those requirements are met, go to the next step.
- Calculate the percentage change in the S&P 500 from the previous Friday's close versus the most recent Friday's close. If the change is positive, do nothing and restart the process with the setup requirements on the following Friday. If it is negative, continue to the next step.
- If the percentage drop is greater than or equal to 5%, invest 50% of your account equity in the bear fund (selected from Table 7.2 or Table 7.3) on Monday. Do not allocate more than 50% of your account equity to this strategy.
- If the percentage drop is greater than 2.5%, but less than 5%, invest 25% of your account equity in the bear fund (selected from Table 7.2 or Table 7.3) on Monday.
- If the percentage drop is greater than 0% but less than 2.5%, do nothing on Monday. You may choose an interim entry if the

S&P 500 Index price continues to drop on any of the next three trading days, however. If the percentage drop for the S&P 500 reaches 2.5% or greater on Monday, Tuesday, or Wednesday (as compared to the Friday closing price from the previous week), invest 25% of your account equity in the bear fund (selected from Table 7.2 or Table 7.3) on the following trading day.

Note that if you only have 25% of your account equity invested in this strategy, you can repeat the setup and entry steps every Friday until you have invested a second increment of 25%.

Exit Rules
These indicators tell you when to get out.

- Calculate the percentage change in the S&P 500 from the previous Friday's close versus the most recent Friday's close. If the change is negative, enjoy the move that is in your favor and do nothing. If the change is positive, continue to the next step.
- If the percentage increase is less than 3%, hold your current position.
- If the percentage increase is greater than 3%, reduce your position according to the following ratio: for every 3% increase in the S&P 500, sell bear mutual fund shares equal to 10% of your account equity.
- With this ratio, if you are fully invested in this strategy (at an amount equal to 50% of your account equity), it would require five increases of 3% to fully exit your position. Note that if there is a 6% increase in a given week, you should sell an amount equal to 20% of your account equity.
- A second exit signal is given any time the S&P 500 closes on Friday at a price higher than it closed five weeks ago. If this happens, exit the balance of your position.
- There is one other time to sell your entire position—when the original CBOE Volatility Index (the symbol is VXO in most quote packages) gets above 50. This index measures how nervous the average investor is, and at extreme peaks it signals major changes

in the market. The VXO has exceeded 50 only seven times since 1997.

Using these rules, this strategy did not give a signal until September 5, 2000. If you had purchased a mutual fund that goes up when the S&P 500 goes down on that date and just held it, you would have had to endure the following drops in your account value:

- 2001 (11.8%)
- Sept.–Oct. 2001 (12.59%)
- July–Aug. 2002 (10.6%)
- Oct.–Nov. 2002 (15.99%)
- March–Aug. 2003 (20.1%)

This is how the exit strategy works. If the exit criteria had been a 15% increase from the highest close, you would not have exited the position until late 2002. You'd have been able to hold your position for nearly two years. However, you would also give back 15% when you exited. Thus, once again, the exit for this strategy will scale out of positions gradually so that you are fully out when the market is up 15%. So, you would have made 50% despite this 15% move against you.

Asset Allocation Rules
These rules explain how much to invest.

- Consider using a maximum of 50% of your account equity for this strategy. This leaves the remaining capital for other appropriate strategies.
- Invest in 25% increments of account equity as described previously in "Setup Requirements." Possible account allocations are 0%, 25%, and 50% for entry into this strategy.
- You can reduce your position in 10% increments according to our exit rules. Because bear markets tend to move down in quick spurts, this strategy positions us to enter quickly and then exit more deliberately to let our profits run.

- Note that at some point in executing this strategy, you may have reduced your position by 10% when you receive a new entry signal to add 25% back into the position. If this happens, just use common sense to add to your position in an increment that makes sense but that does not allow your total position to exceed 50% of your account equity.

Example of How to Apply This Strategy

- *Week 1:* S&P 500 falls 3.23% on the week. You would invest 25% of our portfolio in BRPIX. If you have a $50,000 portfolio, you invest $12,500 in BRPIX.
- *Week 2:* S&P 500 falls 2.64% the next week. Invest an additional 25% in BRPIX. At this point, you'd be fully invested.
- *Week 3:* S&P 500 falls 5.12% the following week. You do nothing because you are fully invested. Again, remember that fully invested is only 50% of your total portfolio.
- *Weeks 4–7:* The market keeps falling (about 6%) for three more weeks and then gains 1.3%. That gain is not enough for you to exit any of your positions but it puts you on alert.
- *Week 8:* The next week the S&P 500 gains 3.1%, so you'd now sell a portion of your position in BRPIX equal to 10% of your account equity. At this point, another weekly decline would probably trigger your sell-all signal.
- *Week 9:* The S&P 500 loses 5.1%. Since the market is still down over the last five weeks, this is a signal to become fully invested again. So, you add back to the position the 10% of account equity that you sold in week 8.

Precautions on Using the Strategy

This strategy should be used only when the 1-2-3 model signals red light mode. You never know what the future will bring, and you won't necessarily have huge bear markets every year in the future. However, using it in red light mode should protect you fairly well.

Second, this strategy can be very risky if you don't follow some of the key guidelines for entry, for how much to invest, and for getting out.

Strategy 2: Profiting from Falls in Individual Stocks

Imagine that everyone has been so excited about a stock that they've bid the price up to $150. It's now selling at 25 times its annual sales. That means that if every penny of sales the company made (*sales* not profit!) was given to you as a shareholder, it would still take you 25 years to get your money back.[3] And, yes, companies do get valued that highly.

What if you could sell a stock like that when it got that high, only to watch it plunge over the next six months, dropping at least 5% every week? Eventually, it starts to sell at $5 per share, or about eight times its annual earnings. You ride the stock down to $5 and then buy it back. Thus, you bought the stock for $5 and sold it for $150—that's a profit of $145 per share—only you did it in the reverse order. You sold it while it was high and then you bought it back later when the price was low. Can you do this? Yes, you can. It's called short-selling. And you are allowed to do it simply by borrowing the stock from your broker, selling the borrowed stock, and then buying it back later.

For example, let's say that you think 3M (symbol: MMM) is expensive at $82 per share. As a result, you ask your broker to sell MMM short. This means your broker will borrow the shares from another account and allow you to sell that borrowed stock. You'll receive the money right now—$82 per share. However, you will also have a debt to the broker that you borrowed the stock from. That is, you'll owe the broker X shares of MMM. Furthermore, one day, you'll have to buy it back. If MMM goes down to $42 per share, you can buy it back at that price. That means you basically bought it for $42 per share and sold it for $82 for a $40 per share profit. You simply did it in the reverse order—you sold it before you bought it.

The Dangers of Selling Short

Selling short can be tricky. First, regulators want to make certain that short-sellers are not responsible for large drops in the market. As a result, you are allowed to short stocks only on an uptick. That means that if MMM is selling for $82 per share, you cannot sell short as it drops to $81.95 per share. You can sell short only when the price goes

- You can only short on an uptick (i.e., when the price is going up), so you might not get as good a price as you'd like.
- You have an unlimited downside and a limited profit if you just sell short and hold. Your debt for the borrowed shares continues to increase if the stock goes up.
- You are borrowing stock, so you must pay out all dividends that come due on the stock you borrowed.
- Market rallies, in a bear market decline, can be violent.

up. For example, you could sell short at $82.05 on an uptick. When you do that, there is no way your sale can be said to have driven the market down.

There is some real danger in putting in a short-sale order. Suppose MMM is selling at $82 per share and you believe the stock is weak. Let's say you are right and the stock starts dropping. It falls to $81.75, to $81.47, to $81.29, and so, on until it hits $77.32. At that price, it shows an uptick to $77.34. You would be selling it at $77.34, not at the $82 price where you initially wanted to sell. Of course, you could put a limit order on it to sell MMM short, with a limit price of $82 (which means you would have to get at least $82 or you will not sell it). However, if MMM dropped straight down to $57.32 without going back up to $82, you would not get filled at all and would miss out on a good drop. (This is an extreme example used to illustrate a point.)

Theoretically, selling short has a limited profit and an unlimited loss. Thus, if you short a stock at $60, you can only make $60 (which you'd make if the stock goes to zero). However, the same stock could go to $600, in which case you would have lost $540. If you follow the principles for cutting losses explained in Part IV, that would never happen for you. However, unlimited losses are still a possibility for someone who sells short and doesn't pay any attention to the investment.

When you sell a stock you don't own, any dividends or rights that are declared before you buy it back are owed by you. Thus, you must pay dividends to the broker who loaned you the "borrowed stock" that you sold.

For these reasons, we urge you not to sell short unless you are a seasoned trader. Richard Russell, the dean of the investment newsletter industry, has observed that very few people make money selling short, even in bear markets.

The short-selling strategy would be best used when you expect a particular stock to have a major fall and the general trend of the market is down (i.e., a red light mode). As a short-seller, you are always a trader, not an investor. Your profits are taxed as short-term capital gains, and corrections (i.e., rallies to the upside) can be sudden and violent. Also short-selling requires a speculator's mind-set. The longer you hold it, the more nervous you are likely to be, so a short position is often difficult to hold psychologically.

Most people believe that short-selling hurts the market, but in reality it puts a break on market crashes. Remember, short-selling cannot contribute to the downside because short-sellers have to do so on an uptick, and they have to buy the stock back. Thus, in a free-falling market, all the people who sold the stock short have to buy it back at some point, which provides a cushion for the market.

A Short-Selling Strategy

The following strategy can be very profitable in a strong red light mode when stocks start to plunge. Use it only in red light mode, and limit it to three to five stocks at one time with no more than 1% risk in each stock (see Chapter 14). Note that your *risk amount* is not the same as your investment amount (or total position). More on this later.

- *Screening stocks.* The first thing you need to do is screen stocks for price-to-sales ratios over 15. For example, a stock priced at $15 per share with only $1 per year in sales would have a price-to-sales ratio of 15.[4] Also look for stocks with a minimum market capitalization of $1 billion so you can be sure they are good short candidates. You can use the Custom Screener from moneycentral.com to find stocks meeting this criterion. You may be shocked when you get your list because these stocks will be some of the darlings of the market.

- *Exception.* Avoid shorting any biotechnology stocks. These stocks have very high price-to-sales ratios. At the same time, some news event could send them skyrocketing overnight.
- *Entry.* You can enter these stocks when we are in red light mode and they have been going down for at least six straight weeks but still have a price-to-sales ratio above 15.
- *Worst-case exit.* If you buy any of these stocks and they start going up, sell them if they rise 25% beyond your short-selling price (i.e., you lose 25% on the price). For example, suppose you sold eBay short at $60 because it met these criteria. If eBay started to rise, you would exit the stock if it increased by 25% to $75 per share.
- *Profit-taking exit.* You would buy your short stock back under two different conditions. First, if our market barometer switched from red light to yellow, you would exit all short positions, whether they were profitable or not. In addition, you would keep a 25% trailing stop of the closing price. This means that if eBay went down in value to $40, you would buy eBay back if it moved up 25% to $50. In other words, whenever eBay goes down in price to a newer low on the

---

ACTION STEPS

➤ When the 1-2-3 model signals red light mode, consider shorting overvalued stocks that have been going down in price for at least six weeks, that have a price-to-sales ratio above 15, and that have a market capitalization of over $1 billion. This chapter shows you how to do the appropriate screens for these stocks.

➤ Keep a 25% trailing stop on the price as an exit. You would also exit all short stocks if our market barometer moves to yellow light. And never risk more than 1% of your portfolio on any one shorting position.

➤ In the red light mode, also consider following the bear market mutual fund strategy or investing in a hedge fund as described in Chapter 6.

close, you would adjust your trailing stop. You do not adjust your stop the other way. Trailing stops are explained in detail in Chapter 13.

- **Position sizing.** You must never risk more than 1% of your portfolio in any of these stocks. Position sizing is explained in much more detail in Chapter 14. However, the basic idea is to make sure that you won't lose more than 1% if your stock moves to your worst-case exit. For example, suppose your account was $50,000. That means that you could risk $500. In our example, with eBay, the worst case movement against us was $15. If you divide that into $500, you get 33 shares. Thus, you can only sell short 33 shares of eBay. If the price was $60 per share you would be paying $1,980 ($60 × 33) for this position, but you're only risking $500 of your $50,000 account. Be sure that you thoroughly understand position sizing as described in Chapter 14 before you use this strategy.

Short-selling can be very profitable during strong bear markets if you follow the guidelines given in this chapter. Develop a thorough plan for how short-selling will work for you, and be sure you understand the risk control strategies outlined in Part IV.

Notes

1. The standard deviation is a statistical measure of the variability. Thus, a higher standard deviation means that the index was more variable than a lower standard deviation. Approximately two-thirds of all samples will fall within ± one standard deviation of the mean.
2. The Spiders (SPY) can be shorted without an uptick.
3. This assumes that sales stay the same for the next 25 years.
4. As we write this book, there are great shorting candidates selling at 20 times sales. At some point in the future, you may have to look for stocks selling at 10 times sales. If that is the case, be certain that they sell for at least $25 per share and that they meet all the other criteria.

BUYING STOCKS SAFELY: AN ALTERNATIVE TO CONVENTIONAL WISDOM

*"The problem with the person who thinks he's a long-term investor
and impervious to short-term gyrations is that the emotions of fear
and pain will eventually make him sell badly."*

—ROBERT WIBBELSMAN

Mary Ellen became very nervous about the stock market when everyone else was excited about it. She also knew that stocks with price-earnings ratios in the 40s were highly overvalued, and she was seeing some popular stocks with price-earnings ratios over 100. To her that meant that if those earnings didn't grow, then every penny of earnings for the next 100 years would have to be paid to her just to get her money back. She wanted no part of that, so she got on the sidelines.

When the market started going down with conviction, Mary Ellen was practicing some of the shorting strategies mentioned in the last chapter. She also found a newsletter with great recommendations that she could follow on a short-term basis. She was making good money from that. She also noticed that some stocks were still going up, so she purchased those and made even more money. And when everything looked gloomy, she noticed that some stocks were selling way below their liquidation value, so she loaded up on those. And sure enough, during the 2003 recovery, she made great money on those stocks. In all, Mary Ellen Williams was pleased with her stock market performance during the bear market. And since she was up nearly 70%, she should have been. How about you? Are you proud of your investments? Are they up? Well, they can be!

This chapter gives you three strategies that will give you an edge in picking the right stocks during the appropriate market conditions. All of these strategies require that you follow the risk control guidelines given in Part IV.

The first strategy involves following the recommendation of someone you trust. You must know how the strategy works in order to know when to employ it. For example, most stock market strategies work well only in our green light mode. However, two authors of this book, D. R. Barton, Jr., and Steve Sjuggerud, have newsletters with strategies that adapt well to red light, yellow light, or green light market conditions. The second strategy of buying efficient stocks, presented in this chapter, tends to work best in yellow or green light conditions, but you can sometimes find good stocks in red light conditions. Two examples are given that occurred during red light conditions. The third strategy, finding stocks that are extremely undervalued, is best used during yellow and red light mode. You could use it during green light mode, but you'd probably have problems finding stocks that meet the required criteria.

Method 1: Following a Newsletter's Recommendations

Most newsletter recommendations fail to outperform the markets, but some are very good. For example, the *10-Minute Trader*, a stock screening service written by D. R. Barton, Jr., has had a great track record.[1] This newsletter's record from the calendar year 2002 will be the basis for our examples as we look at some of the best practices to use when following newsletter selections. At the end of each suggestion, we'll relate the general newsletter advice to specific examples for following the *10-Minute Trader* newsletter. Let's start by digging into the reasons why the newsletter has beaten the averages.

Understand Why the Newsletter's Strategy Works

To be successful in following a newsletter, you have to know why it makes the investment selections it does. Some newsletters use fundamental analysis; some use the judgment, intuition, and experience of the advisor; others use mechanical trading systems. Your job is to see past the newsletter's advertising and learn the true basis for its investment selections. Even if the signals are proprietary, you can still learn the investing style, beliefs, and philosophy. Ask yourself, why is this strategy successful? It's not enough to look at a newsletter's track record. If you want to be successful following the recommendations, you have to know the path you will be following. This takes research on your part.

10-Minute Trader Example

The *10-Minute Trader* strategy scans for stocks that have moved too far in one direction, like an overstretched rubber band. The strategy then requires the stock to reverse and begin its snap-back. If it starts the snap-back with sufficient momentum, we jump on board in the direction of the snap-back on the open of the next trading day, hoping to catch a quick "opening pop." This strategy works because it identifies a useful market condition (a stock that is stretched too far, either up or down) and takes advantage of the situation when it corrects itself.

Make Sure the Newsletter's Investment Philosophy Is Consistent with Your Beliefs About the Market

This is a subtle point for some people, but it is really the root cause for most failures in following an advisory service. Many people subscribe to a newsletter because of its track record or great ad copy. Study the reasons behind your selection. If you don't agree with the advisor's investment philosophy, you'll find it almost impossible to follow his or her recommendations in the long run.

Let's say that through your study you've come to believe that the market moves in cycles and that it corrects itself when it gets out of balance. You believe that the best way to make money in the markets is to follow these cycles—you sell when prices are too high and buy when they're too low. With this belief system, it would be very difficult to make money with a newsletter that trades breakouts or follows long-term trends. The first time the advisor has a few losing trades in a row, that little voice in the back of your head will say, "I knew trading these breakouts would never work. He's always trying to buy when stocks are already stretched too far." And with those thoughts running around your brain, you will eventually find ways to consciously or subconsciously sabotage your success.

10-Minute Trader Example

This newsletter buys stocks when they are stretched too far on the downside and sells them after a quick snap-back. It also sells stocks when they are stretched too far on the upside and buys them back after a quick reaction. If you expect stretched rubber bands to pop back into shape, then this system is a good match for you. On the other hand, those who only look for breakouts at every new high or breakdowns at every new low may have difficulty playing the countertrend snaps recommended. Similarly, if you have trouble shorting the market or playing quick reactions, you'd have trouble with this method. The *10-Minute Trader* examples are best for traders who can trade the first hour of the trading day. If this doesn't fit your style, then you would probably have trouble following these recommendations successfully.

Make Sure the Newsletter Does What It Claims to Do

Before you trade a newsletter, get a list of the last 50 to 100 of the newsletter's recommendations. If the newsletter will not provide this, then avoid that newsletter or wait until you've accumulated 50 to 100 real-time recommendations before you actually trade it. Analyze those trades the same way you would your own system, using the guidelines given in Chapter 15.

Paper-trade the recommendations, whether they are past recommendations or done in real time, following the risk control procedures given in Part IV. Determine for yourself if the track record merits following. Be sure to calculate all of the following information, which we'll describe how to do in detail in Part IV.

- What is the *R*-multiple distribution of the recommendations?
- What is the expectancy of the trade?
- What is the yearly rate of return on your account trading at a 1% position size?

This information is critical, and you should not trade any newsletter recommendations without it. It's easy for a newsletter, through good copy, to trick you into believing that its recommendations are much better than they actually are. IITM has an entire newsletter on this topic.[2]

Take Every Recommendation

Once you've decided that a newsletter merits following, you must decide what you can expect on the downside, and you must take every recommendation. Investment newsletter readers rarely follow this simple, commonsense advice. It seems logical that to duplicate your newsletter's performance, you have to take the same trades—*all* of them! But it's tempting to make up your own rules about when to take the trades and when not to. This is especially easy after the newsletter you're following passes through an inevitable losing streak. When a few trades have gone against you, you'll want to pass up a few trades, or quit the service altogether. But if the approach of the newsletter is sound, it will rebound. And, as you'll see, you're most likely to find your best returns right after a losing streak. Quite often systems or advisors make a big percentage of their gains by having several really big wins or by putting together a long winning streak. Those tend to be the trades you are the least likely to take.

There is one possible exception to this rule. Newsletters often make recommendations based upon fundamental research about the nature of the stock. The newsletters come out on a set date each month and must make their recommendations on that date. Often this is not the best time to take the recommendations. Thus, we suggest one key filter prior to following any recommendations—*be sure the position is moving in your favor*. This is one of the six risk control fundamentals discussed in detail in Chapter 13.

10-Minute Trader Example

The *10-Minute Trader* strategy has one indicator for when the price has stretched too much (either up or down), another one that checks the stock for acceptable momentum in the direction of the potential trade, and one simple entry criterion that keeps you out of trades that never get going in your direction. The strategy uses small stop losses (see Chapter 13) and is very robust and consistent across many different market conditions because of its simplicity. But despite the system's great history of over 100% returns in 2002, people always want to tweak the system.[3] They want to personalize it by adding a filter here, or an extra rule there. But we've yet to have someone say, "Hey, I've added some additional complexity to your strategy, and it's so much better now."

Table 8.1 shows a selection of trades with this system with proper stops and a position sizing algorithm that only risks 1% of your account per trade. You'll learn how that's done in Chapter 14, but for now just look at the nice increase in equity using these safe strategies. And remember that these trades occurred during a huge bear market during 2002.

Notice that we were up 43% in just over a month, despite being in a bear market. However, about half of these trades involve shorting the market. Please be careful because past performance does not necessarily indicate what results this newsletter (or any other) will get in the future. Market conditions could change and impact the newsletter's effectiveness.

Don't Count on the Newsletter to Get Risk Control and Position Sizing Right

The risk control methods given in Part IV of this book are absolutely essential if you want to make money trading. You must know when to exit and how large a position to buy or sell. *If you just do the stock selection part, you'll lose money. It's almost guaranteed.* Before you follow a newsletter recommendation, make sure you understand the principles of risk control and have a plan for using them. As you should have noticed by now, we cannot stress this point enough.

Table 8.1 *10-Minute Trader* Newsletter: September to October 2002

Symbol	Date	Stop Loss Risk per Share	Win or Loss per Share	Risk = 1% of Equity: in $ Risked	Ending Equity with 1% Risk
Beginning Equity					$100,000
MCDTA	9/26/2002	$0.15	−$0.05	$1,000	$99,667
SMTC	9/26/2002	$0.15	−$0.01	$997	$99,600
CAT	9/26/2002	$0.25	$0.38	$996	$101,114
AMR	9/27/2002	$0.10	−$0.10	$1,011	$100,103
AYE	9/27/2002	$0.25	−$0.07	$1,001	$99,823
JNPR	10/2/2002	$0.10	−$0.03	$998	$99,523
FISV	10/9/2002	$0.25	$0.15	$995	$100,120
ANF	10/9/2002	$0.25	−$0.01	$1,001	$100,080
CSCO	10/10/2002	$0.15	$0.15	$1,001	$101,081
MERQ	10/10/2002	$0.25	$0.45	$1,011	$102,901
ISIL	10/10/2002	$0.25	$0.39	$1,029	$104,506
SAP	10/10/2002	$0.20	$0.75	$1,045	$108,425
HI	10/11/2002	$0.25	$3.95	$1,084	$125,556
ELX	10/11/2002	$0.25	$0.84	$1,256	$129,775
TSM	10/11/2002	$0.15	$0.18	$1,298	$131,332
ADPT	10/11/2002	$0.10	$0.05	$1,313	$131,989
CD	10/11/2002	$0.20	$0.85	$1,320	$137,598
CLS	10/11/2002	$0.25	$0.03	$1,376	$137,763
PMCS	10/14/2002	$0.10	−$0.10	$1,378	$136,386
CY	10/14/2002	$0.10	−$0.02	$1,364	$136,113
LSCC	10/14/2002	$0.10	$0.05	$1,361	$136,793
FCS	10/14/2002	$0.15	−$0.03	$1,368	$136,520
GT	10/14/2002	$0.15	−$0.15	$1,365	$135,155
S	10/14/2002	$0.25	$1.31	$1,352	$142,237
TEC	10/21/2002	$0.20	$0.15	$1,422	$143,303
PEG	10/22/2002	$0.25	$0.65	$1,433	$147,029
WDC	10/25/2002	$0.10	−$0.10	$1,470	$145,559
SLE	10/25/2002	$0.15	−$0.11	$1,456	$144,492
GNSS	10/25/2002	$0.20	$0.13	$1,445	$145,431
YHOO	10/29/2002	$0.25	−$0.10	$1,454	$144,849
TMP	10/29/2002	$0.15	−$0.15	$1,448	$143,401

> **KEY IDEAS**
>
> ➤ If you follow the recommendations of a newsletter, you must know the logic behind the recommendations and determine if it fits your beliefs and personality.
>
> ➤ Be sure to put 50 trades through a thorough system analysis as suggested in Chapter 15.
>
> ➤ Once you decide a newsletter is worthwhile, take *all* of its recommendations.
>
> ➤ Follow the risk control and position sizing guidelines in Part IV.

Method 2: Trading Efficient Stocks

Imagine buying a stock that is slowly going up—a little every week. That's the next strategy. In green or yellow light mode, buy stocks that have been going up steadily. It's easy to find them—just look for stocks that are moving up in a smooth (efficient) fashion.

What is efficiency? It's really a way to measure how orderly the stock's price rise has been. In mathematical terms, one looks at the change in price of the stock over a period of time in relationship to its daily price range. For example, if a stock goes up or down very smoothly, say 50 cents per day, then it's probably very efficient. If a stock goes up 10 points one week and then down 7 the next and then up 10 the next and then down 5 points, it will have gone up 8 points,

> **ACTION STEPS**
>
> ➤ If you decide to follow the recommendations of a newsletter, collect 50 past trades from that newsletter.
>
> ➤ Take the 50 trades and do a thorough system analysis of the recommendations as shown in Chapter 15.

but not very efficiently. There is a lot of volatility, or what is sometimes called "noise." You want to buy stocks that are going up smoothly, without a lot of noise.

You can determine the efficiency of a stock by looking at its price change over the period of time under consideration (we'll use a 60-day time frame for our examples) and dividing this price change by the noise. How do you measure noise? A simple way is to use the average daily price range for the last 60 days. The daily range for a stock is simply the highest price for a given day minus the lowest price of that day. (For our stock screening, we actually use the *average true range* of a stock—this is an indicator that is very similar to daily range, but which takes into account the times when a stock has a gap in its price from one day's close to the next day's open.)[4]

Let's say you want to do an efficiency screen for 60 days. You'd first find the change in price over the last 60 days for a particular stock. Take the most recent closing price and subtract the closing price from 60 trading days ago. Let's say the difference was $13.51. You'd then find the average true range of the stock over the last 60 days. Let's say that was $0.83. The stock's 60-day efficiency calculation (or efficiency ratio) would be $13.51 divided by 0.83, which is 16.27. That is a fairly efficient stock. In fact, anything with a ratio over 15 is usually worth looking at more closely.

Thus, the first step is to screen for efficient stocks with an automated stock screening program. AIQ has an excellent stock screening software package that allows users to program their own screens. There are many other packages that would also work.[5]

The next step is to review all of the stocks with a value over 15. What do they look like? A stock that shows a flat line, has a 15-point jump on one day, and then becomes a flat line again would still show up as mathematically efficient on this sort of screen, but doesn't fit the criteria of being a stock with an orderly rise in price. You want to find stocks that are going up very smoothly. For example, both Autozone (AZO) and Deluxe Corporation (DLX) exhibited very efficient increases in price during 2001. A 60-day efficiency screen would have picked up both of those stocks early in the year because, as shown in Figures 8.1 and 8.2, the increases were already evident in the third quarter of 2000. Both

Figure 8.1 AZO Was Very Efficient from February Through June

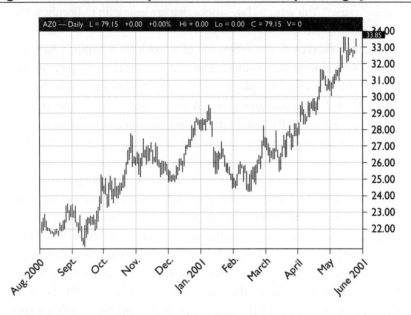

stocks continued to have orderly straight-line price movements throughout 2001, and that included the September 11 disaster (see Figures 8.3 and 8.4). You'd be into Autozone at about $33 per share and Deluxe Corporation at about $28 per share. Thus, while the markets

Figure 8.2 DLX Was Very Efficient from January Through June

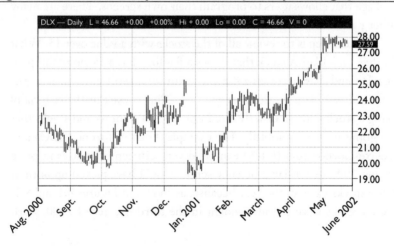

Figure 8.3 AZO Made Great Profits After June

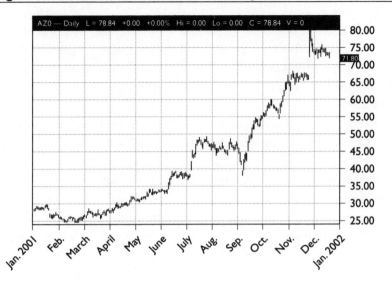

Figure 8.4 DLX Remained Efficient for All of 2001

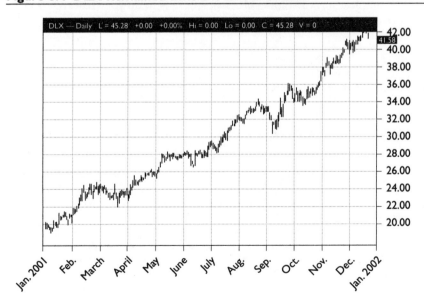

were going down as a whole, you could have made money by owning these stocks.

Every efficient stock you find will not turn out this well, but efficiency is a great screen to pick out good stocks. And if you practice the risk control techniques given in Part IV of this book along with this screen, you'll do much better than the average person in the stock market.

We run a personal screen at the beginning of every month for stocks with positive efficiencies above 15. In early 1999, there were hundreds of stocks that met our screening criteria. During this almost unprecedented run-up in stock prices, many stocks were moving up in an efficient fashion, and any of them would have been good additions to your portfolio at that time. In contrast, during 2001, we could usually find 20 to 50 stocks that met the efficiency number criteria, although there might only be two or three (such as AZO and DLX) that met the other criteria for buying an efficient stock (see Figure 8.5). By mid-2002, only one or two stocks met the efficiency criteria, and these were eliminated by other criteria in Figure 8.5.

Entry Strategy for an Efficient Stock

The simplest way of trading efficient stocks is to do your research over the weekend and enter at the open on Monday. Enter as soon as you

Figure 8.5 Efficient Stock Selection Criteria

- Stock must have an efficiency number of 15 or greater.
- Stock price rise over the last 60 trading days must be relatively smooth and consistent. Eliminate any stocks that have flat price action followed by a huge one- to five-day jump in price and then are flat again.
- Stock must have a 60-day average volume greater than 200,000 shares per day.
- The stock price should be smooth and not parabolic or climactic. In other words, if huge price moves occurred in the last week or month, you may be nearing the end of the run.
- Make sure that the daily price action has not suddenly increased dramatically. For example, if the daily range throughout most of the move was $2–$3, then make sure it stays in that range. Huge changes in volatility could signal an unpleasant surprise.

KEY IDEAS

➤ Consider buying stocks that are moving up efficiently (smoothly).

➤ You can determine the efficiency of a stock by looking at the price change over 60 days and dividing that by the average daily range as defined by its average true range.

➤ Use a software package, such as AIQ, to screen stocks for efficiency on a weekly basis, looking for stocks with an efficiency over 15.

➤ Don't practice this strategy until you are thoroughly familiar with the risk control techniques in Part IV.

---

find a qualifying stock that meets all of the efficient stock selection criteria from Figure 8.5.

Practice Risk Control and Position Sizing

Again, for this strategy it is critical that you understand risk control methods. These include the six guidelines given in Chapter 13 and the

---

ACTION STEPS

➤ If this strategy appeals to you, make sure that you read the risk control methods in Part IV.

➤ Find a stock screening program such as AIQ and make sure you do an efficiency screen as described.

➤ Do your first efficiency screen for stocks above 15 and then find the smoothest stocks. See if any look enticing. If so, buy . the stock with a 25% trailing stop. (Trailing stops are described in detail in Chapter 13.)

➤ Make sure that your risk is no more than 1% of your portfolio should you be stopped out.

---

position sizing guidelines given in Chapter 14. You should also have a written plan for how you will undertake this strategy. These simple precautions will make this a safe strategy.

Method 3: Buying Deeply Undervalued Stocks

Benjamin Graham is the father of value investing. During the Great Depression, when most people were losing their shirts in the stock market, Graham was averaging returns of 17% per year for his clients. You can do that, too, by following his methods.

Warren Buffett is also a value investor. Buffett's prowess in the stock market is legendary, but his biggest secret is that he is a student of Benjamin Graham. He understands when a stock is highly undervalued.

In this section, you will learn how to think like Graham and Buffett. How can you find stocks selling for less than their liquidation value? These stocks are very hard to find in green light or yellow light mode, but they become common in red light mode. Furthermore, we'll show you how to accumulate them for free. That's right, for free!

Undervalued Stocks

At the end of bear markets, stocks historically tend to be highly undervalued—selling at about six to eight times their earnings. Thus, if a stock earns $5 per share annually, it will probably sell for $30 to $40 per share at this low level of market valuation. When you buy stocks in this range, you are typically getting good value.[6] There will be many bargains for you to pick up off the bottom. And, if you've been making money throughout the bear market by following our other strategies that suit bear markets, you'll have the equity in your account to afford lots of these bargains.

One way to look at the value of a stock is to use Graham's number, named after Benjamin Graham.[7] The key to value investing, according to Graham's strategy, is a simple number that tells the strength of a company's near-term financial picture. This number is called the net current asset value (NCAV) of the company. When NCAV is calculated on a per-share basis, many practitioners call it Graham's number.

In basic terms, Graham's number, when compared with the price of the stock, tells us if a company has more liquid value (cash and instruments that can readily be turned into cash within a year) on hand than it has debts to pay. In the language of a corporate balance sheet, NCAV is calculated by subtracting a company's total liabilities from its current assets. When you divide this difference by the total number of outstanding shares, you get Graham's number.

Graham suggests that you can safely buy a stock that sells for two-thirds of its Graham's number. This extra reduction gives you something of a safety net because companies with a very low Graham's number typically have been heading down in price. Once you identify them using this method, they are likely to head a bit lower before beginning their rebound. So holding off on investing in stocks until they are at two-thirds of their Graham's number means that you are getting in at a very low price, or, said another way, at a very good value. Few companies meet this stringent criterion; in fact, most companies have negative NCAVs. *In the spring of 2003, only 30% of the stocks listed on the combined NYSE, AMEX, and Nasdaq stock exchanges had current assets that were larger than their total liabilities.*

However, since 30 percent of the more than 7,000 stocks out there is still a very large number, here are some screening guidelines to help you search for stocks that might have great NCAV numbers. These criteria are given in Table 8.2.

If you screen for the requirements in the table, you can usually find 10 or more stocks that will pass all the tests. There are a variety of Web screeners, but a few that work well are the Quick Stock Search from *Business Week Online* (businessweek.com)[8] and the Custom Screener from moneycentral.msn.com.[9] A screen from spring 2003, after three years of a massive bear market, produced the list of 11 stocks shown in Table 8.3.

Once you have a list of candidates, you can determine which of the selected stocks, if any, meet Graham's requirements for NCAV. You need to find a website with balance sheets for the various companies you've

Table 8.2 Criteria for Screening Stocks Selling at 60% of NCAV

Variable	Criterion	Comments
Stock's price per share	Should be above $3.00	Low-priced stocks are risky.
Price-to-book ratio[a]	Should be below 0.8	Stocks selling below book value are likely to fit our screen.
Price-to-cash flow ratio[b]	Should be positive— greater than 0.1	Requiring positive cash flow eliminates many high-risk companies.
Price-to-sales ratio[c]	Less than 0.3	Most stocks meeting Graham's criteria have price-to-sales ratios below 0.2.
Debt-to-equity ratio[d]	Less than 0.1	Most good NCAV stocks do have some debt.
Average daily volume	10,000 shares per day minimum	A good rule of thumb: stock should have average daily volume of at least 100 times the number of shares you'll buy.

[a]The price-to-book value is the ratio of the price per share to what the company has on its books as its value per share. For example, a price-to-book ratio of 1 means the company is selling for its value. Stocks usually sell for way over book value, but you can occasionally buy stocks that are selling for under their book value.

[b]The price-to-cash flow ratio is the ratio of the price of the stock per share compared with how much cash flows into the company per share.

[c]The price-to-sales ratio is a ratio of the value of the stock per share versus the amount of sales it generates per share. For example, if a stock had $5 in sales per share, the stock may sell for as much as $100.

[d]The debt-to-equity ratio is the ratio of the total debt the company has divided by its equity. Thus, if a company has a ratio of 0.1, it has $1 of debt for every $10 of equity (value) in the company.

selected, and you want those balance sheets to be in a format you can easily read and understand. Two recommended sites are hoovers.com and yahoo.com. Since most people are more familiar with Yahoo!, we'll show you how to get the necessary information there.

Go to yahoo.com and click on Finance at the top. Enter the ticker symbol and click on Balance Sheet under Financials. You can save yourself a lot of time by seeing if the NCAV is at least positive (meaning that current assets exceed total liabilities). This step will eliminate some of the stocks on your list. If the NCAV number is positive, then check the number of shares outstanding by clicking on profile at the top of the page and scroll down until you see shares outstanding. You now need to divide the NCAV by the number of shares outstanding. Your result

Table 8.3 Fundamental Data Scan for Graham's Number

Symbol	Current Price 4/11/03	Price/ Book Value	Price/ Cash Flow	Price/ Sales	Debt/ Equity	Average Daily Volume
CC	5.25	0.8	3.3	0.2	0	3,949,600
TWMC	3.08	0.5	12	0.2	0	112,600
PMRY	6.79	0.6	4.9	0.2	0	76,800
GADZ	2.28	0.6	14.1	0.2	0	48,000
SYX	2.09	0.5	6.6	0.1	0.1	42,200
TPR	4.17	0.7	6.6	0.1	0	40,700
SMF	3.93	0.5	2.2	0.1	0	30,600
TESS	7.00	0.6	4.7	0.1	0.1	18,000
ICTS	4.85	0.4	0.7	0.1	0.1	17,300
BL	23.50	0.7	10.6	0.3	0	15,600
FFEX	2.19	0.7	2	0.1	0.1	13,900

is the NCAV per share, or what we call Graham's number. Your last step is to compare Graham's number with the price of the stock.

Let's look at what happens to this list of 11 stocks when we scan them for their Graham's numbers. In Table 8.4, we have all of the required information to calculate Graham's number: current assets, total liabili-

Table 8.4 Graham's Number Calculation for Screened Stocks

Symbol	Current Price 4/11/03	Current Assets ($M)	Total Liabilities ($M)	Shares Outstanding (M)	Graham's Number	Price/ Graham's Number
CC	5.25	3,103	1,458	207.19	7.94	66%
TWMC	3.08	486	294	38.93	4.93	62%
PMRY	6.79	168	51	12.39	9.44	72%
GADZ	2.28	75	31	9.16	4.80	47%
SYX	2.09	357	234	34.10	3.61	58%
TPR	4.17	132	120	7.10	1.69	247%
SMF	3.93	277	341	29.89	(2.14)	n/a
TESS	7.00	72	46	4.52	5.74	122%
ICTS	4.85	103	70	6.67	4.95	98%
BL	23.50	279	79	8.05	24.82	95%
FFEX	2.19	75	63	16.93	0.71	309%

Table 8.5 Graham's Number Calculation for Screened Stocks, Nine Weeks Later

Symbol	Original Price 4/11/03	Graham's Number	Price/ Graham's Number Basis 4/11	Price on 6/20/03	Price/ Graham's Number Basis 6/20	% Change in Price 4/11–6/20
CC	5.25	7.94	66%	7.50	94%	43%
TWMC	3.08	4.93	62%	4.54	92%	47%
PMRY	6.79	9.44	72%	10.61	112%	56%
GADZ	2.28	4.80	47%	5.82	121%	155%
SYX	2.09	3.61	58%	4.19	116%	100%
TPR	4.17	1.69	247%	4.59	272%	10%
SMF	3.93	(2.14)	n/a	4.74	n/a	21%
TESS	7.00	5.74	122%	7.37	128%	5%
ICTS	4.85	4.95	98%	4.39	89%	−9%
BL	23.50	24.82	95%	20.93	84%	−11%
FFEX	2.19	0.71	309%	2.75	388%	26%
S&P 500	868.30	n/a	n/a	995.69	n/a	15%

ties, number of shares outstanding, and current price. We can see in the last column of this table that four stocks made it through all of the screens on 4/11/2003 and had prices that were at least two-thirds of their Graham's number. These were: Gadzooks, Inc. (GADZ), Systemax, Inc. (SYX), Trans World Entertainment (TWMC), and Circuit City Stores (CC). The fifth-ranked stock, Pomeroy Computer Resources (PMRY), had a price within 50 cents of achieving two-thirds of its Graham's number and could be considered a judgment call for more experienced investors.

It's interesting to note that one stock that made it through our very rigorous fundamental scan still had a negative Graham's number. The seventh stock in Table 8.4 and Table 8.5, Smart & Final Inc. (SMF), had total liabilities that exceeded its current assets. However, this is only one out of 11 stocks, or about 9%. For the whole universe of stocks on U.S. exchanges, about 70 percent have negative Graham's numbers. So from this perspective, it seems that our initial screen, as depicted in Table 8.3,

How to Determine Graham's Number

1. Find a list of stocks meeting the criteria in Table 8.2.
2. Go to finance.yahoo.com. Enter the ticker symbol of one of your screened stocks and click on Financials and then on Balance Sheet.
3. If total liabilities exceed current assets, eliminate the stock.
4. Otherwise, subtract total liabilities from current assets to determine the current asset value (NCAV).
5. Divide the current asset value by the number of shares outstanding.
6. Is the current price of the stock less than two-thirds of the value you obtained in step five? If so, you've found a good stock.

did its job of providing us with a small list of stocks that had a strong chance of generating good Graham's numbers.

What Happened to These Stocks Nine Weeks Later?

Nine weeks after the scans for Tables 8.3 and 8.4 were run, we had the opportunity to look at the performance of the stocks listed in those tables. Table 8.5 shows the interesting price action that resulted for those 11 stocks over the next nine weeks. The S&P 500 cash index has been added as a twelfth entry for comparison. Note in particular that the five aforementioned stocks that either exceeded or were close to Graham's number were the only ones that significantly beat the performance of the S&P 500 (which was up almost 15% during this nine-week stretch). Another key item to note is that none of these stocks meets the Graham's number criteria on 6/20/2003, after the strong market run that occurred in the spring of 2003 (see the next-to-last column in Table 8.5).

The initial screen just happened to be run prior to the start of a large upward movement in the stock market. Don't expect to make 100% as soon as you invest, because it just won't happen. But be patient and you may be able to get your stocks for free. We'll show you how later in this chapter.

How to Accumulate Graham's Number Stocks

When you find a stock that meets these rigid criteria, don't just buy it. Start doing some research on that stock. Look it up on yahoo.com to find out why it is down. For example, Circuit City was down because the earnings had started to dry up. However, there was a reason for that—Circuit City switched to a massive credit program. People started buying on credit with no payments for up to six months, so revenues for Circuit City dropped. However, people have to make those payments eventually, and they may even have to pay interest on the loans. Obviously, Circuit City was a huge bargain.

Once you know why the stock is down and you ascertain that its potential for recovery is good, then start to accumulate the stock when it begins to go up or wait until it has at least been flat for about a month. Then purchase the stock with about 4% to 6% of your capital.

How to Get These Stocks for Free

When you buy a Graham's number stock, it should eventually have a nice rally, as shown in Table 8.5. When the stock gains 50%, start watching it carefully. If it continues to rise, great. However, if it flattens or starts to fall, then immediately sell two-thirds of your position. Notice what you've done. If the stock is up 50% and you sell two-thirds, you have gotten your original capital back. You now have the stock for free.

If the stock continues to rise, even better. When it reaches 100% gain, which the top two stocks in Table 8.5 did, sell half of it. Again, you have the rest of your stock for free.

The bear market could continue for a long time. But if you continue to buy stocks using Graham's number and sell off a percentage of them when they gain 50% to 100% during market rallies, you will start accumulating a lot of quality stock for free. You can actually hold this stock until the next bull market is in full swing. Then you might consider adding a trailing stop as recommended in Chapter 13 in case they go down. You can then stop out and secure the profits that you've made.

KEY IDEAS

➤ Graham's number is the net current asset value of a stock per share. Compare this value per share with the current price. If it is greater than the current price, then the stock is undervalued.

➤ Graham recommends buying stocks selling for two-thirds of their net current asset value. This is best done in red light mode, but it's best to wait for the stock to start going up before you buy unless you must accumulate a lot of the stock.

➤ Never open a position without making sure that it is moving in your favor.

➤ Make sure you follow all of the risk control procedures given in Part IV of this book.

➤ When you can sell one-half to two-thirds of your position for your initial cost, do so. Then you have a great stock for free.

ACTION STEPS

➤ Decide if buying stocks based upon Graham's number is right for you. If it is, then be sure you understand the risk control techniques in Part IV of this book.

➤ Following the guidelines given in this chapter, do your first stock screen for Graham's number.

➤ If you find some stocks meeting the recommended criteria, do a thorough search of them so that you can understand why they are selling so low.

➤ When one of your stocks starts an up move that lasts at least four to six weeks, consider buying it using the guidelines given in this chapter.

Critical Information on Using All of the Strategies

Stock selection consumes the time and creativity of most investors. However, real money is made from knowing how to exit the market and having the proper position size. These are the keys to your success. Do not use the strategies discussed in this chapter until you understand those principles, which are explained in Part IV.

Notes

1. For a copy of the *10-Minute Trader* newsletter track record, and to get a free copy of the special report *Swing Trading Strategies That Work*, go to ilovetotrade.com.
2. "How to Avoid Being Misled by Advertising Hype," *Market Mastery*, April 2003. Call 919-852-3994 or 800-385-4486 for further information, or go to iitm.com.
3. The track record is hypothetical and comes from taking every trade, using the recommended stops, and following appropriate position sizing algorithms. Past results don't necessarily predict future results in such trading strategies.
4. The average true range takes into account the total range of the day plus any gaps. Thus, if a stock's low was 13 and the high was 14, then the daily range is one point. However, if it gapped open by 30 cents (i.e., yesterday's close was 12.70), then we also add the 30-cent gap to the daily range to get a value of 1.30 for the average true range. For our efficiency calculation, we simple take the sum of the true ranges for the last 60 days and divide by 60. Most software packages include this average true range indicator. You can also find the average true range of stocks in the free area of stockcharts.com.
5. For more information about AIQ, contact Steve Hill, P.O. Drawer 7530, Incline Village, NV 89452; sales@aiqsystems.com. TradeStation and stockcharts.com would also work well. TradeStation is a high-end professional package, and stockcharts.com has an easy-to-use online screening capability that is reasonably priced.

6. We are talking about broad market valuations in this section. As you become more familiar with different sectors of stocks (e.g., semiconductors, oil and gas, biotechnology, etc.), you will find that some sectors traditionally have higher or lower historical valuations relative to the broader market.

7. Benjamin Graham and David Dodd, *Security Analysis*, 2d ed. (New York: McGraw-Hill, 2002).

8. Select Investing on *Business Week*'s main page and then select Stock Screeners under Investing Tools.

9. From moneycentral.msn.com, look under Investing and click on Stocks; then under the heading Stock Screener, click on Custom Search.

MORE PROFITABLE STRATEGIES FOR FINANCIAL FREEDOM

In Part I you developed a plan for financial freedom and in Part II you learned about stock market strategies. However, there are many other financial freedom strategies that don't involve the stock market. Part III is designed to give you the background material to understand and be able to use some of these strategies.

Chapter 9 will show the tremendous deflationary forces at work in today's economy, despite the Federal Reserve's promise to do everything it can to fight deflation. You'll learn how to monitor the inflation-deflation scenario for yourself and what to do if either of these factors becomes serious.

Chapter 10 will cover the dollar and interest rates. You'll learn how to assess what your currency is doing and how to profit whether it is going up or down. This chapter is very important because you can lose much of your wealth when your money falls in value. Most Americans lose that wealth without even knowing it is happening. You'll also learn how interest rates impact our currencies and how to profit whether interest rates are low, rising, or high and steady.

Chapters 11 and 12 both cover real estate. Chapter 11 shows you how to assess the factors that impact real estate values. Investing in real estate is one of the best ways to become wealthy, but if your timing is bad, it can also wipe you out. Consequently, we'll show you how to monitor the key factors in Chapter 12. Real estate expert John Burley will show you three strategies that can have a dramatic impact on your financial freedom number. Study this material well because you may make a fortune from it.

CHAPTER 9

THE INFLATION-DEFLATION GAME: HOW TO PROTECT YOURSELF

"A world monetary system has emerged that has no historical precedent: a system in which every major currency in the world is, directly or indirectly, an irredeemable paper money standard."

—MILTON FRIEDMAN

What would life be like if things cost 10% to 15% more every year? Would you keep your money in the bank earning 1%? You'd have to have large salary increases just to maintain your standard of living, and even an investment in the stock market might not keep up with the cost of living. What would you do?

What you just read about happened in the late 1970s, and it could happen again. This chapter explains the forces that drive inflation and its opposite, deflation. More important, it presents a model that will allow you to decide for yourself whether inflation or deflation might be in your future and how to profit no matter what happens. So let's get started.

In January of 1980, nobody trusted anybody in government to man the controls. After a decade of dumb ideas (like price controls) from our political leaders, the Vietnam War, and the OPEC oil embargo, we were stuck with drastic inflation, high unemployment, and no signs of economic growth. Gold hit $850 an ounce. Everything the government touched turned to stone. People didn't want the government to have control over their wealth.

Inflation was considered a permanent condition. It got so bad, singer-comedienne Bette Midler demanded that payment for her $600,000 European tour be paid in South African gold coins rather than in U.S. dollars.

Nobody wanted anything to do with the stock market either. The August 13, 1979, headline in *Business Week* ominously predicted "The Death of Equities."

The Dow Jones Industrial Average of stocks was at 850 in January of 1980, the same value as gold, by coincidence. It fell to a lower level than it was in 1966—14 years earlier. In 1964, inflation was a scant 1.0%. By the end of 1979, it was running at over 13% a year.

During this inflationary time, stocks were an awful investment. Look at the annual returns of various asset classes during the last period of rising prices (inflation) from 1968 through 1979 in Table 9.1. Notice that collectibles ruled.

As you can see, stocks were the worst-performing asset class on the list. The rate of inflation was even higher than the return on stocks. So if you were invested in stocks, you actually lost money over that period, due to the effects of inflation.

How times have changed since the beginning of the 1980s. Inflation fell year after year. By 1998, it was under control, hitting just 1.6%. As

Table 9.1 Yearly Asset Returns 1968–1979

Return	Asset
19.4%	Gold
18.9%	Rare stamps
15.7%	Silver
13.7%	Rare books
12.7%	U.S. coins (not gold)
12.5%	Old masters paintings
11.8%	Diamonds
11.3%	Farmland
9.6%	Single family homes
6.5%	Inflation rate
6.4%	Foreign currencies
5.8%	High-grade corporate bonds
3.1%	Stocks

we all know, over that period (1981–1998) stocks soared. Here are the specifics:

Dow Jones Industrial Average
   Dec. 31, 1981: 875
   Dec. 31, 1998: 9,000+

Over the 17-year period when inflation was falling (some call this "disinflation"), stocks rose dramatically.

Now consider the value of the Dow for the previous 17-year period, when inflation was rising. (Here are prices for the Dow that are 17 years apart.)

Dow Jones Industrial Average
   Dec. 31, 1964: 874.12
   Dec. 31, 1981: 875

The Dow didn't rise by even one point in the course of 17 years. The message should be obvious. You really *want* to own stocks when inflation is falling. And you really *don't want* to own stocks when inflation is rising.

As we write, the inflation-deflation debate is raging. The trend for the last two decades has been toward lower inflation. Many are now worried that if that trend continues, we could enter deflation, or a period of falling prices. The last period of deflation was the Great Depression. Will we have a deflationary bear market in stocks like 1929–1949? Or will we have an inflationary bear market like 1964–1982?

Could a Deflationary Depression Like the 1930s Happen Again?

Deflation basically means that your money will buy more. If something costs $100 and then later costs $90, suddenly your money is worth more. This happens all the time with specific products. When it happens throughout the economy, it really means that money is becoming more valuable. This is called deflation. Deflation is a natural byproduct of progress because as technology improves our ability to produce things cheaply, things start to cost less. For example, every two years $3,000 seems to buy a computer that is three to five times more powerful than the computer you had two years prior.

When you put deflation in this perspective (i.e., your money is worth more), it seems good. But we live in a political society in which people want everything right now. They also want more money every year, which is easy if money is worth less every year. But people also have a huge amount of debt. So, it becomes very important that their debt be worth less every year and the things they buy every year be worth more. This all happens when we have an inflationary environment.

Massive deflation sometimes results in economic depression. One such depression occurred from 1835 to 1843, and a second one occurred from 1929 through the late 1930s. America found these times very painful because many people were out of work and everything was going down in value. Politically, inflation is the more tolerable of the two evils. Based upon market cycles, we are currently due for a deflationary period.

There are five major deflationary forces at work today.

- *First, our manufacturing base is being moved to China.* Large companies have discovered that they can manufacture products in China at a huge discount to other places in the world. And the migration to China is lowering prices throughout the world. Here's how that works. Suppose you own a widget factory in the United States. It costs you $2 to make a widget, and you sell it for $5. Your competitor moves his manufacturing facility to China, where he can make widgets for 30 cents. He now sells them in the U.S. for $1.95, a price you cannot possibly match. You can either get your widgets made in China or go out of business. Even the emerging countries in Asia (Singapore, Malaysia, Thailand, South Korea, and Taiwan) are having trouble with this. They used to be the places people went to make their widgets, but they cannot compete with China either. The net result is that widgets cost less (a deflationary force) and people lose their jobs, which, in turn, reduces consumer spending (also a deflationary force).

- *Second, our service industries are moving overseas to places with cheap labor.* Programmers from India are doing much of the software work for U.S. firms. Even technical support often comes from India. When you call a technology company to get support, you are often routed to someone in India who might be answering your question. In fact, the *New York Times* recently announced that financial services were going to be moved to India, eventually costing America at least a million jobs. We've heard that it could cost Americans up to three million jobs in the early twenty-first century.[1] International businesses are also replacing many of their American executives with executives trained in India. These new executives have better business backgrounds and cost the companies far less money.

  When services and products go out to countries where labor costs are low, the net result is a lowering of prices. But these trends are also costing jobs and, for the companies that cannot compete, they are causing bankruptcies. Both are deflationary factors.

- *Third, rising unemployment and bankruptcies are producing wage concessions.* Several years ago, college graduates in engineering and computer science were determining which high-paid job gave them the most benefits. Today, they are lucky to find a job at all. The overall result is that salaries are going down—which is part of deflation.

- *Fourth, modern retail trends are another factor in today's deflation.* Firms like Wal-Mart and Target are selling products much more efficiently than other stores or even other retail chains. They've mastered the art of effective distribution and that translates into lower prices. However, they face increased competition from the Internet, where people can sell products with very little overhead. Many dealers now sell their new products through eBay or other Internet sources at rock-bottom prices. These trends are going to grow, not diminish.

- *Fifth, other countries don't want their currencies to be inflated with respect to the U.S. dollar because they believe that the U.S. consumer is the primary factor growing the world economy.* If their products increase in price because of a fall in the dollar, they believe they'd have trouble selling to the U.S. consumer. And they

DID YOU KNOW? ABOUT INFLATION
AND DEFLATION

From 1821 through 1933, the U.S. dollar was tied to gold at the fixed rate of $20.67. It kept inflation under control, but we certainly had deflationary periods. In 1934, President Franklin Roosevelt devalued the dollar by making gold worth $35 per ounce. In other words, the dollar was now worth less because it took almost twice as much to buy an ounce of gold.

At the end of World War II, Harry Dexter White from America and John Maynard Keynes from England developed an economic arrangement named after the place where it was crafted, Bretton Woods. In that agreement, the U.S. dollar continued to be tied to gold at $35 per ounce, and other currencies were tied to the U.S. dollar.

Since 1913, when the U.S. government allowed a private bank (the Federal Reserve) to print its money, we could print more dollars whenever we wanted to do so. Bretton Woods was great for America because we could print as many dollars as we liked and inflate our currency. This tactic forced other countries to print money as well, to keep their currencies from rising against their links to the dollar. The bottom line was that America could do what it liked. Other countries could either do the same or devalue their currencies, which would make them less competitive versus United States products. That is, it would be hard to sell their products to Americans if their currency was a lot more expensive.

However, other countries had one other choice—they could present their "surplus" dollars to the Federal Reserve and ask for gold at $35 per ounce in exchange. In 1971, President Charles de Gaulle of France did just that— he asked for American gold. In response, Richard Nixon closed the gold window and said that American currency was no longer as good as gold.

When America dropped the Bretton Woods agreement, it turned economics upside down. Inflation had to accelerate because America continued to print money. More money chasing the same products means that those products cost more, or that the dollar is worth less. Gold had to rise in price and the dollar had to fall in value versus other currencies. And, of course, that was exactly what happened.

During the 1970s, people who owned *things* prospered, especially if they bought them with borrowed dollars. As the dollar diminished in value, the payments were easier and easier to make. Obviously, this was the time to own gold, commodities, and land. It was not a good time to lend money because you got paid back with dollars that were worth less and less. However, the inflationary 1970s were during the heart of a bear market in stocks.

You're probably more familiar with inflation, which means the things you buy keep costing more. The movie that cost a nickel in the 1930s now costs $10. The house that was built in a great Los Angeles location in the 1940s for $5,000 now is worth $500,000 or more. Those are examples of inflation. Inflation also means that your dollar is worth less each year. The bear market that lasted from 1966 to 1982 was an inflationary bear market. America was at war in Vietnam and the presses had to work overtime printing money to pay for that war.

In 1979, President Jimmy Carter decided that inflation had to be stopped. He appointed Paul Volcker chairman of the Federal Reserve with instructions to control the printing presses. Volcker did what was expected and dramatically slowed down the rate at which new money was printed. That brought an end to high interest rates, a cheap dollar, and expensive gold.

Since that time, the Federal Reserve has pursued a policy of opportunistic deflation. It would ease up on the printing press when growth got too strong and push hard when growth started to decelerate. This policy, largely pursued by Federal Reserve Chairman Alan Greenspan, produced a huge boom in the economy. Suddenly the dollar was strong, and stocks boomed. The result was the tremendous primary bull market that we described earlier.

At the turn of the century, Greenspan eased up on the printing press and increased interest rates, sending the economy into a tailspin. When he went the other way, with 11 interest rate decreases in 2001, nothing happened. The economy still fell. Suddenly, inflation was no longer a problem—the problem was deflation. Primary bear markets produced by deflation are even tougher on people than inflationary bear markets.

Is that possible now? See the main text for our conclusions.

fear that if Americans stop buying their products, the results would be disastrous. Consequently, many countries are devaluing their currencies, creating a global deflationary force.

These five factors suggest that we could experience strong deflationary pressures, don't they? Would you rather have a deflationary depression or high inflation?

The 1929 through 1949 bear market occurred under deflationary pressure. Prices generally started going down. On the surface, that might seem great. Your food would cost less, as would your car, clothing, and other essentials. But most of the things you own would also go down in value. Your house, now worth $300,000, might go down to $200,000. That's what happened during the Great Depression of the 1930s. And the United States really didn't recover from it until the end of the 1940s.

The primary bear market the United States is in today appears to be a deflationary one, and that's a scary thought. Are those who predict a nasty period of deflation correct? Or will we have the other enemy of prosperity—strong inflation?

Could We See an Inflationary Spiral Like the Late 1970s Again?

Most people, certainly most politicians, would prefer the inflationary scenario. Because of that preference, and because the Federal Reserve has power to print money out of nowhere, we expect our currency to inflate.

With the amount of debt America has today, we cannot afford deflation. If you owe $240,000 on your $300,000 house, it's fine if your house is going up in value because of inflation. But if your house is going down in value because of deflation, it's a disaster for you. First, your income will drop because you will be paid with dollars that are worth more, so you'll get fewer of them. Second, the value of your debt will increase because the dollar is growing in value. Third, your house will drop in value. When you owe $240,000 on a $200,000 house, will you continue to make the payments? Many people won't, and that's a problem the U.S. government does not want.

Albert Friedberg compiled the most amazing track record we'd ever seen—something like a 40% annual return on his main fund over the dozen years it had been in existence. And with that record to back him, Friedberg flatly stated that "You can't have deflation in a fiat money society."[2]

He's probably right. You see, when the government controls the money, it prints money. Since the government wants to do everything it can to prevent deflation, it will print money—a massive inflationary force—to offset the deflationary trends.

Economic experts like Friedberg call the dollar *fiat money*. The U.S. dollar, for example, is fiat money. It is government-decreed money that has no intrinsic value. It is a piece of paper that has a value simply because we believe it is worth something. It is not valued against anything tangible. That's true of most money in the world today. The opposite extreme of fiat money would be the use of gold or silver coins, where the value of their metal content determines the value of the coins.

In 2003 Friedberg was still pounding the table against deflation. The first sentence in his late-January 2003 newsletter said, "The steady fall of the U.S. dollar juxtaposed against rapid monetary growth [and] massive fiscal expansion make nonsense of the fears of deflation."[3]

Friedberg then pointed out that 15 out of 17 commodities were higher than they were a year ago—the highest reading in almost 20 years. He concluded his inflation talk by saying, "In our view, an important acceleration of inflation is a certainty."

In mid-2003, Martin Barnes of BCA Research (bcapubs.com), another eminently sensible analyst, came to basically the same conclusion in *Barron's*: "Not many people have noticed, but China's inflation rate has turned positive. . . . By the middle of next year, deflation fears will be shifting to worries about inflation and concerns about the Fed raising rates."[4]

The U.S. government is committed to preventing deflation at all costs. And if that means accidentally overshooting and creating massive inflation, chances are that's what we'll see. And at the same time, we have the five major deflationary forces at work in the world.

Who's right in this debate? Nobody knows for sure. Smart analysts like Friedberg and Barnes make a powerful case, based on facts and history. But don't take our word for it—monitor the situation for yourself with our four-star system.

Tracking Inflation-Deflation with Our Four-Star System

Consider monitoring four inflation-deflation vehicles:

- commodity prices (agricultural and industrial raw materials that tend to rise in price during inflationary periods)
- consumer prices
- gold prices
- interest rates

Commodity Prices

Rising commodity prices can be an excellent leading indicator that inflation is just around the corner. During the inflationary 1970s, people made huge fortunes in commodities because there were huge uptrends in most of these products. As a rule of thumb, when commodity prices start rising, inflation will rise. When commodity prices fall, inflation tends to fall to a lower level (say from 5% inflation to 3% inflation).

Our first indicator simply looks at whether commodity prices over time are rising or falling. So we look at the nine-month moving average of commodity prices (or the 200-day moving average, or the 40-week moving average—whatever you have easy access to). If the nine-month moving average is rising (i.e., the line has a positive slope), higher rates of inflation are probably around the corner. The reverse is also true: the steeper the line, the more likely the increase in inflation.

Figure 9.1 shows the best index of commodity prices, the Commodity Research Bureau (CRB) Index, over the last 30 years. Notice what it is doing now. The index is starting to skyrocket. Thus, our first signal says to expect inflation.[5]

Figure 9.1 Big Moves in the CRB Index Can Lead to Inflation

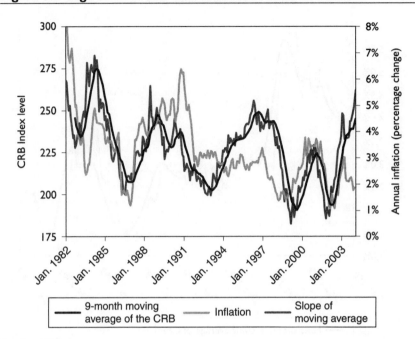

Data from bigcharts.com

Consumer Prices

The government keeps an index of inflation called the consumer price index (CPI). It rises most of the time because we always have a little inflation with our fiat money system. This index is a little dangerous, however, because it is controlled by the U.S. government. The way it is calculated has changed many times, and some say that it is manipulated to hide inflationary pressures. Nevertheless, during strong inflationary periods, expect the CPI to also be above its nine-month moving average.

Yet again, like the CRB Index, the steeper the nine-month moving average, the more likely it is that inflation will continue to trend in that direction.

Figure 9.2 Consumer Price Index

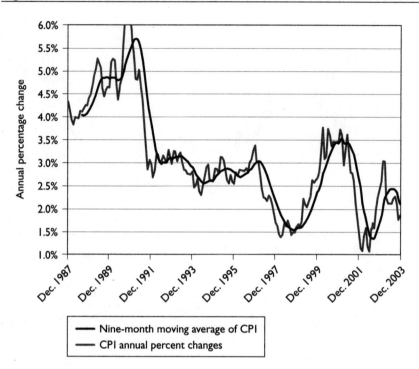

Figure 9.2 shows the current consumer price index. Notice that the CPI is heading down. Should the CPI go below zero, we would be in a deflationary period, and you need to be aware of that as well. Note that such a period does not show up in our graph, which covers the CPI since 1987.

Gold Prices

When fears of inflation rise, gold becomes attractive to investors as a form of real money. As Figure 9.3 shows, the price of gold has been an excellent leading indicator of future inflation. Thus, we suggest the same rule that applies to the CRB and the CPI: when the nine-month moving average is rising rapidly, expect inflation ahead, and vice versa.

Figure 9.3 Big Moves in Gold Tend to Lead to Moves in Inflation

As we write, gold is trading at around $420 an ounce. That is up $160 from its lows around $260 in early 2001. This tells us that inflation should be on the way very soon.

As with the CRB, if gold is falling, the inflation rate will often slow (say from 5% to 3%). We'll still have inflation, only milder. Notice the period from 1979 through 2000 in Figure 9.3. Gold declined dramatically even though we had some inflationary pressure throughout the period. When gold is trending higher, as measured by its nine-month moving average (or its 200-day or 40-week moving average), expect inflation to take off.[6]

Interest Rates

Generally, when inflation is high, long-term interest rates are also high. Think about it. Would you lend someone $100,000 at 5% interest if you knew that at the end of the year (after you had collected $5,000 in inter-

Figure 9.4 Real Interest Rates Versus Inflation

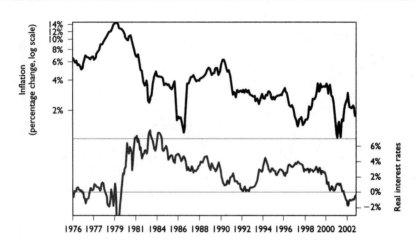

est) your original $100,000 would be worth only about $90,000? Of course, you wouldn't, because you'd lose $5,000 each year in value. That's why interest rates go up when inflation takes off.

However, there is one exception to that rule. The government would loan you money at a low rate knowing there will be high inflation because the government is printing the money. If it loses money to inflation, it will just print more. Nevertheless, loans become much more expensive in an inflationary climate. At the peak of inflation in the 1980s, interest rates were at double digits.

As we write this, long-term interest rates are rising rapidly, suggesting that inflation may be around the corner. However, as a precaution, the government is controlling short-term rates to stimulate the economy.

It's actually very dangerous when the government keeps interest rates artificially low. Our rule (and Figure 9.4 confirms this) is that when real short-term interest rates are pushed below zero and stay there, inflation should soon follow, as it did in the late 1970s.

The term *real* refers to interest rates after you account for inflation. So if short-term interest rates are 1% and inflation is 3%, then the real return on your money will be −2%. The government pushes rates this low to stimulate you to spend money to get the economy going again.

When we all spend, we have too much money chasing too few goods, causing prices to rise—and that's inflation.

We'll discuss interest rates more in Chapter 10. For now, just know that when real rates are pushed below zero and stay there, inflation is likely around the corner.

How to Profit from the Indicators

Figures 9.1 to 9.4 show that three of four indicators are starting to rise out of a long-term downtrend. A majority are pointing toward inflation. We call that a three-star signal. Now let's explore what that means.

Four Stars = Increasing Inflation

When all four indicators are positive (i.e., the model has a score of four), expect rising inflation. Under the four-star mode, expect the stock market to tumble or at least lose purchasing power. Consider keeping at least 40% to 50% of your assets in real estate or in other tangible assets. You'll find that real assets—gold, coins, stamps, silver, art, etc.—perform best under inflation. Paper assets such as stocks and bonds perform poorly. However, be careful to invest only in assets that you know something about. Investing in certain kinds of collectibles can be dangerous even in an inflationary environment, especially if you know nothing about them and end up paying way too much for them.

Gold, gold coins, and gold stocks are also excellent during high inflation. Consider putting up to 25% of your assets here. The easiest gold stock to trade in and out of, one that really moves with changes in the price of gold, is Newmont Mining (symbol NEM). My favorite play in gold coins is Saint-Gaudens from 1924 to 1928 in Mint State condition (MS63s cost about $750, MS65s are about $1,400). Before you buy anything, read *Coin Collecting for Dummies*.[7]

One of the best speculative plays during inflationary times is trading commodities. However, this is a book on safe strategies, and trading commodities can be risky due to high amounts of leverage. If you want to know more about commodities, look into IITM's basic and electronic futures courses.

Three Stars = Inflation Danger

When three of the four indicators are positive (i.e., the model has a score of three) expect rising inflation, but perhaps a little further in the future. The same investments recommended in the four-star mode would apply here, but you might reduce your allocations to 35% or 45%.

Two Stars = Some Inflation Risk

When only two indicators are positive, inflation is still a risk but not as great. Keep only a small allocation in inflation protection assets (25% to 35%).

One Star = Mild or Decreasing Inflation

In the one-star mode, it's time to exit from inflationary assets. Most of these assets decline in value when inflation decreases, so you don't want to be in them any longer than necessary when the indexes shift down to one star.

Zero Stars = Decreasing Inflation

When the signal moves to zero stars, you shouldn't have much more than 20% of your assets in inflationary investments. Be very careful here.

Minus One Star = Deflation

If all four indicators are going down and the CPI drops below zero, you should expect falling inflation and the potential for deflation. This scenario is very unlikely in the long haul because of the existence of the Federal Reserve, but it may be possible. Should this happen, move to a very liquid cash position with as many assets as possible.

At the time of this writing, the model is giving a three-star signal, with three indicators pointing to rising inflation. Inflation will likely follow. Keep up with this by following our free weekly newsletter *Tharp's Thoughts* at iitm.com.

KEY IDEAS

➤ There are currently five deflationary factors influencing the U.S. economy and causing our money to be worth more.

➤ The cost of deflation is too painful for politicians to allow it—especially in a debtor nation like the United States. A more likely scenario is an overshoot by policy makers, leading to inflation.

➤ We present a four-star system to help you monitor inflation. As of January 2004, we were in three-star mode—expect rising inflation.

➤ During rising inflation, invest in gold and hard assets. This is also a good time to speculate in commodities, but that area is not within the realm of our safe strategies.

➤ During a deflationary period (minus one star, all indicators going down, and the CPI below zero), we recommend cash.

➤ When inflation starts to decrease, expect a strong stock market while hard assets decline in value.

ACTION STEPS

➤ Determine the current status of the model and take appropriate action.

➤ Determine how much of your portfolio should be in inflation protection assets and act accordingly.

➤ Subscribe to *Tharp's Thoughts* at iitm.com.

Notes

1. According to Forrester Research in Cambridge, Massachusetts, by 2015, 3.3 million U.S. high-tech and service industry jobs will be moved overseas, most to India. That's $136 billion in U.S. wages. *Christian Science Monitor*, July 23, 2003.
2. You can read about Friedberg at friedberg.com.
3. Friedberg's *Commodity and Currency Comments* newsletter, January 27, 2003.
4. *Barron's* interview, June 5, 2003.
5. You can monitor the CRB index at bigcharts.com by typing in the symbol 20299A01. (We don't know why they use such an odd symbol.)
6. The best place to find gold charts and data for free online is at kitco.com. Gold will also rise as the dollar declines in value.
7. Ron Guth, *Coin Collecting for Dummies* (New York: Wiley, 2001).

CHAPTER 10

THE DOLLAR AND INTEREST RATES: TURNING THREATS TO YOUR WEALTH INTO PROFITS

"The trouble with paper money is that it rewards the minority that can manipulate money and makes fools of the generation that has worked and saved."

—ADAM SMITH (PSEUDONYM OF GEORGE GOODMAN)

What's happening to the value of your currency relative to other currencies? Is it weak or strong? If we have inflationary pressures, then it is probably weak and the potential effect of this pressure on your wealth could be devastating if you don't protect yourself. You could lose half of your wealth without even knowing it. After reading this chapter, you will understand exactly what a crumbling dollar and relative interest rates mean for your wealth. Then you'll be able to position your assets accordingly.

Time after time, governments have shown a willingness to destroy their own paper monies in order to pay their debts. Total wipeouts have happened. Germany couldn't pay its war debts in 1922, so it cranked up the presses to print money. By the end of 1923, prices had risen a trillionfold. The German people had all their savings wiped out.

This same destruction happens all over the world today. For example, you need a wheelbarrow full of money just to buy lunch in Venezuela these days. A decade ago, the exchange rate was about 100 Venezuelan bolivars to the dollar. Today, Venezuela's leader has cranked up the printing presses and the exchange rate has fallen to 1,600 bolivars to the dollar. That means Venezuelans need to make 15 times more money today to buy one dollar than they did a decade ago.

The value of the dollar, and hence your accumulated wealth, is now under the same threat.[1] It's not like what's going on in Venezuela, where the economy shrank by −29% as reported in the first quarter of 2003. Nevertheless, the November 21, 2002, speech by Federal Reserve Governor Ben Bernanke was a watershed event—a tipping point, if you will. And the effects on your wealth, if you don't position yourself properly, could be devastating.

Basically, Bernanke said that the Federal Reserve is willing to sacrifice the value of our money (and hence our wealth) to accomplish its objectives. To show you, here's an excerpt from his November 21 speech:

> *U.S. dollars have value only to the extent that they are strictly limited in supply. But the U.S. government has a technology, called a printing press (or, today, its electronic equivalent), that allows it to produce as many U.S. dollars as it wishes at essentially no cost.*
>
> *By increasing the number of U.S. dollars in circulation, or even by credibly threatening to do so, the U.S. government can also reduce the value of a dollar in terms of goods and services, which is equivalent to raising the prices in dollars of those goods and services. We conclude that, under a paper-money system, a determined government can always generate higher spending and hence positive inflation.[2]*

Not surprisingly, since Bernanke's speech, the dollar has fallen dramatically against the major currencies and the major commodities such as gold. In times like these, you need to spread your risk. You need to have some of your assets outside the U.S. dollar. You don't have to do anything exotic. Try the simple bear market strategies outlined in Chapter 7 and the max yield strategy from this chapter.

DID YOU KNOW? ABOUT U.S. DEBT

The mountain of debt the U.S. government carries has to be considered when you're sizing up future inflation because the best way out of the debt problem is for the government to print money. While paying your debts by printing money sounds like a cop-out, the U.S. government can do just that.

Officially, the government lists its debt at $7.1 trillion. Put in perspective, if there are roughly 100 million American households, then the government owes $71,000 per household. You might think that would be close to the maximum a government could borrow, but it's not. This $7.1 trillion doesn't include future liabilities such as social costs and pensions, which ring the bill up to $31 trillion.

These figures come from the government's own financial report for 2004. Ironically, the government puts a footnote to that, saying that *its power to tax is not reflected as an asset*. If the U.S. government were an investment, you probably wouldn't want to buy it.

The options out of this are simple: tax Americans to death, default and skip out on our debts, or create inflation. The last alternative is the least distasteful.

Sorry, Honey, No More Trips to Europe—
We Can't Afford It

The dollar could lose up to half its value. Said another way, your wealth (in dollars) could be cut in half. However, most Americans won't even realize what is going on, or what happened, once it is over. Most people don't understand what it means for the dollar to fall in value, so here is an example:

Let's say it's March 1985 and you've just landed in Europe for a one-year assignment. You're feeling like a rich American as a banker hands you 28,000 Swiss francs in exchange for $10,000 U.S. dollars. You travel in luxury and pick up a Rolex watch for a steal while you're there.

In March 1988, just three years later, your company sends you to Switzerland again. You hand over your $10,000 again, but this time you get only 14,000 Swiss francs.

"You must be making a mistake," you say to the banker. "No mistake," he says. "The dollar lost half its value in three years." You're flabbergasted. You can buy only half as much stuff this time around, and everything is twice as expensive in dollars as it was on your last trip.

The grim reality is that Europe is not twice as expensive. Prices of Rolexes in Switzerland didn't go up. It just takes you twice as many dollars to buy that same watch. From 1985 to 1988, your wealth was crushed. Your purchasing power was effectively cut in half. Look at Figure 10.1 to see the trends in the dollar over the last 30 years.

But what if you had your money in gold during that time? Gold nearly doubled back then, rising from below $300 to nearly $500 an

Figure 10.1 The U.S. Dollar Tends to Have Megatrends

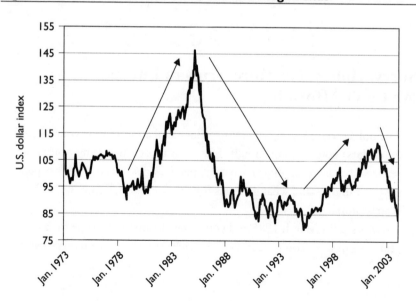

ounce. In reality, gold didn't rise—the dollar fell. It took a lot more dollars to buy one ounce of gold. If you looked at gold in terms of Swiss francs, gold was basically unchanged.

But 1988 is ancient history, right? The truth is, Americans haven't had to worry about the dollar for a long time—the dollar was soaring in the late 1990s. With many years of strengthening under former President Bill Clinton, the dollar is now expensive. It has not only peaked, but it's starting to decline dramatically. It wouldn't be out of the question to see your purchasing power dip significantly again. In fact, it's already happening. A year ago a dollar would have bought 1.7 Swiss francs. Now it's closer to 1.4. What's going on?

The Only Two Things That Affect the Value of Your Money

When you ignore the media and crunch the numbers yourself, you find that only two measurements affect the value of a rich country's currency—its purchasing power relative to other currencies and its real interest rate differentials. People might say that budget deficits and current account deficits matter, but they don't.

The concept of purchasing power parity is simple. Think of it this way. The price of a Big Mac should be roughly the same wherever you are because the ingredients are homogeneous, cheap, and widely available. You shouldn't see a huge difference in Big Mac prices as you cross the border from the United States to Canada, but sometimes you do.

In fact, in the summer of 2003 a Big Mac was US$0.49 cheaper for Americans in Canada than it was in the United States. So if you're planning a trip to Niagara Falls, make sure you spend all your money on the Canadian side.

Should a McDonald's in Niagara Falls, Canada, sell a burger for US$0.49 less than a McDonald's in Niagara Falls, New York? Does this discrepancy in prices in two rich countries make sense? Not in the long run. In the long run, currencies revert back to equal values—to their purchasing power parities. Of course, that long run can be a very long time.

The second force that affects the value of your dollar is the interest rate differential. The underlying principle is that money flows to where it's treated best. All things being equal, if one country is paying 5% interest and another is paying 1%, money will flow to the country paying 5% interest. That flow will cause the value of the 5% currency to increase. It's simple supply and demand.

As recently as 1995–1997, the U.S. dollar was the best deal going. You could make 5% or more on your cash, and there was very little inflation. Big Macs in Denmark and Japan were a full 100% more expensive than in the United States. But no longer.

So based on the only two factors that seem to influence the value of a rich country's currency—purchasing power parity and interest rate differentials—the U.S. dollar is likely in trouble. Our Big Macs are expensive now, and our interest rates are at about 1%.

Tracking the Value of the Dollar

There are three indicators to track if you want to stay profitable:

1. the megatrend in the dollar
2. the Big Mac Index (purchasing power parity)
3. where your money is treated the best

The Megatrend in the Dollar

Currencies seem to move in major trends that defy fundamentals. Once in place, trends in currencies tend to stay in place for long periods of time. Once again, just use the nine-month (or 40-week or 200-day) moving average of the trade-weighted U.S. dollar to determine what the trend is.[3]

When the nine-month moving average is moving up, the dollar is in an uptrend and will often stay in that uptrend. When the nine-month moving average is moving down (when the slope of the moving average is negative), the dollar is performing poorly. This concept is illustrated in Figure 10.2.

Figure 10.2 Tracking the Megatrends in the U.S. Dollar

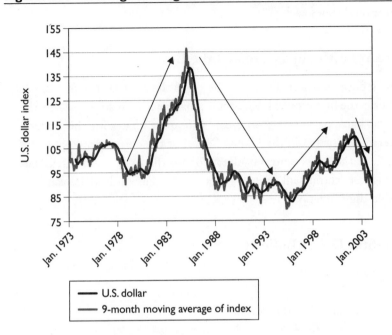

The Big Mac Index (Purchasing Power Parity)
==

The Big Mac Index (Purchasing Power Parity)

When the price of a Big Mac in the United States, which costs about $2.70 at this writing, differs by more than 20% from that of a Big Mac in Europe, for example, an adjustment is likely to occur back toward parity soon.

As of this writing, a Big Mac is 10% more expensive in Europe than in the United States, so there is no fundamental reason for the dollar to move versus the euro based on purchasing power. However, Big Macs in Australia are 31% cheaper than in the States. It should come as no surprise then that the Aussie dollar has been strengthening rapidly against the U.S. dollar. Big Macs are cheapest in China as we write, where they sell for an equivalent of US$1.20. But the Chinese currency is linked to the U.S. dollar and is likely to stay linked for a while. Big Macs cost US$1.86 in both Australia and South Africa. In contrast, they cost US$4.59 in Switzerland and US$2.97 in most countries that use

the euro. *The Economist* magazine publishes an update of this information several times each year.[4]

Where Your Money Is Treated the Best

Money flows to where it's treated best—to the place that is most stable
and pays the highest yield. Right now, that place is Australia, where the
central bank pays 4.75% interest.[5] Compare that with the Federal
Reserve rate of 1% in the United States, or the euro central bank rate
of 2%, or the Swiss central bank rate of less than 1%. South Africa has
the highest central bank rates at about 13.5%, but South Africa can have
double-digit inflation rates.

Three-Star Dollar Indicator

As of September 2003:

1. The dollar is in a downtrend.
2. Big Macs in the U.S. are relatively expensive compared to what
   they cost in some countries.
3. Money is not being treated well in the United States, which has
   one of the lowest interest rates in the developed world.

The dollar looks vulnerable at the moment, but by the time you read
this the picture might be different, so you'll have to make your own
determination. That's not hard to do. You can get a free monthly update
by subscribing to Van Tharp's free e-mail newsletter, *Tharp's Thoughts*.

How Interest Rates Affect the Dollar and Your Wealth

If the bank started paying 12% interest, most people would probably
move their money out of the stock market and into the bank. Why take
the risk of stocks, they'd say, when you can get stock-like returns with
much less risk? So it only makes sense that as interest rates rise, people
sell stocks.

Looking at the reverse situation, as the bank lowers the interest it pays closer and closer to zero, people feel compelled to invest their money somewhere. They usually choose the stock market.

Consider also the two 17-year megatrends we talked about earlier. From 1964 to 1981 interest rates were on a steady rise higher, from 4% to 14%. During that 17-year period, stocks, based on the price change in the Dow Jones Industrial Average, were horrible investments. The next 17 years were the mirror image: interest rates went from 14% to 5%, and the stock market rose by more than 8,000 points.

If you pay attention these interest rate cycles, you can earn large, safe profits.

Interest Rates on Long-Term Government Bonds	*Dow Jones Industrial Average*
Dec. 31, 1964: 4.20%	Dec. 31, 1964: 874.12
Dec. 31, 1981: 13.65%	Dec. 31, 1981: 875.00
Dec. 31, 1998: 5.09%	Dec. 31, 1998: 9181.43

Later in this chapter you'll learn how to use changes in interest rates to your investment advantage, what to invest in when rates are rising or falling, and how to profit from interest rate differences around the world.

The first lessons are that:

• Interest rates can move in long-term trends.
• Stocks do poorly when interest rates are rising and they do well when rates are falling.

Figure 10.3 charts uptrends and downtrends in bond interest rates over a 40-year period.

The Max Yield Strategy: A Safe, Once-a-Year System for Double-Digit Profits

The max yield strategy is the best way to profit from high interest rates. As discussed, you need to have your money in a place where interest rates are high and Big Macs are cheap.

Figure 10.3 Major Uptrend, Then a Major Downtrend

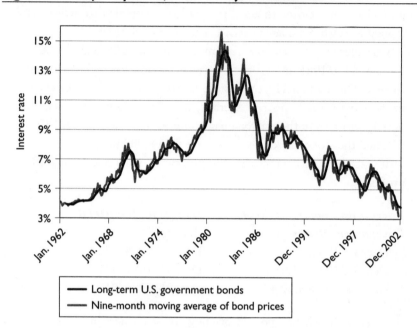

Remember, money flows to where it's treated best. At the time of this writing, it's treated best in Australia and New Zealand. In September 2003, a Big Mac in Australia is an astounding US$0.84 cheaper than a Big Mac in the United States—a 31% discount. Australia also has attractive interest rates. Greenspan has cut short-term rates in the United States to 1%, while the central bank in Australia has maintained interest rates at over 4%. You can take advantage of this information with a powerful strategy based on the idea that money flows where it's treated best.

Currency expert Chris Weber has been so successful investing in currencies he's never had a regular job.[6] He put together Table 10.1 illustrating that if you had put your money each year in a stable country with the highest interest rates, you would have earned double-digit returns on your cash over 33 years—beating stocks with cash.

The strategy here is simple. On January 1 each year you invest in the stable country that pays the highest yield. You collect the highest inter-

Table 10.1 Beating Stocks with Initial Cash Investment of $10,000

Year	Max-Yield	Currency	Interest Paid	Currency Value Increase	Total Return in US$
1970	US	$	10.00%	n/a	$11,000.00
1971	German	DM	7.50%	16.00%	$13,200.00
1972	German	DM	5.50%	1.00%	$14,058.00
1973	British	Pound	9.00%	−6.80%	$14,367.28
1974	British	Pound	16.00%	4.70%	$17,341.30
1975	Japanese	Yen	13.75%	−2.00%	$19,378.91
1976	British	Pound	10.00%	−17.30%	$17,964.25
1977	British	Pound	13.50%	10.50%	$22,275.66
1978	French	Franc	9.25%	9.33%	$26,414.48
1979	British	Pound	12.50%	10.00%	$32,357.74
1980	British	Pound	17.33%	3.60%	$39,130.22
1981	Eurodollars		18.00%	0.00%	$46,173.65
1982	Italian	Lira	21.38%	−13.90%	$49,625.14
1983	Italian	Lira	19.00%	−21.30%	$48,483.76
1984	Italian	Lira	17.75%	−14.75%	$49,938.27
1985	Italian	Lira	15.70%	12.10%	$63,821.11
1986	Australian	Dollar	18.75%	−2.40%	$74,255.86
1987	Australian	Dollar	16.00%	8.70%	$92,597.06
1988	Australian	Dollar	12.88%	18.40%	$121,556.79
1989	Australian	Dollar	16.88%	−7.30%	$133,195.85
1990	Australian	Dollar	15.75%	−2.20%	$151,243.89
1991	Spanish	Peseta	14.49%	−5.45%	$164,916.34
1992	Swedish	Krona	13.75%	−3.00%	$182,644.84
1993	Spanish	Peseta	13.35%	−23.00%	$165,019.61
1994	Spanish	Peseta	7.73%	8.11%	$191,158.72
1995	New Zealand	Dollar	10.02%	2.06%	$214,250.69
1996	Italian	Lira	8.85%	3.50%	$240,710.66
1997	New Zealand	Dollar	7.63%	−17.36%	$217,289.51
1998	New Zealand	Dollar	8.40%	−10.37%	$213,008.91
1999	British	Pound	5.63%	−2.51%	$219,654.78
2000	British	Pound	6.71%	−7.74%	$217,392.34
2001	New Zealand	Dollar	6.52%	−7.15%	$216,022.77
2002	New Zealand	Dollar	4.84%	24.81%	$280,073.52
2003	New Zealand	Dollar	5.76%	25.00%	$366,224.14

Source: Chris Weber

est in the developed world, and you earn gains as that country's currency rises against the dollar. When you add them together, you end up with double-digit annual returns.

It doesn't work every year, as Table 10.1 shows, but it works very well. The times that it doesn't work are during the great dollar bull markets. Chris Weber now believes we are entering the third dollar bear market, so it's time to consider a strategy like this.

The Easy Way to Play the Max Yield Game

Instead of sending your money off to faraway places to play the max yield game, you can work with a U.S. firm that specializes in foreign currency CDs (certificate of deposits) or foreign income-paying investments. You earn the same interest rates on your foreign currency CDs that locals would earn in those countries. Three such firms are:

EverBank (everbank.com): 888-882-3837
International Assets Advisory (iaac.com): 800-432-0000
Peregrine Financials & Securities (pfswp.com): 877-539-1004

EverBank offers a single CD that has four high-yielding currencies in one CD (Canadian dollar, Australian dollar, New Zealand dollar, and South African rand). As of September 2003, a six-month index CD of these commodity currencies was paying 5% (APR).

DID YOU KNOW? ABOUT EVERBANK

Everbank is a U.S. bank. It has been on *Forbes'* Best of the Web lists for 2000, 2001, and 2002. It offers FDIC-insured deposit accounts and CDs. The minimum is only $2,500 for a deposit account and for $10,000 for CDs. The currency-basket CDs, like the commodity currency CD we're recommending, have a minimum of $20,000. Although the CD is FDIC insured, that doesn't mean you can't lose money.

Let's say you put 5% of your money in these CDs and keep the rest in dollars. If the U.S. dollar strengthens by more than the 5% interest you earn on your foreign currency CD, your principal will start to decline by the amount in excess of 5% that the dollar strengthens. There are a few ways to look at this. Let's say you put 5% of your portfolio into an EverBank CD. If it increases in value you're happy, but remember that the other 95% of your portfolio that is in dollars is losing purchasing power. If the 5% does lose some value, be comforted by the fact that the 95% of your wealth that's in dollars is gaining in purchasing power. You're doing this to diversify your risk.

Going Down Under for Big Profits

High interest rates and cheap burgers alone should motivate you to have some money earning interest in Australia. But there is an additional incentive as well. The Australian dollar is what's called a *commodity currency*—a currency that is heavily affected by international commodity prices, including gold. Australia is a gold-producing nation whose fortunes are tied to gold and other commodities. Over the last decade, the Australian dollar has shown a remarkable correlation to the price of gold—with a time lag. In other words, when gold falls, the Aussie dollar will fall afterward. When gold rises, the Aussie dollar will rise in time. See for yourself in Figure 10.4.

Gold hit a five-year high in 2003. It's time for the Aussie dollar to rise. And to capitalize on this, it's time to have a very safe investment that is substantially in Aussie dollars.

A 30% Gain for Every Penny Move

One such investment is the Aberdeen Asia-Pacific Income Fund. It's an Australian bond fund that trades on the American Stock Exchange with the symbol FAX. The fund has a high correlation to the Aussie dollar, but it's more volatile. A 10% move in the value of the Aussie dollar has translated to nearly a 30% move in the value of this fund. This fund isn't perfect. For one, only about 60% of it is in Australia. The rest is

Figure 10.4 The Aussie Dollar Follows the Price of Gold

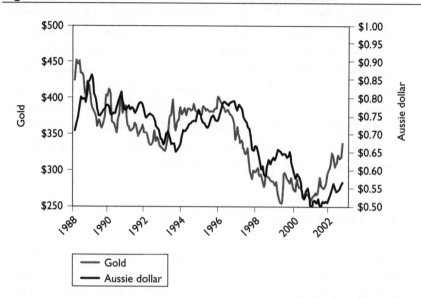

in Asian bonds. It is, however, a good way to get exposure to the Aussie dollar and to collect a nice yield with the potential for significant gains as the Aussie dollar strengthens. With FAX you can earn a high 8% dividend while waiting on a capital gain of 30% or more due to a weaker U.S. dollar.

You would have lost money with this investment under Bill Clinton's strong dollar policy. But now, after seven years of that policy, the dollar is expensive. And at 1%, investors are not being compensated for the risk. The straw to break the dollar's back was Governor Bernanke's speech mentioned earlier.

The Best Strategies in Each Interest Rate Environment

There are two major interest rate environments—rising rates and falling rates. There are two minor ones as well—steady, high interest rates and steady, low interest rates. Let's consider how to invest safely during each:

- *Falling interest rates.* This is the easiest time to invest. Nearly every type of investment works. Both stocks and bonds are generally in rip-roaring bull markets, as the 1982–2000 period suggests.
- *Rising interest rates.* Not much works when interest rates are rising. Tangible assets do the best in this time because rising interest rates often signal a fear of inflation. And when investors fear inflation, they retreat to hard assets. The best-performing assets during the inflationary 1970s, when interest rates were rising, were things like gold, collectibles, and rare coins. Real estate outperformed both stocks and bonds in that time as well.

   A surefire way to succeed in times of rising interest rates is to buy an inverse prime rate fund or an inverse bond fund, like the Rydex Juno Fund (rydexfunds.com). This fund performs the opposite of Treasury bonds, so it will do extremely well when interest rates are rising and bond prices are tanking.
- *Steady interest rates.* When rates are high and relatively steady, bonds are the place to be. The high interest rates will be choking corporate profits, so stock prices could struggle. But bonds will pay you high yields. There's an added benefit here too: when interest rates finally do come down, you will get a capital gain on your bonds in addition to your high interest payments—the best of both worlds.

When interest rates are low and steady, it's a good time to refinance your debt to reduce your financial freedom number, to consider the max yield strategy, and to get things paid off. The goal of low rates is generally to stimulate a struggling economy. Either one of two things will follow: a stronger economy, which means higher rates ahead and poor investment performance, or a still-struggling economy in which the typical investments don't do well. Low rates are a time to clean up your act and play it safe, even though the natural impulse is to stretch for a higher return on your money.

Monitoring Interest Rates on Your Own

The two major interest rate indicators are the Federal Reserve's rate adjustments and the trend in long-term government bond rates.

The easiest way to assess what is going on in interest rates is to notice when the Federal Reserve raises or lowers the rates. The board meets every six weeks, but it doesn't change interest rates at every meeting. When it does make an adjustment, it's all over the news, so this is an indicator that's easy to monitor. As a rule, the coast is clear for most investments if the Fed is either lowering rates or doing nothing. When the Fed raises interest rates—stand aside! Very few investments will appreciate substantially.

To monitor the trend in the long-term government bond, stick with the nine-month moving average (or whatever time period works best for you). You can easily monitor this on the homepage of Yahoo Finance (yahoo.finance.com).

As of February 2004, U.S. interest rates have been trending lower, and they are still below the long-run moving average. It is not surprising that stocks, bonds, and home prices have risen since early 2003. With rates at historic lows, now is a time to play it safe. Pay down debts and consider the max yield approach.

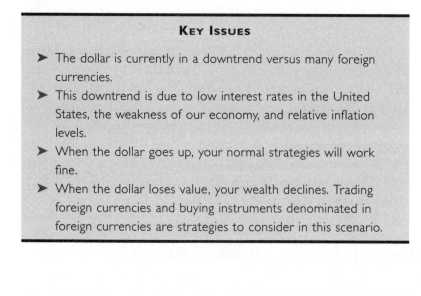

KEY ISSUES

➤ The dollar is currently in a downtrend versus many foreign currencies.

➤ This downtrend is due to low interest rates in the United States, the weakness of our economy, and relative inflation levels.

➤ When the dollar goes up, your normal strategies will work fine.

➤ When the dollar loses value, your wealth declines. Trading foreign currencies and buying instruments denominated in foreign currencies are strategies to consider in this scenario.

ACTION STEPS

➤ If the dollar is above its 40-week moving average, you don't have to take action to protect yourself from a fall in the value of the dollar.

➤ Monitor the situation once a month, or subscribe to IITM's free weekly e-mail newsletter, *Tharp's Thoughts*, and read our thoughts on the big picture every month.

➤ Keep track of interest rates on a monthly basis by following the Federal Reserve discount rate and the 10-year government bond rate.

➤ If the dollar is below its 40-week moving average, consider taking protective action with at least 25% of your portfolio using the ideas suggested in this chapter.

➤ If U.S. interest rates are low, consider paying off debts and using the max yield approach to making money.

➤ When interest rates start to rise, consider a fund that profits when rates go up, such as the Rydex Juno Fund.

➤ When interest rates are high and steady, consider investing in bonds. We are currently a long way away from this environment.

Notes

1. You can monitor this information for yourself by going to the Federal Reserve's website, federalreserve.gov.
2. View Governor Ben Bernanke's speech at federalreserve.gov.
3. Go to federalreserve.gov for data on the dollar.
4. The Big Mac Index is available for a small fee from *The Economist* at economist.com/markets.
5. You can track the interest rates in major countries at bloomberg.com/markets/rates.
6. To order his newsletter, Weber Global Opportunities Report, contact Mt. Vernon Publishing, 105 W. Monument St., Baltimore, MD 21201. Phone 888-384-8339; e-mail customerservice@mtvernonpublishing.com.

CHAPTER 11

SIZING UP REAL ESTATE AS AN INVESTMENT

"Rising real estate markets are what make you rich. Avoiding bad markets is what keeps you rich."

—ROBERT CAMPBELL

More millionaires attain their wealth through real estate than any other type of investment. Doesn't this suggest that at least some of your portfolio should be in real estate? It should, but you also need to be very careful. People can lose a huge amount of money in real estate if their timing is wrong and their leverage is high.

Real estate has generally risen in value during our lifetime, but by how much? After maintenance, taxes, closing costs, and other hassles, is real estate really worthwhile? What place does it have in our investment portfolios, if any? How does it stack up against other investments? These and other questions will be addressed in this chapter. By the end of the chapter you'll know how real estate has performed in the past and you'll understand the arguments for and against real estate today. Equally important, you'll learn how to size it up for the future.

Is Real Estate Really a Good Investment?

Is there a real estate bubble, or is real estate one of the best investments you can make right now? Since real estate is a significant financial freedom strategy, you need to answer this basic question before you think about specific strategies.

Net 2% a year—that's all home prices in America have risen going back as far as we have consistent data (the 1960s), and adjusting for inflation. You're probably thinking that can't be true, but it is. Although home prices have risen about 6% a year, inflation was about 4% over that period. Generally, prices have been up 15.4% across the United States since 2000, but the increase is not equal in all regions. In Los Angeles, the median house price is up 23% in just one year, but in many Midwest towns real estate hardly moves at all.

Most people think housing in America has become overpriced. Many even swear that we're in a "housing bubble" because prices have risen dramatically in recent years. People are flocking to real estate. Some people see this as a sign of a potential top. Many so-called experts like to make comparisons to Japan, where property prices fell 75% since its stock market bubble burst in 1990.

The Negative Side of the Real Estate Picture

Many experts say we are in a real estate bubble that could burst at any time. Some even say the bust has already begun. Their opinions are based on the fact that mortgage debt has grown tremendously and that there is massive speculation in some areas of the country. Let's look at these conditions more closely.

Mortgage Debt Has Grown Tremendously

Mortgage debt grew at an annual rate of more than 10% in each of the last two years. In the last 19 quarters (i.e., just under five years), mortgage debt has increased by $3 trillion, or 58%. Currently, the Federal Reserve lists private real estate equity in the United States at $13.6 trillion. Real estate debt is listed at $7.6 trillion, which means that people have only a 55% equity stake in their houses. During the Great Depression Americans had 85% equity in their houses, so they could tolerate huge price drops in real estate values.

Think about it! Over the last three years, prices have gone up 15% while debt has gone up to 45% of the average home value. It means that people are taking money out of their houses to purchase other things. That is not a sound thing to do during a deflationary bear market. What would happen if prices start to drop?

Massive Speculation in Some Areas

People in Florida were putting deposits on oceanfront condos while they were still being built. By the time a condo was finished, the buyer would turn around and sell it at a nice profit. That sounds like speculative excess—the same sort of thing that occurred in the Nasdaq at its peak.

Florida real estate at the right location can sell in the multimillions. It has a nice climate year-round, and the state allows residents to exempt the full value of their personal home from any debt they owe in legal proceedings.[1] For example, someone who owns a $5 million house and has put down only $1 million on it can still exempt the full $5 million from any lawsuits. Thus, if a person's net worth was under $5 million, that $5 million house with an 80% mortgage would totally protect him from a lawsuit. As a result, people from other states find Florida real estate to be very attractive.

Despite this strong advantage, expensive houses in Florida's Gold Coast are now selling for only about half of what they were selling for three years ago. The houses that sold belonged to people who were willing to drop their prices dramatically. Similar drops have occurred in Las Vegas and Silicon Valley, and they may happen in other hot spots such as Southern California.

When real estate begins to drop, the first thing to go is commercial real estate. Commercial real estate is showing weakness throughout the country. Second homes and expensive homes tend to go next. That's starting to happen as well.

The Federal Reserve says it will do whatever it takes to make sure real estate prices do not fall significantly, but can they really do anything? If they do, the United States will probably see a weak economy for a while—perhaps 15 years. If they cannot stop prices from declining, then we will probably have a debt implosion and watch a strong deflationary scenario play out. The bear market bottom will come much more quickly, but it will be very painful. Watch this carefully!

The Positive Side of the Real Estate Picture

Those who say the United States could have a real estate crash similar to the one that occurred in Japan are not doing their homework. You see, in the boom years of the 1980s, real estate prices in Japan rose by 300%. The current fall in Japanese real estate has simply erased the gains of the boom years. In the United States, real estate did not participate in the stock market boom.

Housing Is More Affordable Than It Has Been in 30 Years

Yes, real estate values have risen in recent years. But as this is being written, the fundamentals for housing have actually improved as prices have risen. Housing in America is more affordable than it has been in 30 years. Back in 1981, it took all you had to afford a median-priced home in America. With mortgage rates of 15%, it took 42% of the median household income just to make principal and interest payments.

Today you only need half as much money to get the same house. Mortgage rates have fallen from 15% in 1981 to 5.5% in 2004. Now the median house payment is about $900 a month and the median household income is about $53,000. So the house payment (principal and interest) takes up only 20% of income. This has made homes more affordable than at any time since the early 1970s, as shown in Figure 11.1.

When Home Prices Are Affordable, Housing Prices Boom

After they were so affordable in the early 1970s, housing prices boomed. Ironically, this occurred during the second worst bear market in stocks of the twentieth century—1973 to 1974. It turns out that the conventional wisdom that home prices must fall because stock prices fell is not based on any "wisdom" at all.

Even though interest rates were going up in the 1970s, home prices continued to skyrocket. New buyers didn't care about high interest rates because homes were still "affordable." It would take an extraordinary

Figure 11.1 Housing Affordability Index (HAI) Versus Home Prices

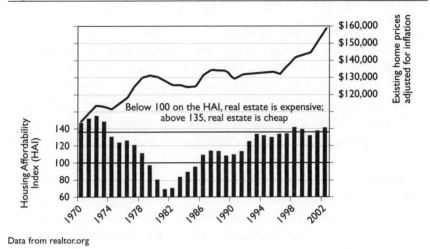

Data from realtor.org

move higher in interest rates for home prices not to be attractive because, for the most part, mortgage payments are cheaper than rent these days.

The Housing Affordability Index that is tracked in Figure 11.1 (available at realtor.org; click on Research and then on Existing Homes) measures the ability of households to purchase housing at prevailing prices with currently available financing. At the time this is written in 2003, homes are more affordable than at any time in the last 30 years, according to this index. Falling household incomes, substantially rising interest rates, or a substantial increase in home prices would cause this index to fall (meaning homes are less affordable).

Where home prices have been is irrelevant. Where they're going is what's important. What you need to consider is the affordability of homes. Today, homes are more affordable (in terms of mortgage payment versus income) than they have been in 30 years. The last time housing was this affordable, home prices (not adjusted for inflation) doubled in six years.

The Housing Affordability Index is a good rough guide for the nationwide picture, but all real estate is local, they say. What's been going on in your area?

The Housing Market in Your Area

Housing prices nationwide have risen an average of 6.5% a year over the last five years. Yet prices have risen by a total of 84.7% in San Diego, California; 81.7% in Nassau/Suffolk, New York; and 51% in West Palm Beach, Florida, in that same time frame. Those numbers are in stark contrast to Springfield, Illinois, where home prices have crept forward at about 1.6% a year on average over the last five years.

The National Association of Home Builders performed its own housing affordability study on local markets. The study compared median incomes with median home prices in hundreds of markets across America. It found exactly what you'd expect—that 9 out of 10 families in Indiana can afford the median-priced home ($64K median income, $125K median home price). On the other hand, 1 out of 10 in San Francisco can afford the median-priced home ($86K median income, $525K median home price). Thus, we may have a bubble in certain sections of the country, but certainly not nationwide.[2]

International Real Estate Opportunities: Five Advantages and Three Ways to Make Money[3]

Most U.S. investors are overlooking a simple truth: *the best deals and the biggest opportunities in real estate today are not to be found within U.S. borders.* You'll have trouble finding a seaside getaway on either U.S. coast that could be called a bargain. But our country doesn't have a monopoly on nice beaches. Indeed, some of the most desirable property in the world right now is outside of U.S. borders. You can find top-shelf real estate in places where economic and political factors allow you to buy at a discount.

International real estate offers five advantages over domestic real estate:

1. Global real estate investments can appreciate faster than U.S. real estate. Because you're buying at a discount, there is higher ceiling for appreciation. With today's technology, many people can work

from anywhere on the planet. Why work in a Peoria suburb when you could work and live just as easily on the beach in Belize?

2. Global real estate offers you a safe haven if things go bad in the United States. Many Americans feel that their constitutional rights are taking a backseat to homeland security. Many governments around the world are less intrusive than ours.

3. Global real estate is an easy way to move some of your assets offshore. Once you own property abroad, it's extremely difficult for the government, creditors, or anyone else to get at it.

4. Your real estate investment can double as a personal retreat, part-time residence, or vacation getaway. You can take enjoyment from it while it's appreciating in value, generating rental returns, and safeguarding your net worth.

5. Global real estate investing can open the doors and broaden your horizon to a new lifestyle. How many investments work like that? Not many.

Today it's possible, even easy, to live, work, relax, or retire anywhere you want. The investors who recognize this trend and identify its path will profit most. So where should you be looking?

Finding What's Right for You Overseas

You need to consider not only geography, but also strategy. As an international real estate investor, you can make money in three ways:

1. By purchasing property (land, a house, an apartment building, etc.), adding value, and selling it at a profit (flipping)

2. By investing in properties (a house, an apartment, a resort unit) that produce rental income (which exceeds holding costs) that can help compound capital appreciation

3. By investing in raw land that you believe will appreciate in value in the coming years; this is a longer-term, buy-and-hold strategy

For some of the best deals in the world right now, look to Nicaragua. The situation there is similar to that in Costa Rica and Belize in the late

1980s, when real estate prices increased by 500% or more in a very short time. And Nicaragua's lakes, volcanoes, two oceans, waterways, and pristine rain forests offer greater potential than the natural resources of its neighbors.

Another recommendation that's in a class by itself: buy an apartment in Buenos Aires, Argentina. The recent crisis in this country has created a serious distortion in the country's real estate market. Centuries-old classic-style apartments (the kind you find in only a handful of cities around the world, including Paris and Barcelona) that sold for $2,000 a square meter or more a few years ago can be bought today for $1,000 a square meter. These are places with intrinsic value—places worth owning. The current market pricing makes them irresistible.

International Living publishes free e-letters and reports that highlight opportunities in locales around the world. To sign up, go to internationalliving.com.

Understanding Real Estate Cycles: The Key to Real Estate Investing

Like interest rates, real estate moves in cycles.

The bottom of the cycle is *depression* in the property markets. This is generally characterized by low prices, no new construction, high vacancies, and low rents. Eventually, the depression bottoms out when you hear people saying that no one will ever make money in property again.

Then the *recovery* materializes. Prices are no longer falling. Neither are rents. Occupancy rates start to rise. Yet there's still no new construction.

Optimism takes over, and the *boom* sets in. Construction cranks up at a furious pace. Prices and rents rise rapidly. You know the top has arrived when everyone thinks real estate is a sure thing.

Suddenly, out of nowhere, the *downturn* arrives. The overbuilding got out of hand, and some bad ideas were hatched in the midst of the frenzy. Returns on real estate start to shrink.

Then the cycle starts all over again. The same sequence just keeps playing itself out.

How You Can Make Money in Real Estate

So how did all the real estate millionaires make their money? While some of them probably followed the three principles we'll talk about here, many of them followed the one strategy we don't advocate—they took extraordinary risks.

If a developer borrows $10 million, the likely outcome is a gain or loss of a few hundred thousand dollars. A loss could put the developer out of business, but a string of winners could make him millions. But there's so much risk—so much leverage.

That leverage is a double-edged sword. After all, you're responsible for every penny you borrow. Japanese real estate investors learned that lesson the hard way, as property prices in Tokyo are still half of what they were a decade ago. If you borrow $500,000 and your house falls in value to $250,000, you still owe the $500,000. It's the leverage, not the real estate investing, that gets people into trouble.

Ultimately, there are two factors that determine risk and reward in real estate investing: leverage and diversification.

You're already familiar with leverage in real estate, so let's talk about diversification. You really can lower your risk substantially by diversifying across many properties and sectors.

Real Estate Looks Good Compared to Other Assets

While the price of homes may have risen by only 6% a year (or only 2% a year after inflation), your total return on most real estate investments (including rental income or dividends on real estate stocks) has actually been pretty good. If your house increased by 6% a year and you collected 7% in net rental yield, you're competing with stocks.

Commercial real estate in particular has been excellent. Take a look at the chart of total returns in Figure 11.2. Note that there has been only one down period in the last 25 years. And real estate during this period has been much less volatile than stock prices.

When you consider the current income (in the 6% range) and the potential for appreciation, property deserves a place in your portfolio. But most people can't go out and buy a big office building, much less a handful of buildings, to get some diversification. And you wouldn't want to because buying buildings in your hometown wouldn't provide you with much diversification. Furthermore, you are not a professional property manager. A better way to diversify is through real estate investment trusts (REITs), which are real estate stocks.

You can also diversify by yourself with the help of John Burley's strategies, which he will share with us in the next chapter. John would probably walk away from a real estate deal that paid 20%. He thinks much bigger, and you should consider his strategies for your own situation.

How You Can Monitor the Real Estate Picture for Yourself

So far you've seen both a negative and a positive picture for real estate. How can you determine if the real estate market is good for you? There are three key rules to follow.

Rule 1: Don't Fight Interest Rates

When the Fed is hiking rates, when mortgage rates are rising, or when interest rates have been rising in general, housing prices suffer. It makes sense—people can afford a particular mortgage payment. If interest rates go up, the amount of house you can afford for that same mortgage payment goes down.

You can think of mortgage rates like the tides. The tide is going to come in—there's no holding it back. Housing prices will suffer under rising interest rates. If the tide is rising, don't fight it. Fortunately, like the tide, interest rates will eventually recede.

Figure 11.2 Annual Total Return in Commercial Real Estate

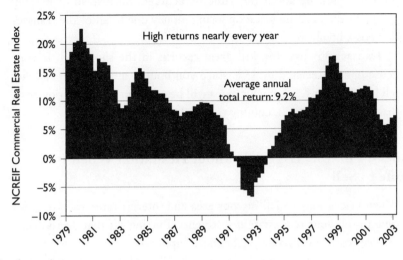

Data from realtor.org

As a rule of thumb, if the most recent 10% move in mortgage rates is against you (rates going up), there's no hurry to buy. However, once mortgage rates have moved 10% in your favor (lower), prices will start moving higher. Fortunately, housing prices move glacially. The best place to follow mortgage rates on the Web is at bankrate.com. Do your homework ahead of time, and be ready to act swiftly when the interest rate environment improves.

Rule 2: Don't Fight the Price Trend

Some family members bought two oceanfront lots in Florida for $20,000 back in the 1970s. After owning the lots for 20 years, they sold one and built a house on the other. Today, the lot they sold is probably worth a half a million dollars or more. Unfortunately, they sold in the early 1990s, when prices just started to move, so they received only $84,000 or so.

One of the keys to making money in real estate is not to sell too early—let the price trend run its course. As soon as most people see a profit in their home, they immediately consider selling it. They don't think about the fact that every other house in the neighborhood has probably risen by about the same percentage. So instead of making money in the deal, they end up losing money due to all of the transaction costs involved.

Transaction costs can kill great returns in the short run. If your house has appreciated by 15% since you bought it a year ago and you sell it today, nearly all of your gains will be eaten up by transaction costs that you paid going in, coming out, and going in again.

Rule 3: Pull the Trigger Without Hesitation When It's Time to Sell

When prices start to fall in your area and interest rates are rising, it's time to sell your real estate investments. Putting off that decision can be very costly. Real estate crashes have happened in many areas over the last 50 years, and you don't want to be holding a lot of real estate when it happens.[4]

Summing up these three rules:

Don't fight the interest rates.
Don't fight the price trend.
Pull the trigger without hesitation when it's time to sell.

As this is being written, interest rates are low but have started rising, and the price trend has been higher. When you combine low rates, the price trend, and the affordability of homes (according to the Housing Affordability Index), it looks like real estate may survive any bad times in the near future. However, if the price or interest rate trends change, it will call for a change in strategy.

Monitoring Real Estate Strategies

Two of John Burley's strategies in the next chapter, *quick cash* and *buy and hold*, will work best in depressed markets that are starting to move or in rapidly appreciating markets. For example, you could buy a home for $200,000 and rent it out for $1,500 per month. If you did so, you

---

KEY IDEAS

➤ Although many people suggest that we might have been at the top of a real estate bubble in 2003, it is probably just a local bubble in certain parts of the United States.

➤ For most Americans, housing is more affordable than it has been for a long time. As a result, real estate prices should rise.

➤ Real estate returns in many overseas markets may be higher than domestic returns in the near future.

➤ You can monitor how good real estate might be doing in your area by keeping track of mortgage rates, price trends, and the affordability of housing in your area.

---

might have a negative cash flow of $500 or more per month. However, that's not significant if this hot property is appreciating by 15% per year because this means that your property is gaining about $2,500 per month in appreciating value. You can afford to lose $500 per month in negative cash flow if you are making $2,500 per month in appreciation. Strategies like these will not work when real estate markets are falling in value. If you attempt them when prices are falling, banking on price appreciation, you will lose your shirt.

Burley's *cash flow* strategy works fairly well in most markets and gives you a lot of protection on the downside.

Notes

1. They cannot use the mortgage amount to offset other debt in bankruptcy, and they can still lose their home to the property lender.
2. You can track local trends through Home Price Index available at ofheo.gov.
3. This section was written by Kathleen Peddicord, longtime editor and publisher of *International Living* and owner of real estate in six countries. *International Living* reports on the best

> opportunities for living, retiring, investing, traveling, and buying real estate overseas.

4. Robert Campbell, *Timing in the Real Estate Market* (San Diego, Calif.: Robert Campbell, 2002). Campbell describes four indicators to keep track of real estate cycles and sells software to help you do so. See realestatetiming.com.

CHAPTER 12

REAL ESTATE STRATEGIES YOU CAN USE FOR PROFIT

JOHN R. BURLEY

"There have been few things in my life which have had a more genial effect on my mind than the possession of a piece of land."
—HARRIET MARTINEAU

During the late 1980s I made a deliberate decision to move into the realm of real estate investing. Up until that time I had been a successful financial planner with my own very lucrative practice. At the same time, I wanted to move from the corporate world into a situation where I would be creating passive income that would allow me to experience true financial freedom and personal fulfillment. I realized that investing in real estate actively and aggressively would generate the passive income and positive cash flow that I was looking for. I moved to Phoenix, Arizona, and began to actively invest in real estate.

I began with very little money and the simple belief that my investment plan would work. A few years later, at the age of 32, I was in a position to retire comfortably for the rest of my life. Rather than retire, I decided to continue investing in real estate and to share my knowledge of investing with others so that they, too, could experience financial freedom. Today, I have well over one thousand real estate transactions under my belt, and I have spoken to thousands of people on three continents about their financial habits and the techniques I've used to invest successfully in real estate. The crowds of people who attend my seminars have convinced me that this is an even more popular investing strategy than it was when I began. People are beginning to realize that real estate is a safe investment that can produce consistent cash flow.

In real estate investing there are three primary strategies. I'll review their specific characteristics and tell you which is most effective in which types of markets.

Choosing Your Strategy

When choosing your real estate investment strategy, begin by answering these three questions:

1. Would you like to develop an appreciating portfolio that others will pay you to own? This is the *buy-and-hold* strategy.
2. Do you want to make some quick cash, say $10,000 or more in the next 90 days? This is the *quick cash* strategy.
3. Are you looking to have substantial monthly income for the next 10 to 30 years? This is the *cash flow* strategy.

All three strategies produce results, but where you apply them and the way you implement them are quite different. I've used all of these strategies at various times. The one I chose for a particular situation depended on what I wanted to accomplish at that time.

Strategy 1: Buy and Hold

This is a well-known strategy that has been taught for many years. While it is applicable in most markets, it can be challenging to apply in some regions of the country. It will be most difficult to implement the buy-and-hold strategy in regions where property prices are the highest.

The basis of this strategy is simple. Buy a good property, rent or lease it, and wait for the property to appreciate (go up in value). It is the most talked-about real estate technique of all time. While it is still a viable option, I believe this strategy is a bit tired and was more effective in the 1970s and 1980s than it is today.

Imagine if you had used this strategy in California in 1970, when you could buy a nice house for around $30,000. Today that same house, in a major population center, is worth well over $500,000. If you had acquired just a few houses a year from 1970 to 1980, you would now be a millionaire many times over.

One of the keys to this strategy is that the rents must cover the debt service and expenses. In the 1970s, 1980s, and even up through the early 1990s, that could be done in most areas of the country without great difficulty. Today, in areas like California and the Northeast, it is often difficult to have rents high enough to cover the expenses. There are some areas of the Southwest, the South, the Mountain States, and the Midwest where you can still successfully buy and hold.

Let's go over the advantages and disadvantages of the buy-and-hold strategy.

Advantages
- *Outstanding profit potential.* If a $200,000 house rises in value by 15% per year, you make $2,500 per month in appreciation. If you put a 20% deposit down on the house ($40,000), you are making a 75% return on your investment of $40,000 in the first year ($2,500 × 12 = $30,000).
- *Steadily increasing cash flow.* As prices rise, you can raise the rents on your properties by 3% to 5% per year in a good market.
- *Great tax deductions.* You get to write off your costs (to the extent that they are greater than your income from the property), and you also get to write off a small percentage of the total value of the property every year as depreciation.

Disadvantages
- *Heavy property management costs.* You are likely to have all sorts of expenses, including repairs, vacancy costs, and even the cost of having someone manage the place for you.

- *Cash intensive.* You tie up a lot of cash—as much as 20% of the value of the property. Plus you periodically have to make large outlays of cash for repairs.
- *Very long-term cycle.* Real estate cycles can be as long as 20 years. You might not see much cash from the property until you finally sell 10 or 20 years later.

In today's market, the barriers to this strategy are obvious. Property prices have increased faster than rents. Expenses such as debt service, maintenance, repairs, and management costs have gone up accordingly. In recent years, many investors have foolishly become involved in properties that have negative cash flow (the property costs money out of their pocket), or they have put large amounts of cash into the property to reduce the payment so that the property would show a positive cash flow.[1]

I do not recommend either of these solutions to the negative cash flow dilemma. If the property cannot be bought in a way that will realistically allow it to carry itself (i.e., pay for itself fully), then I will not buy it, and you shouldn't either. If the property won't provide cash flow with a 10% or less down payment and with realistic market expenses applied, you should not acquire it for a long-term hold.

What are realistic market expenses? In addition to your payment of principal, interest, taxes, and insurance (PITI), you can expect an additional 15% to 40% or more of your income to be eaten up by expenses. No matter how well you manage the property, you will not keep 100% of your projected rents. You will have vacancies, legal fees, management costs, vandalism, general maintenance, capital improvements, and repairs. A lot of investors put themselves in a difficult cash flow situation by failing to plan for these expenses.

Don't give up hope. Keep looking until you find properties that will provide positive cash flow without significant down payments. The harder you have to look, the more profit you'll make. Generally, lower-priced properties are easier to turn into a positive cash flow than higher-priced ones because you can get a much higher rental rate on lower-priced properties. For example, someone investing in the Dallas, Texas, area (where prices are low) could buy a $100,000 property for 80% or 90% of its value ($10,000–$20,000 instant equity). They could probably rent it out at $1,200 per month and have a positive cash flow (i.e., money coming into their pockets every month after paying all expenses). In contrast, someone living in San Jose, California (where prices are high), would have to find and buy a $200,000 property for 60% to 80% of value ($40,000–$80,000 instant equity) to cover the expense with rent. The person in California would have to look at more properties to make a deal, but the effort would offer a greater return. In the long run, it all evens out. The person in Dallas finds more opportunities but has to make a lot more deals to make the same money as the person in San Jose.

When you're looking to buy, there are many good sources of sale properties to start with:

- Veterans Administration (VA)
- HUD/FHA
- Farmers Home Administration (FmHA)
- Bank REOs
- Internal Revenue Service (IRS) sales
- sheriffs' sales
- U.S. Marshals Service sales
- trustee sales
- U.S. bankruptcy court sales
- probate sales
- for sale by owner (FSBO)
- builders
- MLS Realtor® listings

Let me explain how I used the buy-and-hold strategy to purchase a property on Bascom Avenue in Los Gatos, California. Los Gatos is just outside of San Jose, about 50 miles south of San Francisco. This market includes some of the most expensive real estate in the country.

At the time, I was renting an apartment. Like many people, I did not have the money for a big down payment, but I was frustrated with paying rent. I scoured the newspaper for a couple of months. I made several phone calls and a few written offers. Then it happened. A dentist and his father owned a condominium in Los Gatos and were tired of the negative cash flow. They said the government had given them a bum deal by changing the tax laws and taking away most of their depreciation and tax write-offs. They were tired of the vacancies and the property management. They wanted out.

We agreed on a price of $119,000 although the market value of the property was about $138,000. They suggested that I put down 20% and take out an 80% loan with them paying the costs. It sounded like a great deal. The only problem was that I didn't have $23,800 for the down payment. When they asked what I had, I told them the truth. I earned a good living, but I only had a few thousand dollars in the bank. They were disappointed because they were sure we needed the down payment money to make the transaction fly.

Rather than give up, I asked them what they were going to do with the down payment money when they got it. They said they we're going to put it into CDs paying about 7.5%. I suggested that we create a note for $23,800 at 10%. They would make more than 7.5% and Uncle Sam would give them additional tax benefits for providing owner financing.

From there it was smooth sailing until the escrow[2] company decided that I couldn't provide money to the seller out of escrow. Escrow companies make a deal work by protecting both parties, but sometimes they work to your disadvantage when they won't let you do what both parties have agreed to. The escrow company wanted to see the cold hard cash. I couldn't believe it. This sweet deal had just blown up in my face. Fortunately, adversity often brings opportunity. The next morning I stopped feeling sorry for myself and got busy. I called everybody I knew who could get his or her hands on $25,000 in less than 48 hours. I offered them $500 interest for just one week. They didn't even have to give me the money. The loan had been approved. The agreement with the seller to return the money and carry the loan was signed. All that was needed was a cashier's check made out to the escrow company. I found a money partner, and he didn't lose. A week later he got his money back, plus $500, and I was the proud owner of a new home.

Here's how the monthly cash flow worked out.

1st trust deed[3] (my mortgage payment to the bank)	−665.65
2nd trust deed with seller	
(my mortgage payment to the seller)	−198.33
Homeowner's association dues	−97.12

Property taxes	−119.93
Total property, interest, taxes, insurance, and homeowner's association dues	−1,081.03
Tax savings ($918.00 × .33%)	302.94
Rent (2nd bedroom)	450.00
Total income/tax savings	752.94
Net cash flow out of pocket	**−328.09**

In the end, I was paying only $328.94 per month. The fair market rent was $550 per month, and I had the master bedroom and the garage. On top of that, I was now in the business of long-term gain, or appreciation. I had acquired the property with none of my own money down for 87% of its value. I resold the house 29 months later for $220,000. The property had gone up an average of $3,482.76 per month. When escrow closed, I had a cashier's check for more than $93,000. That's how the buy-and-hold strategy works when things go well.

Let's review the buy-and-hold strategy before moving on.

- The property must be able to pay for itself. High-priced homes rent for a smaller percentage of their value than do low-priced homes. Thus, the higher the price of the home, the bigger the disparity between the rents and the payments. Therefore, *you are going to have better success in areas where prices are lower.*
- Make sure you understand the cash flow numbers for every deal. *With this strategy you make your money on the buying, not the holding.*
- The buy-and-hold strategy will work better in some areas than others. *Look for locations where prices are fairly low and have been appreciating.*

Strategy 2: Quick Cash

The key to the quick cash strategy lies in the buying. You need to act as if you are the buyer for a retail store. Your objective is to buy a product (real estate) at a wholesale price and then quickly resell it for a profit. You become the middleman. You acquire properties at a price that allows them to be quickly resold for a higher price. That's why it's called quick cash.

Quick cash properties must be purchased at or below wholesale and resold at or just below retail. Generally, you must acquire the property for no more than 80% of real (not appraised) value. By acquiring the property at this wholesale level, you are able to resell it quickly and still make a good profit.

Let's go over the advantages and disadvantages of the quick cash strategy.

Advantages

- **Produces cash immediately.** You want to turn these houses over as quickly as possible, but when you do, you get immediate results.
- **Short time frame.** If you can make 15% in two months, you make an annual return of 90% per year.
- **Few hassles.** You don't have to worry about repairs, collections, vacancies, phone calls in the middle of the night, or any of the other problems that people who rent properties have.

Disadvantages

- **High turnover.** You must constantly find deals and new buyers.
- **Often cash-intensive.** You might have to put up $25,000 immediately to do a deal worth $10,000. However, if you did that you'd get a 40% return in a month or two.
- **Properties often require repairs.** To sell quickly for a reasonable price you might need to do some repairs.
- **Often high tax rate.** Your income from these transactions may be taxed like regular income.

I completed my first real estate transaction in 1982. It was a quick cash deal. After reading a couple of popular real estate investing books, I decided to go out and see if I could do it myself. I needed to find a distressed situation because I didn't have any money for a down payment.

I looked through the newspapers, called Realtors®, and let people know I was interested in buying real estate. About six months later, I was representing a small construction company at an energy conservation trade show when I found a great quick cash deal. I was talking with a man who sold solar heaters. Eighteen months earlier he had tried to begin a career in home building. He had acquired a 2½-acre plot of land and built an 1,800-square-foot ranch house on it. The house had an appraised value of $89,000.

There was nothing wrong with the house. The only problem was the interest rate. Interest rates were incredibly high in 1982, so fewer people were buying houses. The builder was having a hard time covering his construction loan payments. If he didn't sell soon, he would lose everything. Once he found out I was interested and that I could qualify for a loan, he told me he would do anything to sell it. In the end, he agreed to sell me the house for $75,000 and to pay all points, loan origination fees, and closing costs.

I also asked him to write the transaction up for $89,000 with a forgivable $9,000 earnest money note to be held outside of escrow. In other words, I could get a loan for $80,000 if the lender thought I was paying $89,000 for it. However, the extra $9,000 that was supposed to be my deposit was not held by a third party (i.e., the escrow company). It was just a theoretical sum, which the seller agreed to drop.

Once I financed the house for $80,000 (with no money down), the seller gave me a rebate check back for $5,000 when the escrow closed. Here's how it all worked out:

Contract purchase price	89,000
Forgivable earnest money deposit	−9,000
Loan amount	80,000
Buyer rebate	−5,000
Total purchase price	**75,000**

At the close of the transaction, not only did I have $5,000 in my pocket, but I also had an instant equity profit of $9,000. Putting $5,000 in my pocket at the close of escrow is what I call quick cash. I didn't have to wait to resell the property. I just collected the money and moved in. What could be better than that?

The only drawback to the deal was the financing. Financing rates were atrocious in the early 1980s compared to today. Back then, a fixed-rate FHA loan would run 16% to 18% per year. That would be like buying a house on your Visa or MasterCard. When I look back at the interest rates and those points, I feel great about the financing that's available today.

Let's review how the cash flow worked out.

Principal and interest (mortgage payment)	−754.32
Property taxes	−74.17
Property insurance	−24.42
Private mortgage insurance	−29.34
Total payment	−882.25
Tax savings ($828.49 × .30%)	248.55
Rent income (3rd bedroom)	350.00
Total income/tax savings	598.55
Net cash flow out of pocket each month	**−283.70**

The end result of this transaction was that I paid a little less than $300 a month to live in a very nice house out in the country on a couple of acres with a stream running through it.

Properties acquired for less than 80% of market value can often pay for themselves immediately. Even on a non-owner-occupied basis, these properties can often be financed or refinanced for 90% to 100% or more of your purchase price. In many cases, you can finance up to 100% of the appraised value on an owner-occupied property.

One variation of the quick cash strategy is to purchase property for 50% to 75% of value (not uncommon at cash foreclosure sales) and then refinance. This enables you to take cash out quickly without having to resell the property. You can then resell the property to someone else with favorable terms, thus making even more money. Let's look at more techniques you can use to make quick cash.

Assignment of Contract

One of the best techniques available for quick cash is the assignment of contract. This technique is unbelievably simple. When done properly, you don't even take title to the property. You don't have to put up any down payment, fill out any loan applications, or file a credit report. Yet you still make money. Here's how it works.

You offer to buy a property. Once the offer is accepted, you sell, or assign, your right to buy that property to someone else. When the other person closes escrow, you receive a check directly from the escrow company. You don't even have to be there. They'll mail the check to you if you prefer. The two main points to remember about this technique are that you need to develop a database of buyers and you need to find property for enough under market value that you can easily add to your profit.

The easiest way to develop a database is to run ads asking for exactly what you want. My ads look something like this:

- By owner. I sell houses in Northwest Phoenix for 92% of value. Must qualify. No Realtors®.
- Desperate. By owner. Only $1,900 down. Owner will carry with no bank qualifying. Affordable monthly payments.
- Minor fixer. Only $3,500 total move-in. Easiest qualifying in town.
- If you can qualify for a new loan, I will sell you a home in Glendale for 90% of FHA appraisal.

As people call in, I find out what they're looking for and what their time frame is. I ask them how much money they have to work with and other questions to prequalify them for a loan. After a short time, you will be surprised by how many prospective buyers you have for properties you haven't even found yet! Now you can make offers on houses at way below market. A small percentage of those offers will be accepted. And as your offers get accepted, you show the people in your database the properties you have available. Here are some key points to remember when writing the offer on an assignment of contract:

- Always place "and/or assigns" after your name. This gives you the right to assign, or endorse, the contract to another buyer.
- Always ask for enough time (at least 60 to 90 days) to remarket the property.
- Always request (in writing) the right to show the property to prospective occupants and remove existing signs. It's important to use the term "occupant" because this allows you to show the property to prospective tenants or buyers without having misled the seller.

- Consider using contingencies that give you the right to get out of the deal. A common contingency clause added to this type of contract states: "This offer is subject to written approval of buyer's partner within 60 days of acceptance of offer." Instead of "partner," you can substitute "attorney," "accountant," "CPA," "financial advisor," or "investment advisor." However, keep in mind that the more contingencies you place on an offer, the less likely the offer is to be accepted.

- Structure the transaction so there will be enough money in the deal for you. For example, purchase the property for a very low down payment and then resell for a larger down payment. If the seller needs money, arrange for him or her to create a note (i.e., a loan) and then sell the note to a third party. The seller can keep the proceeds from the sale of the note and you can keep the down payment from the new buyer who came from your database.

- Negotiate to buy the property for enough appraised value that your new buyer can get a loan for more than what is owed. This would be like the example described earlier, in which I bought a house at $80,000 but asked the owner to write up the transaction for $89,000 with a forgivable $9,000 earnest money note to be held outside of escrow. Thus, I was able to get a loan for the full purchase price of $80,000. If you do this negotiation up front, you can sell the house to a new buyer, who will be able to get in for little to no money down, and then pocket the difference in exchange for putting the deal together.

You will have to make several wholesale written offers for each one that gets accepted when using this technique. So you will need to shotgun offers right and left until you find a seller who has a property with financing that can be flexible enough to get the job done.

Many people get started in their investing efforts by using the assignment of contract technique. Because of its flexibility and minimal cash or credit requirements, it is one of the best ways for someone to start a real estate investing career.

Strategy 3: Cash Flow

When I first started investing in real estate, I concentrated on the buy-and-hold and quick cash strategies. I used the buy-and-hold strategy because I wanted to develop assets for the future and I didn't know any other way. I used the quick cash strategy because, like many people, I needed money immediately.

When I first moved out to the Phoenix area, I planned to use the buy-and-hold strategy indefinitely. My strategy consisted of buying properties from the government and other distressed sellers and holding them as rentals. However, I quickly realized that this strategy was not for me.

I didn't like putting-up my hard earned cash and leaving it there for merely breakeven cash flow. I hated working for my tenants. I didn't enjoy doing repairs, and I wasn't very good at it. I'd had it with landlording. I enjoyed making the deals, but the repairs and tenants were making me crazy—and broke. I was at my limit. I needed a way to make the properties generate income without all the work. I didn't really want to own real estate—I just wanted the money. So I started marketing properties on an *agreement for sale*, or *wrap*. In these deals, I keep the original mortgage and sell it to another person with another mortage "wrapped" around it. As I'll explain later, when I do these deals I usually get a cash-on-cash income that amounts to 60% or better per year.

As an alternative I also marketed properties on a lease with a separate option to purchase. With this technique you acquire a property and then remarket it to a new occupant, giving that person an opportunity to own the property sometime in the future. The new occupant makes one lump sum payment to the seller (you) that covers all the costs of ownership. The occupant takes care of the home and does the necessary maintenance. The payments increase as things such as taxes, insurance, or homeowner's association fees go up. You continue to pay on any underlying loans and make your profit by keeping the difference in the payments between your original loan and the new loan that the occupant is paying you. This is known as the *spread*. I like this investment strategy because all I do is collect the money and count the profits. I can develop a substantial monthly income without the burden of property management.

For cash flow transactions I prefer to acquire bread-and-butter-type homes in a "Lunch Pail Joe" neighborhood. In other words, I look for homes that are priced at least 10% to 20% below the area's median home price in a middle-class to lower-middle-class neighborhood. The type of property I invest in can be best demonstrated by walking through one of my first cash flow properties.

North 68th Avenue, Phoenix, Arizona

The property was located in west Phoenix, Arizona. It was a 1,150-square-foot, three-bedroom house with 1¾ baths, a fenced yard, and a two-car garage on a cul-de-sac. The back of the property was a triple lot because of the pie-shaped lots that occur in a cul-de-sac. The house was built in 1978. The living room had a vaulted ceiling and a conversation pit area.

I acquired the property for a purchase price of $47,000 with monthly payments of $476 PITI. This was a foreclosure and I was able to acquire the property with no down payment. I paid only the closing costs. My total investment was only $1,025.

The property was in fairly good condition. I turned on the utilities and checked everything out. The heat pump worked, and the water heater was fine. I spent $348.50 having a handyman paint a living room wall and the bedrooms. I also repapered the kitchen.

I sold the 68th Avenue house a few weeks after I bought it. The price was $63,900 with a down payment of $1,500 and monthly payments of $650. This produced a total contract profit of $16,900, which broke down to a monthly cash flow of $174 for the next 30 years, with no landlording. I liked that a lot.

Incidentally, the people who bought the house told me that the first two things they were going to do were tear down the wallpaper and repaint the house! I learned an important lesson. Most buyers don't mind doing a few cosmetic changes themselves, especially if they can get in for a low down payment.

Let's go over the advantages and disadvantages of this strategy.

Advantages

- *Immediate contract profit.* You sell the home for a lot more than you paid for it and usually at a higher interest rate. My $47,000 house in the first example sold for $63,900.
- *Long-term cash flow.* The sale gave me a positive cash flow of $174 per month for the next 30 years. ($650 payments per month − my payments of $476 per month = $174)
- *Runs on autopilot.* The new "owners" take care of their house and make their payments because, as far as they are concerned, they are the owners.
- *No renters.* I have no vacancy issues, no calls in the middle of the night, and no repairs to worry about.
- *Nominal repairs.* At best, I might have to do some minor repairs to get the initial house ready to sell.
- *Few hassles.* These deals are easy to do.

Disadvantages

- *Collections.* Sometimes people are late with their payments. I then have to collect the money, but I also get late fees.
- *Short-term negative cash flow potential.* If I cannot sell the house immediately, I might need to make payments for a couple of months.
- *Take-backs.* Sometimes people default on their payments and I have to take the house back. I welcome this because my cash flow goes up. I "resell" it and get a new deposit and probably sell the house for even more, because it has gone up in value.

Today, I emphasize the principle of long-term cash flow. Let me give you a couple more examples.

West Kerry Lane, Phoenix, Arizona

We acquired this property in October 2002 from a distressed seller who just wanted out. It was a very nice house in good condition. We purchased it for $104,000 with $7,500 for the down payment; the house had outstanding back payments that we made up. We then took control of the loan and began making the payments of $911 per month.

We had just over $9,500 invested in the property as our down payment and closing costs. The PITI was $911 a month. We remarketed for $119,900 in less than a month. We received a total move-in fee of $4,150. The new monthly payment is $1,250 (since we carry the financing on the house). That comes to a $339 per month spread for 360 months, which adds up to $122,040. Notice that for a cash investment of $5,350 ($9,500 − $4,150), I make $339 per month in passive income. That amounts to a return of 76% ($5,350 divided into the annual income of $4,068). You can reduce your financial freedom number rapidly with deals like this.

North 30th Drive, Phoenix, Arizona

A money partner and I acquired this three-bedroom, two-bathroom house with a swimming pool for the fantastic price of $69,513. The previous owner had been in the process of remodeling, so the master bathroom had been completely removed. We put just over $7,500 into the property as our down payment and closing costs. The PITI was $522 a month. We remarketed the property three weeks later as a handyman special and sold it for $87,900. We received a total move-in of $2,725. The new payment to us was $825. That comes to a $303 monthly spread for 360 months, which adds up to $109,080. Thus, for $4,775 ($7,500 − $2,725) we receive an annual return of $3,636, or 76.1%.

One thing happened on this property that does occur from time to time. After living there for a few years, the people stopped making the payments and moved out. This returned the property to us according to the contract we had on the deal. People often do this willingly. They simply call the office and ask if we will take the house back. With some occupants we negotiate a move-out settlement (usually $500 to $1,500). With others we need to use the legal process to move them out for nonpayment. This can take three weeks to three months, depending where you live and the expertise of your representation.

After getting back the property on North 30th Drive, we remarketed it. This time we got an even better return on our investment. We received a selling price of $112,900, which was more than $50,000 in contract profit. Our new occupant gave us a readjusted monthly payment of $1,075, which brought in more than a $550 per month paper profit.

These examples are not special deals or fantastic wraps. They are typical of the transactions I complete on a daily basis. Certainly, I have some cash flow transactions that make less than a $200 monthly spread. I also have many that bring in more than $500 a month in positive cash flow. Most are between $250 and $350 per month.

I love the cash flow strategy because it's easy to do and quick, and it provides substantial income. The cash flow strategy takes care of one of the biggest problems with money—it gets spent! Have you ever noticed that no matter how much you make per month you find a place to spend it? To me, that is the major drawback with the quick cash and the buy-and-hold strategies. Every time you do a deal, you have to do another one to keep the money coming in. What happens if you hit a cold streak or get burned out? The money you worked so hard for will soon be spent and you'll be asking your boss for your old job back.

Key Ideas

➤ Study the buy-and-hold, quick cash, and cash flow strategies presented in this chapter. Be sure you thoroughly understand the advantages and disadvantages of each.

➤ Buy and hold is best used when prices are low and appreciating rapidly.

➤ Quick cash is best used when you find bargains and turn them over quickly. Be sure to have your buyers lined up before you start making offers.

➤ The cash flow strategy provides you with a steady return over many years.

➤ In the current environment, I prefer the cash flow strategy. It has allowed me to accumulate lots of little deals. Our properties produce a five-figure income per month in positive cash flow.

ACTION STEPS

➤ Assess the real estate situation in your area.

➤ Develop a long-term perspective, deciding what will work to improve your situation and help you toward financial freedom. Then develop a plan. Each big deal in real estate might require a separate plan.

➤ Choose your strategy from the three mentioned in this chapter and take action.

➤ For more information on building an investment plan using one of the real estate strategies mentioned here, visit johnburley.com or call 800-561-8246. IITM can also give you further information.

Most people think wealth is cash. It isn't. Real wealth is cash flow—money consistently coming in every month—using it to reduce your financial freedom number to zero. The only way you are going to get cash flow is by owning a piece of every deal. That's why I like cash flow transactions so much. They give me the opportunity to own all or part of every deal. I own the asset. Real wealth is owning assets that other people pay you to own. That's how you achieve financial independence.

We suggest that you thoroughly research anything you do with real estate. If you are doing your own deal, make sure you understand the cash flow numbers and have accounted for important considerations such as repairs and vacancies. If you are working with some sort of joint venture, be sure you understand what you are getting into before you sign anything.

Notes

1. The more you put into the property, the smaller the principal and interest payments will be. Thus, if you put enough money down on a rental property, it will have a positive cash flow. For example, if you bought a $100,000 house and put $90,000 down, you would be paying principal and interest on a $10,000 loan of

less than $100 per month. Even if you add in repairs, vacancies, and taxes, it would still be easy to rent the house for a positive cash flow. However, let's say your positive cash flow was $500 per month. That means you would be making $6,000 ($500 × 12) per year on your $90,000—not a very good rate of return.

2. *Escrow* is defined as the documents, real estate, money, or securities deposited with a neutral third party (the escrow agent) to be delivered upon fulfillment of certain conditions, as established in a written agreement.

3. The first trust deed is the first mortgage on the house. The primary lender has the first right to get his or her money back if you default on the loan. The second trust deed has the second right to be repaid should you default.

PART IV

SAFEGUARDING YOUR FINANCIAL FREEDOM

In Part I you developed a plan for financial freedom. In Parts II and III you learned several strategies to lower your financial freedom number. Part IV is about how to turn them into safe and profitable strategies through the proper use of risk control. This part of the book is a little more complicated than the others, but this material is the most important. Read it several times if you need to, but be sure to understand these concepts.

Chapter 13 presents six keys to investment success. These include protecting your equity by having clear exit points, keeping your losses small, letting your profits run, understanding expectancy, knowing the effect of investment frequency on your bottom line, and opening only positions that are moving in your favor.

Chapter 14 covers position sizing, or determining how much you will risk. This is one of the most important factors in achieving the results you want while making your strategies safe.

Chapter 15 explains how to determine if your strategy is working. You'll learn how to keep up with the macroeconomic factors that can affect the outcome of your strategy. We'll tell you about a number of free resources for doing so.

You'll learn how to assess which market types will work best for your strategy, how to plug the risk-reward profile of your strategy into a simulator so that you can know exactly what to expect, and how to assess your strategy. These aspects of risk control are very important if you want to sleep well, knowing that what you are doing is safe.

SIX KEYS TO INVESTMENT SUCCESS

"It's only when the tide goes out that you learn who's been swimming naked."

—WARREN BUFFETT

History is full of one-hit wonders in music, sports, and other endeavors. Sure, there are people who take shortcuts and catch a temporary windfall. But the truly great ones all share a mastery of the fundamentals, the building blocks of success in their chosen fields. Learn them well.

Whether it's a golfer stroking hundreds of putts, a pianist rehearsing countless scales, or a speaker practicing clear enunciation, top achievers master the fundamentals. The fundamentals we'll cover in this chapter are applicable across all types of investments: real estate, stocks, futures, business ventures, or collectibles. These core principles are what make the strategies given in Parts II and III safe.

This chapter will bring these key investment principles to life. If you already have investment experience, here's a challenge to learn these fundamentals anew—you may find a gold nugget that enhances your understanding. And if you are new to the investing world, embrace this chance to start your journey on a firm foundation. With these elements fully understood, you'll be prepared to build safe, winning investment strategies.

Fundamental 1: Protect Your Equity

If you want to protect the equity in your investments, you have to understand the nature of risk and the relationship between risk and reward. You also need to have a reliable exit strategy in case the market moves against you.

Set Up an Escape Hatch Before You Enter an Investment

Never enter into a new investment without determining your worst-case exit point. We call this exit point a *stop loss* because that's what it's designed to do—stop the money from going down the drain when things go against you.

Your stop-loss point should be the first thing you establish when you're considering a new investment. We have had the opportunity to work with many outstanding traders. Without exception, when we look at a specific trade with one of them, the first thing he or she looks for is a safe place to exit. Whether they're trading Nasdaq stocks on five-minute bars or Treasury Bonds on weekly bars, they all think about safety before they look at potential rewards. They look at the potential risk and then the potential reward. And if the reward-to-risk ratio is not high enough, they won't open the position.

This is in sharp contrast to most beginning traders. The typical beginner is mesmerized by the thought of huge profits, doesn't understand the risk involved in a position, and certainly doesn't understand the ratio between the two.

Just look at the direct-mail ads for investment "opportunities" that hit your mailbox. They all promise spectacular gains, but few, if any, mention how the strategy will get you out of a losing investment if it goes against you. Your challenge is to transform your mind-set from "the sky's the limit" (profits first) to "protect my cash at all costs." In other words, *defense wins in the long run*.

Defining Your Worst-Case Loss

The money you can lose in an investment if it goes against you is what we call the risk amount, indicated by an *R*. We call this the worst-case loss because this is the point at which you'll know that the investment didn't work out as planned. When you start defining each investment in terms of your amount at risk, or *R*, you will make a quantum leap in your investment thought process. You will begin to look at every investment in terms of reward-to-risk ratios. You already do this in many other areas of your life.

Thinking in Terms of Reward-to-Risk Ratios

When faced with two choices, how do you decide? For example, your commute home has two choices: choice one is a busy interstate that can whisk you home in 30 minutes if all goes well but will take two hours if there's an accident. Choice two is a less-traveled road that has many traffic lights and almost always takes 45 minutes regardless of traffic conditions. You probably choose your route by weighing the reward of a shorter trip home versus the risk (and aggravation) of sitting in traffic on an interstate. The same thought process applies to successful investing: we weigh the potential profit against the possible loss to see if that ratio makes sense.

Top investors describe their market opportunities in terms of reward-to-risk ratio. These investing pros think about multiples of their risk amount, or *R* multiples. If the investment is likely to make three times the risk amount, then it is a 3*R* opportunity. We can use this shorthand to describe all of our investments, whether they are in stocks, mutual funds, real estate, or other instruments. A 2*R* profit means the same thing in stocks as it does in real estate—you made two times the amount you risked. Let's look at a couple of examples.

In the first example, you're looking to buy a house for a bargain price and just want to flip it (sell it) for a quick profit. It's a quick cash deal. You make the purchase of an $80,000 home with a predetermined risk amount, *R*, of $5,000—that's the most you're willing to lose on the deal.

You hope to sell the property for $100,000, or a $20,000 gain. This would be a 4*R* opportunity because your projected profit ($20,000) is four times larger than your risk amount ($5,000). In our example, the housing market is softer than you expected, and you end up selling the house for $90,000—a $10,000 profit. This turned out to be a 2*R* investment for you; you made twice what you risked.

Now let's look at a stock example. Microsoft is trading at $25, and your trading strategy says that it is a short-term buy. Your strategy says that if the price drops to $23 you should get out, so *R* is $2 per share. Remember your risk is $2 per share at the planned exit point. You have a profit target of $33, so your profit potential is $8 or 4*R*, four times your risk amount. However, Microsoft's price just can't seem to get above $29, so you decide to take your profits at that price and move on

MONEY-MAKING TIP: USE THE STOP LOSS TO PROTECT YOUR EQUITY

The stop loss is a tool that defines the point where you'll get out of an investment if it goes against you. Here are some important points that will help you make better use of this important tool.

- Before you enter any investment, decide where you'll get out if things go against you—this is your stop-loss point.
- Once you set a stop loss, never move it farther away from your entry point, no matter what happens. Moving the stop closer (also called *trailing the stop*) is fine.
- For a stock you want to hold for several months or longer, set the stop loss so that you'll exit if the stock price drops 25%. This method is described in detail later in this chapter.
- For a real estate investment, get out of the position if the property loses half of your initial deposit (hopefully not more than 10%). Never lose more than your original cash investment in your real estate holdings. If you have real estate holdings, do you know how much your initial cash deposit was?

to the next opportunity. Your actual trade turned out to be a *2R* investment, again making twice what you risked.

You'll see the *R* multiples used many times in this book. You couldn't
make a more important shift in mind-set than to start analyzing investment opportunities in these terms. The next several fundamentals build
on this idea as we form core building blocks for safe and successful
investing.

Understand the Initial Risk in Your Investment Strategy

Now that you understand the importance of limiting your risk in any
investment strategy, let's review some of the strategies we've covered
and look at what you might use for your initial risk.

- *Chapter 6—mutual funds.* The key worst-case scenario exit strategies might be: (1) if the market is down 2% on the week, get out of
  25% of your position; (2) if another fund is performing better than
  your fund, move to that fund. This sets your worst-case risk at about
  8% of your portfolio, which is very unlikely.
- *Chapter 6—hedge funds.* Don't commit more than 25% of your
  portfolio to any one hedge fund. If it declines by more than 15%,
  get out. This limits your total portfolio risk to about 3.75%. Also,
  be sure to do your due diligence before investing in any hedge fund.
- *Chapter 7—bear mutual funds.* When the market goes up 3%, exit
  one-fifth of your position. If the market is higher than it was five
  weeks ago, exit all of your position. If the VIX Index (option volatility) hits 50 or higher, take your profits immediately. These exits set
  your worst-case risk at about 10%, and this size loss is very unlikely.
- *Chapter 7—shorting overvalued stocks.* Don't invest more than 4%
  of your portfolio in any one stock, and set a 25% stop. This limits
  your maximum risk per position to 1% of your portfolio (25% of a
  4% risk is 1%).
- *Chapter 8—following a newsletter's recommendation.* Again, don't
  invest more than 4% of your portfolio in any one recommendation and set a 25% stop. This again limits your exposure to 1% per
  position.

- *Chapter 8—trading efficient stocks.* Again, don't invest more than 4% of your portfolio in any given efficient stock. Make sure you have a 25% stop so that your total initial risk is only 1%.
- *Chapter 8—buying undervalued stocks.* Do not invest more than 2% of your portfolio in a stock at 0.6% of Graham's number initially, and do so only when the stock is rising. You may add another 2% if the stock eventually goes down and reaches 0.5% of Graham's number as long as it's rising when you buy it. Add another 2% if the stock reaches 0.4% of Graham's number and starts rising. However, if the stock retreats and goes to 0.3% of Graham's number, something is seriously wrong. Sell your position. You will have lost 2.4% of your portfolio should this worst-case scenario happen.
- *Chapter 9—inflationary investments.* Although you might have 25% to 50% of your portfolio in inflationary investments, follow the guidelines recommended elsewhere for each individual investment.
- *Chapter 10—interest rate strategies.* If interest rates are going up, buy an inverse bond fund (e.g., Juno) with about 10% of your portfolio. Don't lose more than 20% here so your total risk would be about 2%.
- *Chapter 10—max rate game.* When buying foreign bonds in appreciating currencies, don't risk more than 10% of your portfolio per bond and keep a 25% stop. Here your total risk per bond would be 2.5%.
- *Chapter 12—real estate strategies.* Never risk more than your initial down payment on real estate. Many of John Burley's strategies, if properly structured, have zero or very little risk.

For each of these investments, you should now have some idea of what a 1*R* loss might be.

MONEY-MAKING TIP: THE GOLDEN RULE OF TRADING AND INVESTING

Keep your losses small (1*R* or less) and let your profits run (become large multiples of your initial risk).

Fundamental 2: Keep Losses Small

Once you begin to think about all of your investments in terms of *R* multiples, you can focus on the first half of the golden rule of trading: cutting your losses short. One bad habit that keeps investors from reaching their potential is allowing their investments to run through their stop-loss points (or failing to establish those points in the first place). Even if you have the best investing strategy in the world, you won't succeed if you don't follow its rules. Sticking with a plan that cuts your losses and lets your winners run is the only path to consistent, long-term profits.

Investing is a lot like gardening—if you pull the small weeds every day, like the woman in the story, you end up with a wonderful garden full of beautiful plants. Small weeds haven't had time to grow big roots and so it takes very little effort to remove them from your garden. However, if you ignore the weeds and let them grow large, they become very hard to pull out. The time you spend dealing with these tough weeds diverts your attention from the plants that are bearing fruit, making the time spent weeding even less productive. Worst of all, the big weeds can ruin your garden. In a similar way, losing positions are the weeds of your investment portfolio. If you consistently eliminate these losing investments while they are still small, you can maintain a beautiful and profitable portfolio.

THE OLD WOMAN'S GARDEN

There is a story about a woman who took over an abandoned lot and spent a year fixing the fence, preparing the soil, planting, and weeding. The local pastor came to visit and, upon seeing the remarkable transformation and true beauty of the place, he remarked, "You and God did a wonderful job with this garden." The woman answered, "You should have seen it when God had it all to Himself!"

Taking Small Losses Keeps You in the Investing Game

Losses are just another expense in the investment business. They are going to happen, so take them in stride. Like the weeds in your garden, losses are much easier to take when they're small. And like weeds growing large roots, as a loss grows bigger, they become harder to eliminate. Few traders ever say that taking lots of small losses blew out their account. Many former traders will tell you stories about one or two big losses that drained all the cash from their trading accounts. Big weeds can ruin gardens; big losses can wipe out your investing capital. Don't give them the chance to grow.

Proper Investing Psychology Is the Key to Keeping Losses Small

It seems logical that if you constantly eliminate losing investments and let the winning ones grow, your portfolio will grow nicely. So why don't more people just do it? Letting losses grow is all about your investing psychology—it's the way people think about their losses that leads to trouble.

Let's look at the two main issues that keep people from pulling their investment weeds when they should—the need to be right and the counterintuitive problem that arises when we classify things like profits and losses as either good or bad.

Being Right

The need to be right is ingrained in us at an early age. This is most evident in our educational system, which rewards correct answers, chastises wrong answers, and discourages nonconformist thinking. Children in school learn that if they are not right 70% of the time, they are a failure. Certain careers—engineering, medicine, accounting, and law, for example—accentuate the need to be right. This mind-set might be useful in some endeavors, but it can make an investor concentrate on being right instead of being profitable.

Suppose you buy a $100,000 rental property with $10,000 down and the belief that real estate prices in that area are going to boom because a new hospital is proposed for construction nearby. You'll collect enough rental income to make the property cash flow neutral, but your real reason for investing is that as soon as the hospital project is approved, your equity value will jump and you'll be able to sell quickly for $150,000.

You're willing to risk half of your cash investment, or $5,000, in hopes of making $50,000, or a 10$R$ investment opportunity. However, the hospital approval process runs into bureaucratic snags and it looks like the project will be delayed three years, if it is approved at all. On this news, the value of your rental property drops to $95,000. But instead of selling the property and taking your $5,000 loss, you decide to wait and see if some positive new development takes place. You have a feeling that the minute you sell the hospital approval process will be accelerated and the real estate values in the area (including your property) will skyrocket; you can't risk being wrong at the bottom of the market.

Unfortunately, the hospital approval drags on and the value of your property drops to $90,000. You're now down two times your initial R value, or $10,000. But you know that if you can just hang on for a while longer, things will turn your way. However, a competing site for the hospital suddenly emerges across the county. The value drops another $5,000.

Now you're so far in the hole that you just have to wait and see if things will turn around. You tell yourself that it's only a loss on paper and that when the project is finally approved you'd kick yourself if you got out now. Alas, the cross-county site is approved and you're holding a property that's now down $30,000 from where you bought it. When you finally sell, not only do you lose your initial $10,000, but you also have to shell out an extra $20,000 to pay off the loan. You've lost $30,000, or six times your worst-case loss of $5,000. This is a painful example of what can happen when you act on your need to be right instead of on the need to follow your investment strategy.

Good Profit, Bad Loss
Focusing on the concept that losses are bad and profits are good is another issue that affects an investor's ability to stick with the plan of cutting losses short. If you dwell on the thought that losses are bad, you'll concentrate consciously and subconsciously on avoiding losses. When a position moves against you, your thought process tells you that

losses are bad, and you'll want to avoid taking the loss. Instead of closing out the position at a small $1R$ loss, you leave it alone because you
rationalize that "it's not real," meaning you don't have to acknowledge
it until you close it out. And once you run a stop, it becomes harder to
take the loss because a bigger loss means that you have to deal with a
bigger dose of something you consider bad.

The flip side of this mind-set also works against you. As soon as a
profit shows up, your mind kicks into the "I love profits" mode and the
urge to protect your profit becomes irresistible. So instead of letting
your profits run, you grab them quickly before they slip away. As you
can see, this good-bad paradigm can lead to results that are the opposite of what you want: you'll cut your profits short and let your losses
run.

What can you do if you hold on to losses because your need to be
right kicks in? What if you are staying with a losing position because
you hate losses and can't stand the thought of actually executing the
trade? Begin by making permanent changes in your investment psychology (the way you think when you're investing). That requires commitment and a plan that uses proven techniques. Enabling this type of
positive change in investors' psychology has been at the heart of our
work for more than 20 years. To help you, we recommend two tools.

- *IITM's game.* One suggestion is to practice taking small losses in
  IITM's position sizing game. The first three levels can be down-
  loaded for free at iitm.com. Playing this game over and over will
  really help you with this concept.
- *A written plan.* Before every investment, make a *written* plan that
  will guide you during the whole course of the transaction. This can
  be as simple as a one-line entry in a trading log for a stock day trader
  or as complex as a business plan for someone investing in an apartment complex or a start-up business. While your plan can have some
  areas of flexibility, the stop loss—the price at which you'll exit the
  investment—must be in writing and firm. This is the second tool that
  will make a real difference in your ability to stick to a stop-loss point.
  When you write something down, it becomes more real for you. The
  only way you'll ignore a stop loss is through deliberate self-sabotage.
  Try writing it down for 30 or 60 days and see what impact it has for

---

KEY IDEAS

➤ Remember that taking small losses keeps them from growing bigger, thus allowing you to continue participating in the investment game.

➤ Most people want to be right, and that means taking profits quickly. They also hate to be wrong, and that means holding on to losses in the hope that the investment will rebound, which usually leads to an even bigger loss.

➤ To fix these problems we recommend that you practice the IITM trading game and that you develop a written plan to guide you during each investment.

---

you. The plan is right—it will protect your capital and make you some nice profits if you follow it. With this mind-set, you'll be focused on carrying out the plan, not on the results of the investment.

Until you get to the point where you always set stop-loss points and consistently get out when you hit them, all the other aspects of investing become almost insignificant. But once you develop the discipline to cut your losses, you can turn your attention to the area where top traders and investors spend most of their time: letting profits run.

Fundamental 3: Grow Big Winners

The section on cutting losses short was about discipline in carrying out a plan. It is one of the more straightforward parts of investing. In contrast, letting your profits run requires more creativity and a more thorough understanding of your investing strategy.

Suppose your system requires you to buy a stock when it breaks out of a flat period and makes a new high. Your stop is very small because if it goes back into the base, you were wrong in this trade. After five trades you have four 1*R* losses and one large (8*R*) profit. If you look at the net results of the five trades, you are up by 4*R* even though you were right on only one trade out of five. That shows the power of letting your profits run. One 8*R* profit will wipe out four 1*R* losses and give you a net profit. You can be wrong four out of five times (80% of the time) and still come out in front.

In the late 1990s, when the stock market seemed to trend for extended periods of time, letting your profits run meant catching a trend and holding on until you were sure it was no longer moving in your direction. It was easy to get the 8*R* profit. In today's volatile markets, you need to give a broader interpretation to the phrase "letting your profits run." Let's look at how the investing fundamental of growing big winners plays out in several different investing scenarios.

Growing Big Winners with Long-Term Investments

The following strategies, which were explained in Parts II and III, usually appeal to investors who are looking for long-term appreciation (value investors) or who want to capitalize on major market trends:

- Buying the strongest mutual fund and not exiting until there is either a stronger fund or the market starts going down (Chapter 6).
- Purchasing a well-run hedge fund and holding it as long as it outperforms the market (Chapter 6).
- Shorting bear market mutual funds when the S&P 500 is down for five weeks and continuing the position until the market is up over five weeks or the downturn reaches an extreme (Chapter 7).
- Shorting overvalued stocks and not buying them back until a 25% trailing stop is hit (Chapter 7).
- Buying highly efficient stocks and not selling them until a 25% trailing stop is hit (Chapter 8).
- Buying stock at two-thirds of its short-term liquation value (selling half to get all your money back) and then keeping the stock until the next bull market starts to get overvalued (Chapter 8).

- Purchasing inflationary assets when we have a four-star signal and holding on to them until inflation starts to recede (Chapter 9).
- Using the max yield strategy when the dollar is falling and keeping our investment for one year or until the dollar starts a significant uptrend (Chapter 10). Or purchasing the Aberdeen Asia-Pacific Income Fund (FAX) and holding it while the dollar is in a downtrend (Chapter 10).
- Purchasing low-priced real estate in an area with a good chance for appreciation. This is the buy-and-hold strategy (Chapter 12).
- Using the cash flow strategy with real estate and keeping the real estate as long as you have a positive cash flow. Evaluate your cash flow yearly (Chapter 12).

The key to all these strategies is keeping your losses small and holding on for large profits when you are right. When trading for longer-term profits, you need a strategy that allows you to stay with your investment through the occasional pullbacks that will happen. We recommend using a trailing stop in many of these strategies because it allows you to stay with your position as long as it goes up and it locks in profits.

Understanding the Trailing Stop

You've already learned about the stop loss. Now let's just extend the concept a little to develop your profit-taking exit. The simplest ways to do this is to have a trailing stop. A trailing stop is one that moves when the investment moves in your favor, but not when it moves against you. One example is the 25% trailing stop. This means that you put your stop 25% below the current price and continue to hold it at 25% below the current price as the stock makes new highs (for longs) or new lows (for shorts).

Table 13.1 shows how this works. Suppose you buy a stock, let's say QCOM, at $40. Your initial stop is 25% away, at $30. QCOM moves to $44 and you move your stop up so that it is again 25% away, this time at $33. In other words, whenever the stock makes a new high, you move the stop up so it trails the new high by 25%. If you want to make this really simple, then use the closing price each day to adjust the stop. Thus, if QCOM moves to $45, but closes at $44, you'd adjust the stop to $33.

What happens if QCOM stock moves down to $36? Do you adjust your stop 25% away from that price? No you don't. If you own the stock, you only adjust the stop upward (on new highs). You never move it away from you. If the stock were to move down to $36, your stop would still be at $33—$3 away from the current price.

If the price starts to climb and QCOM reaches a new high of $64, then you'd again adjust the stop so that it is 25% away, at $48. If the stock starts to move down from there, you'd eventually get stopped out at $48. However, since we bought the stock at $40, we now have an $8 profit when we are stopped out. And since our initial risk was $10, our locked-in $8 profit is a 0.8R profit.

You may look at these figures later and say, "I wish I had gotten out at $64." However, you didn't know at that time whether the stock was going to fall or keep going up. This is the greed factor and another key in the psychological process. Do not look at the highest price after the fact and think that you could have made $24. Be content with the $8 profit that you did make. You followed sound principles and made a profit. Continue to do that consistently and you'll be a winner in the markets.

Too many people boast about their "profits on paper," which can be their downfall because it isn't real and a big win with no plan can cause overconfidence in their own abilities. They then err by trying to beat the market instead of planning effectively.

Table 13.1 Example of a Trailing Stop

Price	Stop	Action to Take
$40	$30	Buy and set initial stop
$44	$33	Move stop up on new high
$36	$33	Don't adjust stop down when the stock price drops
$64	$48	Move stop up on new high
$52	$48	Stop remains the same
$45	$48	Stopped out at $48 for an $8 profit

KEY IDEAS

➤ When you begin an investment, keep in mind that you want it to profit by some multiple of your initial risk. You are looking for big profits, and those sometimes require patience.

➤ The trailing stop is easy to use with any investment. A 25% trailing stop is a good substitute for buy-and-hold investing.

➤ Be happy with the profit that you make, rather than looking at what you could have made.

Fundamental 4: Understand the Relationship Between Risk and Reward

The next fundamental allows you to understand all of your trades based upon the amount of risk (R) you initially take in a position. We call this variable *expectancy*. It's an important concept to understand because it gets you to think about every trade as a function of the initial risk involved. Until you understand the application of expectancy, your investing will never reach its full potential. So have some fun as you learn this useful concept.

Imagine that you happen upon a lamp while you're cleaning out the basement. As you dust it off, a genie appears. But instead of wishes, the genie offers you two alternatives. On the fifth day of every month for the next 10 years, you will spin a wheel (which mysteriously appears in your basement as the genie speaks) and, based upon the spin, you either will or will not receive a set sum of money for that month. The genie offers the following options:

Option 1
80% chance that you'll get
$10,000 for the month
20% chance that you'll get
$0 for the month

Option 2
5% chance that you'll get
$200,000 for the month
95% chance that you'll get
$0 for the month

Make your choice before reading further.

Most people are drawn to the high-probability choice (option 1), much as they are drawn to high-probability investing strategies. For example, each week we get about a dozen offers in our mail or e-mail to buy incredible trading systems. All of them claim to have "unlocked the secret" to winning 70%, 80%, or 90% of the time. This high-probability bias feeds our general need to be right as well as our love for profits, no matter the size. We have yet to receive an offer that promises we'll win 40% of the time, where the average winner is five times bigger than the average loser.

If you chose option 1, you were probably comforted that you would get some cash, on average, four out of every five months, and discouraged by the relatively infrequent payout of option 2, where you get money only once every 20 months, on average. If this was your thought process, remember that the genie's offer was for 10 years, or 120 spins of the wheel. With that in mind, and the fact that the key is the most profitable outcome, let's look at a mathematical evaluation of the offer.

To determine the total payout for each option, simply multiply its payout times its probability of occurrence. Then add up all the values to determine its total expectancy. The formula looks like this:

Average payout per month =
(Percent chance of possibility A × payout for possibility A) +
(Percent chance of possibility B × payout for possibility B)

Total payout =
Average payout per month × Frequency (number of months)

For the options our genie gave us, the calculation would look like this:

Option 1
80% × $10,000 = $8,000
$8,000 + (20% × $0) =
   $8,000 Average payout
   per month
$8,000 × 120 months =
   $960,000 Total payout

Option 2
5% × $200,000 = $10,000
$10,000 + (95% × $0) =
   $10,000 Average payout
   per month
$10,000 × 120 months =
   $1,200,000 Total payout

If you have an option with more than two possibilities, just continue summing the possible payouts until you account for all of them. If any possibilities have negative payouts (you lose money), you subtract that amount instead of adding it.

What does the math tell us? If you chose option 1, you would have a better chance of getting a payout each month, but the average payout would be lower. At the end of 10 years, you would receive almost a quarter of a million dollars less ($240,000 to be exact) by choosing option 1.

Many investors fall into the trap of choosing the higher probability investment option instead of the higher profitability option. As an investor you need to concentrate on what makes a difference in your investing—profits—instead of concentrating on what makes you feel comfortable and smart, like how often you're right. To move your thought process away from a concentration on probability (percentage of winners) and toward the concept of profitability (whether or not you're making the most money over the long run), let's look at one more example.

Imagine that you have just finished your 10 years of genie-granted cash windfall. Because you had read *Safe Strategies for Financial Freedom* many years ago, you chose the option that allowed you to pocket a quarter of a million dollars more over the last 10 years. As you put away that wonderful lamp, the genie reappears and tells you that because you have been so gracious he is going to offer you another set of alternatives as a going-away present. Every month for the next 10 years, you are going to have money put into or taken out of your bank account. Your choices are as follows:

Option 1	*Option 2*
50% chance that you'll get $50,000 added that month	**90% chance** that you'll get $100,000 added that month
50% chance that you'll have $10,000 removed that month	**10% chance** that you'll have $750,000 removed that month

This choice is a tough one, but only if you ignore the math! Getting that huge payout 9 out of 10 months is alluring, but you have to endure a huge hit every 10 months. And remember, this is not a one-time deal. It repeats itself 120 times, so the overall profitability of your choice is what we're interested in. Let's look at the calculations for this set of choices:

Option 1
  50% × $50,000 = $25,000
  $25,000 + (50% × −$10,000)
    = $20,000 Average payout
    per month
  $20,000 × 120 months
    = $2,400,000 Total payout

Option 2
  90% × $100,000 = $90,000
  $90,000 + (10% × −$750,000)
    = $15,000 Average payout
    per month
  $15,000 × 120 months
    = $1,800,000 Total payout

So once again the math favors the less-frequent payout, with your patience rewarded by an extra $600,000 from the genie.

Hopefully you have returned from our world of genies with a good foundation in the simple math required to understand a key tool for evaluating investment performance. This tool is called expectancy, and it can be used to evaluate any strategy, whether it involves short-term commodity trading, long-term stock investing, real estate, or other business investments in which you risk a set amount of money in order to make a profit. Expectancy is calculated using the same math that we used to evaluate the genie's options.

When evaluating investment strategies, you are usually faced with one of two types of data: either a record of individual trades (investments) or overall averages. You'll learn how to calculate your strategy's expectancy for both types of data. If you have a history of each trade that was taken, the simplest way to calculate the system's expectancy is to add each trade's R multiple, and then divide by the total number of trades. This easy calculation will give you the system's expectancy for that series of trades. Let's look at an example of this type of expectancy calculation. Table 13.2 shows a series of 10 trades.

Our 10 trades gave us a total gain of $7R$ and an average gain of $0.7R$. The average gain, or expectancy, tells us what we can expect to make on the average over many trades in terms of our initial risk. In our example, we average 0.7 times our risk on every trade.

Table 13.2 Sample Expectancy Calculation

Trade No.	Risk R	Profit or Loss in $$	R Multiple
1	$1.50	$3.00	2R
2	$3.00	$3.00	1R
3	$2.00	−$1.00	−0.5R
4	$2.50	$10.00	4R
5	$3.00	−$3.00	−1R
6	$2.00	−$3.00	−1.5R
7	$1.00	$3.00	3R
8	$4.00	−$4.00	−1R
9	$2.50	−$2.50	−1R
10	$2.00	$4.00	2R
Total			**7**
Expectancy			**7R ÷ 10 trades = 0.7**

Expectancy reflects the amount, on average, that you will make for each dollar that you risk. If the strategy's expectancy is a negative number, it represents the amount that you would lose for every dollar risked. Given this definition, the 0.7 expectancy of the system means that the system would return, on average, $0.70 for every dollar risked—and you'd get your original dollar back![1] This second definition of expectancy is really the same as the prior one, but perhaps one of them is easier for you to grasp than the other.

As mentioned earlier, there is a second way that you can calculate the expectancy of an investment system. This method is useful if you have projected numbers for a given strategy. For example, if you know your system's projected winning percentage, the predicted size of the average winning trade in terms of *R*, and the size of the average losing trade in terms of *R*, you can approximate the expectancy for the system using this calculation:

**Expectancy =
(% Winners × *R* multiple of average win) −
(% Losers × *R* multiple of average loss)**

You can also use this formula when you don't have trade-by-trade data but have overall results or predicted values. As an example, let's calculate the expectancy for the trades in Table 13.2 using this method. Only let's assume that we only know that the system wins 50% of the time and that the average winner is 2.4 times as big as the average loser. Here is how to calculate the expectancy:

Expectancy = (50% × 2.4R winners) − (50% × 1R losers)

$$\text{Expectancy} =$$
$$(0.5 \times 2.4R) - (0.5 \times 1R) =$$
$$(1.2R - 0.5R) = 0.7R$$

The result is exactly the same as before, 0.7R. It's that easy.

Following are four problems to test your understanding of expectancy. Solve them for yourself and then check your answers in the notes at the end of this chapter.[2] All the tools you need to solve the problems are in the preceding paragraphs on expectancy.

Example 1: If the following trading systems had the same number of trades per week, which would you choose?
  A. a system that is right 40% of the time with average winners that are three times bigger than the average losers
  B. a system that is right 70% of the time and has equal size winners and losers

Example 2: If the following trading systems had the same number of trades per day, which would you choose?
  A. a system that is right 50% of the time with average winners that are 1.5 times bigger than the average losers
  B. a system that is right 80% of the time and has winners that are half as big as the losers

Example 3: Two real estate strategies are designed to buy depressed properties and resell them for a quick profit. Tables 13.3 and 13.4 show results that are typical of each system. Which would you choose?

Table 13.3 Sample Expectancy Calculation 1

Trade No.	Risk R	Profit or Loss in $$	R Multiple
1	$5,000	$5,000	
2	$2,000	−$2,000	
3	$4,000	−$4,000	
4	$2,500	$10,000	
5	$3,000	$9,000	
6	$6,000	$12,000	
7	$1,000	$8,000	
8	$4,000	$8,000	
9	$2,000	−$2,000	
10	$2,000	$8,000	
Total			= _____
Expectancy		_____ R ÷ 10 trades = _____

Example 4: If the following long-term trading systems had the same number of trades per year, which would you choose?

A. a system that is right 30% of the time with average winners that are seven times bigger than the average losers

B. a system that is right 50% of the time and has winners that are three times as big as the losers

Table 13.4 Sample Expectancy Calculation 2

Trade No.	Risk R	Profit or Loss in $$	R Multiple
1	$5,000	$5,000	
2	$2,000	−$2,000	
3	$4,000	$4,000	
4	$2,500	$5,000	
5	$3,000	$6,000	
6	$6,000	$12,000	
7	$1,000	$2,000	
8	$4,000	$4,000	
9	$2,000	$2,000	
10	$2,000	$4,000	
Total			= _____
Expectancy		_____ R ÷ 10 trades = _____

KEY IDEAS

➤ Expectancy really tells you how much you'll make on average, over many trades, in relationship to your initial risk. Thus, an expectancy of 0.5 means that over many trades you won't lose money, but will make half of your initial risk.

➤ Expectancy reflects the amount, on average, that you will make for each dollar you risk.

Fundamental 5: Understand How Investment Frequency Affects You

When you know an investing strategy's expectancy, the only other piece of information you need in order to compare that strategy to any other is the frequency of investment. How many opportunities per week, month, or year will you have to use the strategy? Certain real estate investing strategies may provide only three or four opportunities per year, while a stock or futures day trading system may have a frequency of 200 trades per month or more. With information on frequency and expectancy, you can compare strategies. Perhaps the real estate strategy has an expectancy of 25 (you make $25 for every dollar you risk) and gives you two opportunities per year. For each transaction, you risk $1,000. Your average annual profitability would be calculated like this:

Expectancy × Opportunities per year × Risk per opportunity = Annual profit

25 × 2 × $1,000 = $50,000 Annual profit

Now we'll do the same calculation for the high-frequency stock trading system. A system that trades 10 times a day may have a very low expectancy, like 0.04 (you make four cents for every dollar risked after

---

ACTION STEP

Be sure to work through all the examples so that you understand this important concept.

---

commissions).[3] This system trades 200 times per month, so to compare it to the real estate example above, we'll annualize the monthly rate, multiplying it by 12 to arrive at 2,400 trades per year. If your risk is $1,000 for each trade, the annual profit calculation would be:

0.04 (expectancy) × 2,400 (times per year) × $1,000 (at risk) = $96,000 annual profit

This comparison highlights the importance of the number of opportunities a strategy provides you, per time period. Despite the real estate strategy's very high expectancy, its low frequency makes it less profitable than the low-expectancy, high-frequency stock trading system. However, two factors must be taken into account when evaluating high-frequency systems. Most high-frequency strategies require significantly more of your personal time, so take that into consideration when comparing investment strategies. Also, higher-frequency strategies usually bring higher transaction costs, so be sure to include these extra costs in your calculations as well. You also may have software and equipment costs that you might want to subtract from your final calculation to get your actual return in your account.

Let's close this important section on expectancy with a quick review. Expectancy is a key concept to understand when designing or evaluating investing strategies. It tells you how well you'll be rewarded, on the average, for each risk you take. When combined with the frequency of opportunities a strategy provides, expectancy tells us the profitability of the strategy. This allows us to compare strategies, even ones that invest in different instruments or different time frames (intraday trad-

---

KEY IDEAS

➤ When you multiply the average gain per trade (i.e., expectancy) by the number of opportunities you get, you'll have an overall idea of how profitable an investing or trading method might be.

➤ Multiplying expectancy times opportunity for several strategies will give you an overall comparison of the strategies in term of profitability.

---

ing versus 10-year real estate projects). Expectancy is a flexible tool that allows us, as investors, to concentrate on the important aspects of our strategies—profitability and reward-to-risk ratios.

Fundamental 6: Make Sure a Position Is Moving in Your Favor Before You Enter It

Table 13.5 shows 21 real stock recommendations made through an advisory service, the Oxford Club, from January 1999 through April 2000.

ACTION STEPS

➤ If you are considering several strategies, determine the expectancy of each strategy.

➤ Multiply the expectancy of each strategy by the number of opportunities it gives to determine how good it is.

➤ Be sure you've accounted for transaction costs when you calculate expectancy.

Despite the high expectancy from buying those stocks, only 11 of them made money. In fact, only 8 of the 21 stocks made as much as the initial risk (i.e., there are only 8 gains of 1R or better). The expectancy of the picks was 2.5R, which was excellent, but it's possible to do much better. And one key factor will give us that better performance—only buying stocks that are moving in our favor (for at least a month) prior to buying them.

Table 13.5 Oxford Club Trades from January 1999 Through April 2000

Symbol	Rec. Issue	Recomm. Price	Initial Stop	I R Value is Equal to	Date Sold or 4/15	Sale Price on 4/15	Profit/ Loss	R Multiple
ALA	I Jan 99	23	17.25	5.75	4/5/00	38.5	$2,635.65	2.64
JDSU	I Feb 99	11.95	8.96	2.99	4/5/00	110.25	$32,843.77	32.84
MTA	I Feb 99	30.94	23.21	7.74	4/12/00	40.75	$1,208.26	1.21
NXLK	I Mar 99	24.38	18.29	6.10	8/15/99	82	$9,393.65	9.39
ABX	I Mar 99	17	12.75	4.25	6/15/99	17.06	($45.88)	(0.05)
LVLT	I Apr 99	72.25	54.19	18.06	7/1/99	69.75	($198.41)	(0.20)
ATHM	I May 99	115.43	86.57	28.86	5/15/99	112.81	($150.79)	(0.15)
MO	I May 99	34.5	25.88	8.63	11/1/99	31.81	($371.88)	(0.37)
ADBE	I May 99	30.9	23.18	7.73	1/31/00	55.05	$3,066.21	3.07
CX	I May 99	23.6	17.70	5.90	4/12/00	22.56	($236.27)	(0.24)
LMT	I Jun 99	41.25	30.94	10.31	10/15/99	31.5	($1,005.45)	(1.01)
TWFC	I Aug 99	7.18	5.39	1.80	10/1/99	6	($717.38)	(0.72)
DCFT-SI	I Oct 99	4.45	3.34	1.11	1/5/00	9.25	$4,254.61	4.25
PCS	I Oct 99	35	26.25	8.75	4/12/00	51.68	$1,846.29	1.85
PETM	I Dec 99	4.63	3.47	1.16	2/14/00	4.01	($595.64)	(0.60)
0416-HK	I Dec 99	0.89	0.67	0.22	1/5/00	0.94	$164.72	0.16
NETA	I Dec 99	25	18.75	6.25	4/5/00	26.31	$149.60	0.15
PEB	4 Feb 00	74.82	56.12	18.71	3/14/00	104	$1,500.01	1.50
CY	I Mar 00	45.5	34.13	11.38	4/12/00	48	$159.78	0.16
NTAP	I Mar 00	91.53	68.65	22.88	4/4/00	67	($1,132.00)	(1.13)
LHSP	I Apr 00	103.75	77.81	25.94	4/12/00	99.625	($219.04)	(0.22)
							Total	**52.53**
							Expectancy	**2.50**

Table 13.6 Recommended Stocks Moving Up When Purchased

Symbol	Date Recommended	Trend at Purchase	R Multiple
ALA	1 Jan 99	Up	2.64
JDSU	1 Feb 99	Up	32.84
NXLK	1 Mar 99	Up	9.39
LVLT	1 Apr 99	Up	(0.20)
ADBE	1 May 99	Up	3.07
PCS	1 Oct 99	Up	1.85
PEB (now ABI)	4 Feb 00	Up	1.50
CY	1 Mar 00	Up	0.16
		Total R Profit	**51.25**
		Expectancy	**6.41**

What would happen if you had bought the same stocks, but only if they were moving in your favor? Table 13.6 shows eight stocks that were in clear uptrends at the time they were purchased (i.e., they had been going up for at least 40 days). Seven of those eight ended up as winning stocks, and the only loser (LVLT) showed only a $0.2R$ loss. The total R multiple of those winners was 51.25, accounting for almost all the total portfolio gain of $52.53R$. But since the group only had one loser, the expectancy of these eight stocks was 6.41—more than twice the expectancy of the entire portfolio.

If you had just purchased these stocks and risked about 1% on each one, your portfolio would have been up about 60% from January 1999 through April 2000. That doesn't seem so significant considering what was happening in the market from 1999 to 2000. However, you would have used less than 40% of your portfolio to make that 60%. You would still have had another 60% of your portfolio to make money in other things.

Table 13.7 shows the nine stocks that were in clear losing trends at the time they were purchased or recommended. Of those nine stocks, seven were losers. And neither of the winners was a big winner. Those nine stocks had a total R value of -2.67 and a negative expectancy of -0.30.

Table 13.7 Recommended Stocks Moving Down When Purchased

Symbol	Date Recommended	Trend at Purchase	R Multiple
MTA	I Feb 99	Down	1.21
ABX	I Mar 99	Down	(0.05)
ATHM	I May 99	Down	(0.15)
MO	I May 99	Down	(0.37)
LMT	I Jun 99	Down	(1.01)
TWFC	I Aug 99	Down	(0.72)
PETM	I Dec 99	Down	(0.60)
NETA	I Dec 99	Down	0.15
NATP	I Mar 00	Down	(1.13)
		Total R Profit	**−2.67**
		Expectancy	**−0.30**

The message is very clear here. *Open positions only in stocks that are obviously moving in your favor.* Many value players may object to this proposition, saying you want to buy stocks that are out of favor. However, what if you bought out-of-favor stocks only when they had been moving up for a while as we recommend in this book? You'd probably save a lot of money and do very well.

Incidentally, we've been talking mostly about purchasing stocks. However, if you want to sell stocks short, the same lesson applies. Wait to short the stock until it forms a clear base and then breaks it to the downside. Make sure it's moving in your favor before you enter the position.

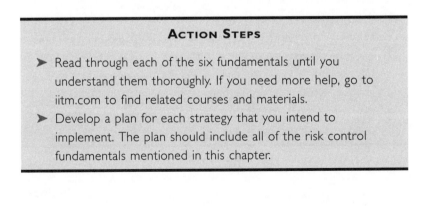

ACTION STEPS

➤ Read through each of the six fundamentals until you understand them thoroughly. If you need more help, go to iitm.com to find related courses and materials.

➤ Develop a plan for each strategy that you intend to implement. The plan should include all of the risk control fundamentals mentioned in this chapter.

KEY IDEAS

➤ Establish a worst-case exit point for every investment you make (defense first). This defines your risk in the investment.

➤ Think about all investments in terms of their reward-to-risk ratio.

➤ Make your average loss 1R or less. Be willing to get out.

➤ Keeping losses small allows you to stay in the game.

➤ Proper psychology is the key to consistently cutting losses.

➤ Having a written plan and writing your stop losses down will help you keep your losses small.

➤ Growing big winners means that your strategy generates investments that have bigger wins when compared to losses.

➤ You can let winners run by going with the market's trend until it reverses.

➤ You can get big winners by having a profit target that is many times bigger than your risk amount.

➤ Make sure your average gain is much bigger than 1R.

➤ Profitability is your goal. Choose higher profitability over higher probability.

➤ Expectancy represents the amount of money you make for each dollar you risk.

➤ Expectancy also represents your average gain in terms of your initial risk.

➤ You can calculate the profitability of your strategy only if you know how many times in a month or a year it signals an investment.

➤ A higher-frequency strategy can have a lower expectancy and still be as profitable as lower-frequency strategies.

➤ Higher-frequency strategies can require more time and higher transaction costs, so be sure to include these considerations in your investment evaluations.

➤ Make sure the market is moving in your favor before you open a position.

Notes

1. We have not included the cost of investing (commissions) in these calculations, but you probably should do that. To do so, subtract the cost of each trade from the profit/loss in column 3 of Table 13.2.

2. The calculations for the four examples are below. Note that the third example used the simpler calculation of summing the R multiples and then dividing by the number of transactions.

Example 1

A: $(0.4 \times 3) - (0.6 \times 1) = 0.6$

B: $(0.7 \times 1) - (0.3 \times 1) = 0.4$

Example 2

A: $(0.5 \times 1.5) - (0.5 \times 1) = 0.25$

B: $(0.8 \times 0.5) - (0.2 \times 1) = 0.2$

Example 3

A: $21R \div 10 = 2.1$

B: $13R \div 10 = 1.3$

Example 4

A: $(0.4 \times 7) - (0.7 \times 1) = 1.4$

B: $(0.5 \times 3) - (0.5 \times 1) = 1.0$

3. Notice that we included trading costs in this example.

CHAPTER 14

USING POSITION SIZING TO MEET YOUR OBJECTIVES

"Over 91% of the performance variance of 82 retirement plans over 10 years was due to asset allocation."

—BRINSON, SINGER, AND BEEBOWER

Once you have set appropriate objectives and adopted one or more low-risk strategies that you like, you need to use position sizing to meet your objectives. This is the seventh fundamental key in your journey to financial freedom.

Understanding Position Sizing Through the Marble Game

In some of our talks, we have participants play a marble game to simulate real trading experience.[1] One typical game represents a trading system in which you win 20% of the time and lose 80% of the time. However, when you win, you win big, $10R$, or 10 times what you risk. The $10R$ winners are represented by two yellow marbles. And when you lose, your losses are small, just the amount you risk. These are represented by seven black marbles. However, there is one $5R$ loser (i.e., you lose five times the amount of your risk). This simple game represents a trading system that doesn't win often but wins big when it does. Would you like to play a system like this? Think about that before you read on. You should be able to calculate the expectancy of the system easily by now.[2]

Let's look at a typical 30-trade sequence that might arise from such a game, shown in Table 14.1. The sample there is a little better than average. The first 10 trades include three 10R winners and produces a total payoff of 23R. Trades 11–20 include two 10R winners and produce a total payoff of 12R. And trades 21–30 produce a zero payoff because of the three 5R losers. Thus, the total payoff of the sample is 35R (23 + 12 + 0). And, recalling our discussion in Chapter 14, the expectancy of the sample is its total payoff divided by the number of trades. When you divide 35R by 30 trades, you get a sample expectancy of 1.17R. This means that over the 30 trades you should make an average of 1.17 times the amount you risked. If you determine the average payoff of the marbles in the game, you'll find that it is 0.8R, so our sample is better than what one might expect from the game.

How you play the game will depend upon your objectives. Let's assume that your objective was to win the game and not go bankrupt. Table 14.2 shows a sample of the final equities of 20 people who played the game with that objective. They all started with $100,000, and their

Table 14.1 30-Trade Sequence from the Marble Game

Trade No.	Payoff Ratio	Trade No.	Payoff Ratio	Trade No.	Payoff Ratio
1	1R Loser	11	1R Loser	21	1R Loser
2	10R Win	12	1R Loser	22	1R Loser
3	10R Win	13	1R Loser	23	10R Win
4	1R Loser	14	1R Loser	24	5R Loser
5	1R Loser	15	10R Win	25	1R Loser
6	10R Win	16	1R Loser	26	1R Loser
7	1R Loser	17	1R Loser	27	10R Win
8	1R Loser	18	10R Win	28	1R Loser
9	1R Loser	19	1R Loser	29	5R Loser
10	1R Loser	20	1R Loser	30	5R Loser
Totals	**23R**		**12R**		**0R**

only objective was to win the game. There was no penalty for going bankrupt except that they would be out of the game. Notice the tremendous variability in the final returns in the table. The winner had $431,500, while the worst loser was down by $1.8 million. The only ending equity duplicated among the players was zero—four went down to zero and three went well below zero. Eight people (40%) ended up with less money than they started with, despite playing a game that was 35R in their favor.

The first player in our sample game risked $1,000 on each trade. Since the game was up by 35R, he ended up with $135,000. Player 15, nervous about a game with only 20% winners, risked the minimum of $10. As a result, this person ended up with $100,350. Players 6, 9, and 13 went below zero because they risked 20% or more on a trial when one of the three 5R losers was drawn. They probably risked everything on the last marble in an attempt to win the game.

The marble game shows the tremendous variety of results that position sizing produces in one's final equity. Everything else in the game was constant. Everyone played the same game. Everyone made the same simulated trades (i.e., they bet on the same marbles). The only difference was their position size, or the amount they decided to bet or risked per trade.

Table 14.2 Equities of 20 People Playing the Marble Game

Player No.	Final Equity	Player No.	Final Equity
1	135,000	11	62,400
2	0	12	431,500
3	141,000	13	(1,300,000)
4	325,000	14	180,000
5	207,850	15	100,350
6	(1,800,000)	16	0
7	0	17	161,000
8	220,500	18	148,000
9	(430,000)	19	123,000
10	0	20	189,400

MONEY-MAKING TIP: POSITION SIZING

- Position sizing is the key factor in determining the variability and profitability of your portfolio.
- Even with a positive expectancy system, people lose money trading because they don't understand position sizing (how much to risk on any given trade).
- Your position sizing strategy is largely dictated by your objectives.

Another reason the variability between the game participants is so large is that we give a prize for whoever has the most money at the end of the game. There is no penalty for drawdowns (losing money) or for going bankrupt (except that those who go bankrupt are out of the game). These guidelines set the objectives for the game, and these particular guidelines encourage people to take big risks.

We could construct the rules differently, charging a $50 penalty when a player's final equity is down more than 20% and a $500 penalty for going bankrupt. If we did this, the results would be quite different because the players' objectives would change. There would still be a significant variability among players, but the results would fall into a much narrower range.

The message here is twofold. First, the most important factor in playing a positive expectancy game is your position sizing strategy—the part of your system that dictates how much you are willing to risk per trade. Second, your position sizing strategy is largely dictated by your objectives. When the objective is to win the game with no penalty for losing money, there will be a huge variability in performance and many people will go bankrupt because they'll take more risks. When there is a penalty for losing 20% or more (even if the objective is still to win), most people will scale back their positions and a much smaller final equity will win the game. They'll play it much safer.

The quote at the beginning of this chapter underscores the impact of position sizing on performance. Brinson and his colleagues analyzed the performance of 82 pension fund managers over a 10-year period.[3]

KEY IDEAS

➤ Position sizing tells you how much to invest in any one position or investment. It is one of the most important factors in any investment strategy.

➤ Position sizing accounts for most of the variability in the results of any system and is the key factor in achieving your objectives.

➤ The size of any investment should be determined by your objectives—what you want to achieve from that investment; the result.

They looked at how much each manager had in cash, how much in stocks, and how much in bonds. They called this "how-much" decision *asset allocation* and showed that it accounted for 91% of the variability in the performance of pension fund managers.

When you play the marble game described in Table 14.1, you need to make an asset allocation decision on each trade—you need to decide how much you will risk on the next marble draw and how much you will keep safely in cash. In other words, what *we* call position sizing is the same thing that professional managers call asset allocation—it's a "how-much" decision.[4] In the remainder of this chapter we will recommend some basic strategies for both position sizing (how much to risk on a trade) and asset allocation (which we'll call how much to risk on a strategy). However, they are different parts of the same decision—how much to risk per investment.

Now let's look at some practical steps to determine how big a position you should have when you enter the market.

ACTION STEP

Make sure you set clear objectives for each of your strategies.

Calculating Your Own Position Size

A good, but simple, position sizing strategy is to risk a percentage of your trading capital on every trade. When you enter a position in the market you need to know three things:

1. How much money do you want to risk? We'll call this C, for cash.
2. How much do you want to risk per share? In other words, how much will you allow the stock to drop per share before you exit? Call this R, for risk.
3. How many units (e.g., shares of stock) do you want to purchase? Call this P, for position size.

The net result is CPR for traders and investors.[5] You can solve for any of the three variables if you know the other two:

$$\textbf{Cash = Risk} \times \textbf{Position size}$$

or

$$\textbf{Position size = Cash} \div \textbf{Risk}$$

or

$$\textbf{Risk = Cash} \div \textbf{Position size}$$

Here's how it works. First, you must decide how much trading capital you have (your equity); then decide what percentage of your equity you want to risk, or how much cash will be at stake. Unless your position (or your trading system) is exceptional, I wouldn't recommend risking more than 1% on any single position (or trade). In other words, if you have an account with $30,000 in it, you would risk, at most, $300 on a single position. That's the C in your equation. Please note that this is *not* how much the position is going to *cost* you. You may invest $5,000 of your $30,000 equity, but you're only "risking" $300 of it.

Now you must determine how much you want to risk per share. For long-term positions, we typically recommend a 25% stop loss, or risk, because the trade has room to move and that amount will keep you in a position for a long time. When a stock moves down 25%, it's probably not going to move in your favor for some time. And even if you lost 25% of your starting investment, you only have to recover 33% of the remaining investment cash to break even again. However, if a stock goes down 50%, it has to double in value (i.e., 100% recovery) to break even, and that's a big discrepancy that's much harder to achieve. Thus, 25% is a fairly good initial risk amount.[6]

Let's look at an example. Say you want to purchase Boeing stock (BA) that is priced at $32. Your worst-case exit would be a price drop of 25% of that amount, or $8. Thus, when the stock drops to $24, you will be out. Your risk per share is $8.

Now plug two known factors into the equation to determine how many shares to buy. Remember that:

Position size = Cash ÷ Risk

In our example, your hypothetical account has $30,000 in equity and a 1% risk per position is calculated as $300. If you do the division to find the position size ($300 ÷ $8), you find that you need to buy 37.5 shares of BA. Since you cannot buy a half share, you would purchase 37 shares (always round down). Notice what you've done at this point. You can let your stock fall 25%, to $24, and you will have lost only 1% of your portfolio, or $300. Your risk here is only 25% of the value of the stock. You are buying 37 shares at $32 per share for a total cost of $1,184. However, you will get out if the stock drops 25%, so you are risking only about $300, or 1% of your portfolio.

Most people risk much more than 1% on their investments. And most fund managers, who equate asset allocation with selecting the best asset class, do not even understand how critical position sizing is to their performance.

With our formula, when you lose 1*R* you've lost $300, or 1%, and if you gain 10*R* you will make $3,000, or 10 times your risk. That's a 10% gain in your portfolio.

Too many traders and investors, especially those new to the game, believe the hype and think that winning in the markets is getting huge gains or doubling their portfolios quickly. Seasoned traders and those that *stay* in the game know how to really play it. Take heed and learn, don't take greed and burn. Rather than wanting to double your $30,000 portfolio, change your thinking and be happy with consistent profits while protecting your initial capital. Only then will you be able to stay in the game and become a trader who really does double your portfolio consistently.

Here is another example. Suppose you want to purchase Sun Microsystems (SUNW) at $4. Again, you want to risk only $300, or 1% of your portfolio (*C* = $300). You use a 25% stop, so if the stock drops to $3 per share you will exit the position (*R* = $1.00). Now let's plug these two known values into our position sizing formula: $300 ÷ $1.00 = 300 shares. So, you'll be buying 300 shares of SUNW. Those shares will cost you $1,200, but your risk is only 25% of that, $300, which is 1% of your portfolio.

Position Sizing Equalizes Risk (*R*) Across Investments

Notice in both of the foregoing examples that we had different risk values. In the first example, with BA, your risk was $8 (1*R*). In the second example, with SUNW, 1*R* was $1.00. But when we decided to risk 1% of our portfolio, or $300, we equalized the risk. We bought 37 shares of BA and had about $300 at risk. We bought 300 shares of SUNW and had about $300 at risk. Thus, our 1% position sizing means that a 1*R* risk is equal to 1% of our portfolio.

Using Position Sizing to Meet Your Objectives

What objectives might you have in the marble game? One might be to win the game and avoid going bankrupt. That's the most common

---

KEY IDEAS

➤ Position size is equal to cash divided by risk, so if you know any two variables you can solve for the third. If you determine how much of your portfolio to risk (Cash) and how much to risk per unit (Risk), you can determine how much to buy (*Position size*).

➤ If you always risk 1% of your portfolio, then 1R means the same for every investment you make (i.e., you equalize your exposure or risk to 1% per investment).

---

objective. Let's define it as having the highest ending equity. With this objective, you don't care how probable it is that you win, as long as you have the most money at the end of the game.

Another objective might be to win the game with a realistic gain of, say, 50% after 30 trades. This is an entirely different objective. (You could have picked any size gain, not just 50%.)

You might also have a very conservative objective of not losing much money so that you won't look foolish. This objective might be defined as minimizing the probability of a drawdown of 20% or more.

And what if your objective was something in between—you want to optimize your chances of making 50% and minimize your chances of losing 20%? You'd like to meet your goals, but you want to minimize your chances of a loss of 20% or more.

Notice that four totally different objectives were presented—two focusing on minimizing certain kinds of drawdowns and two focusing on winning the game. If you wanted to maximize the probability of various gains or minimize the probability of various losses, you could develop a huge number of objectives. Later in this chapter we'll go over some simple and very effective guidelines for safe position sizing strategies. But first, let's look at state-of-the-art position sizing.

IITM has a simulator called Know Your System™ that will calculate the optimal percentage risk for whatever objectives you have.[7] Know Your System is a custom-designed software package that simulates trading results based on a user's unique trading history. It does this by generating years of potential outcomes and then interpreting the results. We enter your *R*-multiple distribution (in this case, the marbles in the bag), your idea of ruin (down 20%), and your goal (up 50%). We then set an increment factor, say .02%, that we want to increment by, up to a top risk percentage, say 20%.

The simulator will start with the increment factor as your initial risk (.02%) and run 10,000 simulations. It will then add the increment factor and run another 10,000 simulations at the new percent risk level (.04%). It will keep doing this until it reaches the maximum risk percentage (20%). The simulator will then tell you the chances of meeting your goals using each of these risk percentages. Figure 14.1 shows this information entered into the simulator. Once we run the simulation, we send out a report with screen shots similar to the one shown in Figure 14.2. This gives the optimal percent risk for each of your objectives.

Figure 14.1 Plugging Your Goals into the Optimizer

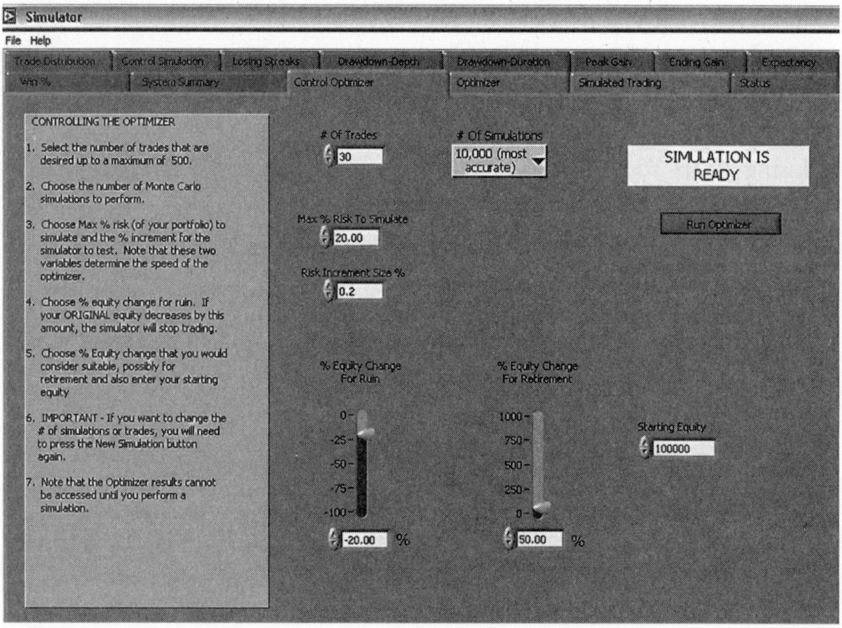

The maximum risk was set at 20% because this is the total ruin point. Why is this the point of total ruin? As soon as the 5R loss is drawn, you become bankrupt if your position size is set at 20% (i.e., 5 × 20% = 100% loss), so there is no point in risking more than that percentage. However, Know Your System's report suggests that risking 19.8% will give you the highest average ending equity (which essentially was your first goal—winning the game). Notice that there is a 98.7% chance of ruin (being down 20% when you risk this amount). Incidentally, Know Your System stops trading as soon as you are down 20% or more; whatever equity you have when it stops is your final equity. Of course, if it didn't stop, there is a chance that you could hit a hot streak and still make a fortune and a much more likely chance that you'll lose even more. At 19.8% risk, Know Your System shows that there is only a 1.5% chance of meeting your goal—being up 50%. Nevertheless, on some runs (i.e., perhaps one that has mostly 10R gains and no 5R losers) you'll make so much money risking 19.8% that you'll still

Figure 14.2 Simulator Results on Optimal Bet Size

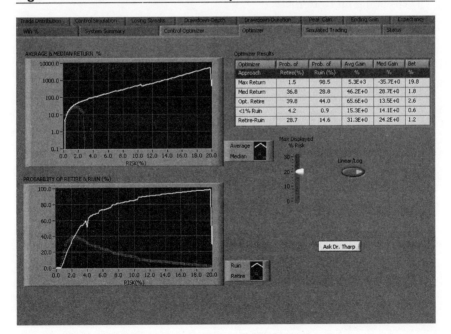

come out with the average highest ending equity. This happens even though the simulator averages in all of the runs that stop when you are down 20% or more. In fact, the average ending equity is up an average of 5,300% when you risk this amount. However, Know Your System proves why this sort of shooting-for-the-stars objective is rather fruitless in the long run—most of the time you'll fail. In fact, the simulator shows that your median gain (the point at which half of your gains will be higher and half will be lower) is actually negative when you risk 19.8%.

Figure 14.2 also shows what percent risk produces the highest average median gain with the simulator. That gain, shown in the second line of the table, is 1.8%, producing an average gain of 46.2% and a median gain of 28.7%. Notice that the average highest ending equity was produced by risking 19.8%, whereas the median average ending equity was produced by risking 1.8%.

The top graph in Figure 14.2 shows the average ending equity as a function of your risk. Notice that it hits 100% when you risk 4% and hits 1,000% at 14% risk. However, also notice the bottom graph. The probability of ruin (being down 20%) hits 60% when you risk 4% and keeps going up from there.

So what about the objective of gaining 50%? What risk percentage gives us the maximum probability of meeting this goal? The table in Figure 14.2 suggests that this optimum percentage is 2.6%. Risking 2.6% gives us a 39.8% chance of meeting the goal of making 50% after 30 trades. However, as the table shows, it also gives you a 44% chance of being down 20%. Thus, while risking 2.6% gives you the optimal chance of meeting your goal, it holds an even bigger chance that you'll hit the ruin mark. Incidentally, the average ending equity when you risk 2.6% is up 65.6% at the end of 30 trades, but the median gain is up only 13.5%. The bottom graph in Figure 14.2 shows that if you want to make a 50% return on equity, you have a 40% chance of this happening if you risk between 2% and 2.5% of your equity per trade. Your probability of reaching your objective of a 50% return drops off sharply as your risk increases beyond that level.

How about the risk percentage that gives you less than a 1% chance of being down 20%? Perhaps that is optimal? Well, Know Your System suggests that this percentage risk is achieved when you risk 0.6% of your equity. If you do that, you have only a 0.9% chance of being down 20% after 30 trades. It also suggests that your average ending equity after 30 trades would be up about 15.3%, which is not a bad gain for 30 trades. However, you only have a 4.2% chance of meeting your goal of being up 50% when you risk 0.6%.

Perhaps you are not happy with any of these results. Instead, you decide that you want the percentage risk that gives you the biggest difference between meeting your goal of 50% and being down 20% after 30 trades. The last row on the table in Figure 14.2 shows that this percentage is 1.2%. It gives you a 28.7% chance of being up 50% and only a 14.6% chance of being down 20%. Thus, we have a 14.1% better chance of meeting our goal than we have of suffering a 20% loss.

When you run simulations with higher percentage goals—such as being up 100%—you discover that you need to risk about 4.5% to get the highest probability of achieving that goal. However, the chances of ruin are much higher at this risk percentage. Furthermore, there was no risk percentage that gave you a better chance of making 100% than it did of being down 20%. Thus, the goals plugged into Know Your System must be realistic for the *R*-multiple distribution you have and for the number of trades in which you want to achieve your objectives. Being up 100% would be much more realistic after making 200 trades with this *R*-multiple distribution.

One other caution is that simulation in not an exact science. The optimal percentages can vary slightly from one set of 10,000 simulations to another. However, it does give you a fairly realistic idea of what

---

KEY IDEAS

➤ There are innumerable ways to define optimal position sizing, and each definition produces a different position sizing amount to best achieve the goal.

➤ Be sure to determine exactly what you want and how you will use position sizing to achieve that goal.

to expect, provided that you estimated your *R*-multiple distribution correctly. If your *R*-multiple distribution is inaccurate, so is your position sizing estimate, so it is always safer to be conservative.[8]

Safe Strategy Position Sizing

The goal of this book is to help you achieve financial freedom, and that is best done by having good, consistent returns. As a result, the goal in our position sizing discussions will be to make a minimum 10% return each year, and hopefully much more, while minimizing the chances of loss.

Strategy 1: Don't Risk More Than 1%

Our general advice is that if you cannot tolerate drawdowns, you probably should never risk more than 1% per position, no matter how good your system is, because you will experience drawdowns. For many of you, 1% might even be too high, especially if you're just starting in this area.

We studied the Oxford Club's stock picks from January 1999 through April 2000.[9] That was a great time period because it included a roaring bull market and the beginning of the current bear market. By May 2000, they were stopped out of all of their positions. During that 14-month period, 21 stock picks were made, with 11 of them making money. The selections were shown in Table 13.5.

Remember that the expectancy of those trades was 2.5*R*, which reflected the great bull market at the time. Also remember from Chapter 13 that long-term stock investors get better results if they only purchase stocks that move in their favor at the time they are recommended. In the current example, you would have eliminated 10 losers and increased your expectancy to 6.41*R*. However, the examples that follow will not eliminate those 10 losers and will use all of the recommendations to illustrate the effect of position sizing.

Table 14.3 shows the monthly performance of these picks if you simply risked 1% on each. This example began with $100,000, so the initial risk per position (the cash exposed in our equation) was $1,000. Notice that the portfolio was down only 5% between mid-March and mid-April 2000, a time period that included a huge drop in the market. Overall, it was up 55% during the 14 months while never having more than 59% of the portfolio exposed to the market.

When these data were recalculated using a 2% position sizing strategy, the results basically doubled. The portfolio was up 111% and had a drawdown in April of 8%. The 2% strategy resulted in the portfolio being 83.5% invested at the peak. And with this riskier strategy, there were three down months instead of two. (The strategy is riskier because putting more money into each stock creates extra volatility in the portfolio.) Remember that these returns occurred during the height of one of the greatest bull markets in history and even though all positions were stopped out at the end, giving back only a minimal amount of the gains, these results are not likely to repeat in the near future. Don't ever risk as much as 2% if you want to have a safe strategy.

Table 14.3 Monthly Values at 1% Risk

Date	Cash	Equities	Total	Gain/Loss	% Change
Feb 99	88,000	12,000	100,000		
Mar 99	80,000	20,352	100,352	352	0.0035
Apr 99	76,000	25,856	101,856	1524	0.0150
May 99	60,000	45,602	105,602	3,746	0.0368
Jun 99	59,909	42,349	104,258	−1,344	(0.0127)
Jul 99	63,923	46,206	110,129	5,871	0.0563
Aug 99	63,379	52,800	116,179	6,050	0.0549
Sep 99	76,836	39,018	115,854	−325	(0.0028)
Oct 99	67,568	49,785	117,353	1,499	0.0129
Nov 99	74,475	54,658	129,133	11,780	0.1004
Dec 99	62,667	71,865	134,532	5,399	0.0418
Jan 00	62,667	89,095	151,762	17,230	0.1281
Feb 00	71,685	82,042	153,717	1,955	0.0129
Mar 00	70,989	92,863	163,851	10,134	0.0659
15 Apr 00	130,232	25,152	155,383	−8,468	(0.0517)
			Total	**0.4613**	
			Average monthly gain	**0.0330**	

Strategy 2: 1% Risk with up to Four Scale-Ins

Another way to use position sizing is to increase your share amount for those stocks that are working for you. This is called *scaling into the position*. Use this strategy only when the stock market is in a green light mode as per Chapter 5. Apply this scale-in position with great caution in yellow light mode, and then use it only if your experience level warrants this aggressive strategy. Avoid scaling into a position in red light mode.

The Oxford Club during this period was using a 25% trailing stop as described in Chapter 13. This means that every time the stock made a new high, a new stop was placed 25% below the new high. The stop always went up, never down. Thus, if you bought a stock at $40, your initial stop would be 25% away at $30. If the stock moved to $60 per share, hitting a new high, you would move your stop 25% away to $45. If the stock then dropped to $45, you'd be stopped out at a $5 profit. In other words, you wouldn't move your stop down as the price dropped, only up.

When you have a 25% trailing stop like this, your stop moves to your entry price when the stock goes up 33.3%. For example, if you buy a stock at $40 a share, when the stock price goes up 33.3% to $53.33, your new stop is now at the entry price of $40. This is a strong enough move to scale into the stock with another position. As a result, another 1% position is added whenever the stop moves to breakeven. Up to four scale-ins were allowed for any given stock. Table 14.4 shows how this aggressive strategy might work.

Your original buy price is $40 with a 25% trailing stop at $30. When the stock goes up 33.3% to $53.33, your stop is now at breakeven and

Table 14.4 Breakeven Scale-In Strategy

Stock Price	Stop Price	Action	Total Position Size
$40	$30	Original entry	1% position size
$53.33	$40	Scale-in one	2% position size
$71.11	$53.11	Scale-in two	3% position size
$94.81	$71.11	Scale-in three	4% position size
$126.41	$94.81	Scale-in four	5% position size

you enter with another 1% position. When the stock goes up another 33.3% to $71.11, your first position is profitable and your second position is now at breakeven. You now enter your second scale-in with a 1% position. When the stock goes up another 33.3%, to $94.81, your second position is now profitable and your third position is breakeven. Now you add your third scale-in, another 1% position. You add your last 1% scale-in if the stock goes up yet another 33.3%.

What is the effect of this scaling-in on the 1999 to 2000 Oxford Club positions? The results are shown in Table 14.5 on a monthly basis. Now the portfolio is up 160% over the 14 months. The April drawdown is now 7.3%, which is less than the drawdown with the 2% risk. And the portfolio is basically 100% invested just before the crash starts. However, even with this large exposure, the portfolio is down only 7.3% on the first month of the crash. By April 15, our stock exposure going into the teeth of the bear market was only about 25%. And by May the portfolio was in total cash with only a 10% total drawdown from its peak in March.

Table 14.5 Monthly Positions with the 1% Scaling-In Model at 1% Risk with Scale-In at 25% [up to 5% Total]

Month	Cash	Equities	Total	Gain/Loss	Net Change
Feb 99	88000.00	12000.00	100000.00		
Mar 99	80000.00	20351.75	100351.75	$351.75	0.0035
Apr 99	72000.00	29856.50	101856.60	$1,504.85	0.0150
May 99	55702.96	54470.28	110173.24	$8,316.64	0.0817
Jun 99	55702.96	53866.05	109253.53	($919.71)	(0.0083)
Jul 99	46313.11	71655.99	117979.10	$8,725.57	0.0799
Aug 99	40736.38	99863.10	140599.48	$22,620.38	0.1917
Sep 99	74520.38	68442.08	142962.46	$2,362.98	0.0168
Nov 99	52596.50	129697.79	182294.29	$33,375.41	0.2241
Dec 99	5242.23	188744.88	193987.11	$11,692.82	0.0641
Jan 00	5242.23	242283.97	247526.20	$53,539.09	0.2760
Feb 00	24670.93	228408.41	253079.34	$5,553.14	0.0224
Mar 00	391.12	279916.79	280307.91	$27,228.57	0.1076
15 Apr 00	195455.71	64350.72	259806.43	($20,501.48)	(0.0731)

| | | | | Total percent gain | 104.3% |
| | | | | Average monthly gain | 0.0745 |

Strategy 3: Position Sizing Based upon Your Worst-Case Drawdown

Another way to do safe position sizing is to determine how big a loss you would be willing to tolerate in your original equity. Let's say you are trading $40,000. You would be willing to risk $8,000 of that $40,000 in a trading strategy like the marble game described earlier. How much could you risk? We have suggested that 1% would be a fairly safe place to start as a rule of thumb. Know Your System suggested that you should risk only 0.4% to keep this 20% drawdown from happening. Let's look at it one additional way.

Know Your System can play the marble game that we have been using as our example 10,000 times and keep track of all sorts of information. For example, you can calculate the expectancy of the system to be $0.8R$, but not all games have that expectancy. In fact, it would be interesting to determine what percentage of 30-trade games will even have a positive expectancy. Certainly, with 80% losers we know that some 30-trade blocks will lose money. We can also determine the worst-case drawdown in terms of R. In other words, how many times your basic risk are you likely to lose (as a worst case) in a down period during the 30 trades? And what's the worst-case drawdown over 10,000 simulations?

The first statistic that stands out from the simulations is that the game has an 82.5% chance of making money in 30 trades. That means if someone were to make 30 trades per day, he or she would make money on four out of five days (80% of the time). Superb system. A person doing 30 trades per month would make money in four out of five months. Great system. And someone doing 30 trades every year would make money in four out of five years. Good system.

Another interesting statistic is the losing streaks one might experience. These are shown in Table 14.6. The left column shows the size of the losing streak and the right column shows the probability of getting a streak that big or bigger. Notice that in 30 trades you have 100% chance of getting at least 6 straight losers and a 43% chance of getting at least 10 straight losers. Most people would think that a system was broken when they got 20 straight losers, but it apparently would happen about 2.6% of the time. Imagine the psychological impact of 20 losing trades in a row! But knowing that you had a 43% chance of 10

Table 14.6 Losing Streaks in Sample Marble Game

Streak Size	Cumulative Probability
6 straight losses	100%
8 straight losses	72.8%
10 straight losses	43.0%
12 straight losses	25.2%
14 straight losses	14.7%
16 straight losses	8.4%
18 straight losses	4.6%
20 straight losses	2.6%

losses ahead of time would make it easier to take and understand. Clarity equals power. Without this knowledge, you could become extremely upset if this happened, but knowing that it is a possibility lessens the impact. Actually, I've played this game about 150 times before various groups. I've seen one losing streak of 24 straight losses and another losing streak of 30 straight losses. The game with 24 straight losses actually made money at the end of 30 trades, but the 30 straight losses was a disaster.

Now let's look at the most critical information for safe position sizing—how big the losses might be in terms of R. This is shown in Table 14.7. The left column shows the size of the drawdown (cumulative loss) in terms of R and the right column shows the probability of getting a loss that big or bigger.

Table 14.7 Maximum R Drawdown in the Marble Game

Maximum R Drawdown	Cumulative Probability
$-10R$	85.1%
$-15R$	53.2%
$-20R$	28.2%
$-25R$	13.9%
$-30R$	5.8%
$-35R$	2.4%

The simulations showed that the average drawdown was 14.6R and that the maximum in 10,000 simulations was 60R.

So how do you use this information to determine position sizing? Let's assume that you decided you were willing to lose up to 20% of your starting equity, as mentioned earlier. If you divide 20% by the average maximum R multiple drawdown of 14.6, then you'd be able to risk 1.2%. However, this would give you about a 50% chance of a 20% drawdown in your equity somewhere in the 30 trades. If you use the maximum drawdown of 60R, you would get a 0.3% allowable risk. That's very close to the 0.6% risk percentage that the simulations suggested. Risking 0.3% would give you about one chance in 10,000 of losing as much as 20% of your starting equity. And if you were willing to tolerate a 5.8% chance of losing 20%, you could probably risk 0.67%— almost at the original 1% estimate.

Once again, remember that simulator results are accurate only when you really know your R-multiple distribution. You know the R-multiple distribution of the marble game, but you can only estimate what it is for your system, so it is always better to be conservative.[10]

Strategy 4: A Safe Strategy Allocation

In Chapter 7 you learned a mutual fund strategy that involved using asset allocation in the strategy instead of position sizing. So when do you use an asset allocation strategy as opposed to a position sizing strategy? And since position sizing and asset allocation both indicate how much, what is the difference?

A position sizing strategy is used when all of your other decisions are made. For example, you might decide to buy XYZ with a stop set if it falls 25% in price. Those are your entry and exit decisions, but they say nothing about how much. You need to add a position sizing strategy, which might be to risk at most 1% of your portfolio.

In an asset allocation strategy, the decision to buy and the how-much decision are one in the same. Suppose, for example, that you think one mutual fund best represents the position you'd like in the market. You think this sector will do better than the market as a whole, and you want to take a major position in it. If you risked only 1% on this fund, you would risk a very small portion of your total portfolio. An asset allocation strategy might be more appropriate.

Here's how an asset allocation strategy works. Suppose you invest in an index mutual fund that represents the S&P 500 Index. You decide that you will enter the fund with a certain position size (determined by your asset allocation parameters) when certain criteria are met. You might decide that if the S&P 500 is up over the last five weeks and is up at least 2.5% on the week, you will purchase a position equal to 20% of your portfolio.[11] If you have a $25,000 portfolio, you would buy $5,000 worth of this mutual fund. On subsequent weeks, you might decide that if the market moves up another 2.5%, you will buy another 20% position. Conversely, you might decide that you will exit the entire

---

KEY IDEAS

➤ If you have a good strategy, the key to meeting your objectives is your position sizing method.

➤ Portfolio variability is due primarily to position sizing and psychology.

➤ Position Size = Cash ÷ Risk

➤ Risking more than 1% of your portfolio on any one idea can be hazardous to your financial wealth.

➤ During very good market conditions you might be able to risk 1% on an original position plus four scale-in positions.

➤ If you know the R-multiple distribution of your system, you can determine what position sizing algorithm to use through many trading simulations.

➤ You can also use a worst-case drawdown in terms of R, to determine position sizing, as described earlier in this chapter. Divide that R drawdown in the amount of portfolio drawdown you wish to avoid to determine your position size.

➤ Asset allocation means that your position sizing decision is a part of your entry decision.

> ### ACTION STEPS
>
> ➤ Determine your objectives for yourself.
> ➤ How much would you like to make in your portfolio (and at what level of certainty), and how much are you willing to lose (and at what level of certainty) in order to do so?
> ➤ Using your objectives, simulate your system's *R*-multiple distribution many times to decide what position sizing strategy to use. If you want to be conservative, simply risk 0.5% or less per position.
> ➤ If you want reliable information about position sizing for your system, go to iitm.com. You can download a free example of a Know Your System report or learn more about position sizing in-depth through a variety of products on this topic.

position if the market moves lower than it was five weeks ago. Thus, your entire decision to buy incorporates an element of "how much," which is the essence of an asset allocation strategy.

Answering Your Questions on Position Sizing

Position sizing is a complex topic, and many questions arise when it is presented. The following section responds to some typical queries.

Let's say I have a $20,000 portfolio and I want to risk only 1%. I can't buy much stock with $200.

You are risking $200, but that's not how much stock you buy, which is determined by your stop. When are you going to get stopped out? If you use a 10% stop, you'd buy $2,000 worth of stock because you'd be risking 10% of what you bought (10% of $2,000 = $200 risk). Remember that position risk and your stop go hand in hand in determining how much stock to buy. This was calculated in the CPR formula given earlier in this chapter. Here's another example: If you use a 25% stop, you could buy $800 worth of stock (25% × $800 = $200 risk).

Position sizing sounds easy, but buying only 37 shares or 20 shares—that's not very much.

You are risking 1% of your portfolio, and that's the most you should risk. Doing so will keep you out of danger and in the market longer. If you had 10 stocks going into a bear market with 1% risk and you suffered the worst-case loss on each of them (i.e., 1%), you'd only be down 10% in your portfolio. So after 10 losses, you still have 90% of your capital. Imagine if you'd risked 10% on each trade (10 × 10% = 100%). Good-bye to trading because all your money is gone.

Buying odd lots: isn't that much more expensive, and wouldn't my broker laugh at me?

If you care about your broker's response, then you have a personal issue to deal with. In today's competitive market, there is typically one fee whether you buy 400 shares or 14 shares. Thus, buying an odd lot should not be much of a problem. Yes, a $30 commission is ⅒ of your risk, but that's one of the disadvantages of being small. But unless you want to risk losing way too much, 1% is all you should risk per position in your portfolio. And you can trade stock online through Schwab, eTrade, or Ameritrade. You don't have to talk to a broker. No one will know what you do except you.

But this is so simple. Don't the professionals do something much more complex?

Some do, but many of them have never heard of position sizing. In fact, if you are invested in a mutual fund, chances are your fund manager is fully invested (with perhaps only 3% to 5% cash). That's one reason most fund managers fail to outperform the market. If the Dow Jones Industrials were to go down 50% in one year, your fund manager would probably be down 52% because he must be fully invested and portfolio managers seldom outperform the market averages.

What if I only want to risk a dollar per share when I get into a stock?

Then you'd plug in $1 as R in the equation. If your total risk was $300 (1% of your $30,000 account), you would be buying 300 shares, and that would be the same whether it was BA at $32 or MSFT at $60. Remember that using a 1% position sizing model means that a $1R$ loss is always just 1% of your portfolio. With BA at $32, you'd buy 300 × $32, which is $9,600 (and you'd get out if it went down to $31 per share). With MSFT at $60, you'd by 300 × $60, which is $18,000 (and you would sell and be out if it went down to $59 per share). Only $300 was risked in each scenario.

I'm a little confused by R. If it means risk per share, how is that different from the total risk or cash position, C?

C is your total position risk, while R is your risk per share. When you calculate expectancy, it's much easier to refer to total risk as R instead of C. You simply take your total profit or loss on the position (after commissions are subtracted) and divide that by your total initial risk (C). The net result will then be expressed as an R multiple of the total position risk. When you do it this way, R is always 1% of your portfolio (or whatever percent risk you are using). Again, the percent risk model has the advantage of equating the risk for all investments.

Let's say you risk $300. If your eventual profit is $600, you made twice your risk, or a $2R$ gain. You might have risked $30 on 10 shares of stock (i.e., a $300 risk) and watched the stock go up $60. You also might have risked $3 on 100 shares of stock (i.e., also a $3 risk) and watched the stock go up $6. In both price-per-share examples, your total profit was twice your risk (i.e., $600), or a $2R$ gain.

Okay, so how do I use position sizing to meet my objectives? This sounds like one formula for everything.

With different objectives, you risk different percentages of your equity. We covered that topic in this chapter.

Does position sizing apply to all investments, even real estate?

This material is crucial to all investments. It doesn't matter whether you risk $5,000 on stocks, gold, futures, bonds, or real estate. You've still risked $5,000 and that's your position size. However, sometimes it is difficult to limit your risk in an illiquid investment like real estate. That is, if real estate prices fall, you might not find a buyer. Your loss could easily be much bigger than $1R$.

How can I get a good feeling about position sizing?

Try simulating a trading system (i.e., a set of R-multiple distributions that you might represent with a bag of marbles) with different position sizing strategies. It doesn't take too long to get a feel for it. And we do it for you in our free position sizing game (at iitm.com). Keep playing with different amounts and risk different percentages of your overall equity to see what happens. How often do you go bankrupt? Could you do that in real life? In addition, we produce reports via our trading simulator, Know Your System. This will help you to achieve a total understanding of what your trading system (with a particular R-multiple distribution) is likely to produce in terms of results.

Please explain again the difference between asset allocation and position sizing.

Both decisions involve how much. The asset allocation decision tells you how much you'll risk for the overall strategy, which you will keep either until your model says you will no longer apply the strategy or until you've lost enough money to suggest the strategy isn't working. The position sizing decision tells you how much you'll risk per trade when the strategy requires that you trade many times. You use position sizing to determine how much you could lose per trade. You use asset allocation to decide how much you will lose with the strategy before you stop trading it.

Let's look at an example of each. Asset allocation is used when your strategy is simply a decision to buy a large amount of something such as a mutual fund or a commodity, because one of your models says that's what you should do. For example, if you decide that you should invest in a technology mutual fund (because it is the hottest fund) or gold (because inflation is heating up) or FAX (because you think the dollar is going down), you will want an asset allocation strategy. You might decide you want 25% of your portfolio in gold. In this case, you might be willing to lose 8% of your portfolio if the model was wrong about inflation. (This would be equivalent to buying eight stocks with a 1% risk in each and being wrong on all of them.) You would sell the position if it was down about 30%, which would cost you 7.5% of your portfolio.

In contrast, a position sizing strategy comes into play when you decide to do individual trades in a particular area. For example, you might decide to buy gold stocks (instead of gold) because inflation is heating up. You decide that you will continue to trade gold stocks unless you draw down your portfolio by 25% or your model about inflation changes. You trade many gold stocks with a 25% trailing stop, risking 1% on each. Your decision to risk 1% on each is a position sizing decision.

Is this what portfolio managers do in terms of asset allocation in mutual funds?

Some might, but most don't. Most just decide to invest some percentage of their portfolio in a particular type of asset, and they call that asset allocation. If they do that, then asset allocation is just a selection decision and has nothing to do with risk or how much they are willing to lose. If the market dropped 50%, they would probably still stick with their positions.

That's why it is so important that you accept total personal responsibility for any money that you have invested. Although the manager might let it ride down to a 50% loss (or more), if you know that you were only willing to tolerate a 20% loss, you could move your money away from that manager when necessary to do so.

Notes
1. Much of this chapter is based upon Van Tharp's experience consulting with investors, traders, and market professionals on the importance of position sizing.
2. Hint: Add up the *R* multiples of all the marbles in the bag and divide by 10, the number of marbles. You should get an expectancy of 0.8*R*.

3. Brinson, Singer, and Beebower, "Determinants of Portfolio Performance II: An Update," *Financial Analysts Journal* 47 (1991):40–49.

4. Unfortunately, because the name "asset allocation" implies that selecting the appropriate asset class is the key variable, the impact of position sizing is totally lost on most portfolio managers. Most of them must be nearly 100% invested in long positions all of the time. As a result, most portfolio managers cannot practice position sizing at all. This is one of the huge dangers of mutual funds in today's market climate.

5. Ron Ishibashi came up with the idea of CPR for traders. He also made excellent suggestions when reading the first version of this book.

6. A 25% risk position is not appropriate for highly leveraged positions such as foreign exchanges, futures, or options. These topics are not covered in this book, which is about safe strategies.

7. For more information on the Know Your System simulator and on receiving a free sample report, go to iitm.com.

8. If you have a portfolio of highly correlated positions, then your risk per position needs to be even more conservative.

9. Steve Sjuggerud was the investment director of the Oxford Club at the time and made many of the stock picks. Van Tharp was on the investment advisory board for the Oxford Club and was looking for a good position sizing strategy for its members.

10. If you are trading multiple correlated sustems or have many trades at one time, you need to be much more careful because Know Your System does not account for this correlation.

11. This is basically the reverse of the short strategy given in Chapter 7.

CHAPTER 15

KNOWING YOUR STRATEGY

"People who lose money in the market say, 'I just lost money and now I have to do something to make it back.' No, you don't. You should sit there until you find something."

—JIMMY ROGERS

You now know most of the fundamentals of a safe and profitable strategy. However, there is one more key ingredient—knowing when your strategy works and when it doesn't. This chapter will give you a framework for making that determination.

To protect yourself from using a strategy that no longer works, we recommend that you take three steps.

First, you must know what will happen to your strategy when key major (macro) economic factors change. You must understand the relationship that your strategy has in that overall background and have a way to keep up with changes in the macroeconomic climate.

Second, you must understand that the markets you are trading will change even if the macroeconomic conditions remain constant. Laws change, rules change, and the way "big money" plays the money game changes. All these changes can affect your strategy. For example, as we submitted the manuscript for this book, mutual fund families started to prohibit the type of weekly switching that Ken Long recommends. As a result, we had to update that material in a special report for you as opposed to presenting it in this book. This is a great example of what happens to investment strategies all the time. You'll learn specific ideas for how to keep up with changing trends in this chapter.

Third, you'll learn about the six types of markets and how your system will perform in each. The best way to understand what to expect is to collect the *R*-multiple distributions from 50 to 100 trades in each type of market and then feed each of those distributions into a simulator. In this chapter we'll demonstrate the Know Your System simulator more thoroughly to demonstrate the kind of information you can gather.

Once you understand what to expect from your system, you'll have to decide if you are comfortable trading it. For example, the max yield strategy given in Chapter 10 allowed you to increase your account from $10,000 to $322,817 in 34 years. When you heard those results, you probably wanted to start using the system. However, it lost money in four out of five years from 1997 through 2001. Are you willing to trade a system that has made money in only three of the last seven years? Could it behave even worse? Of course, the max yield system is only appropriate when the dollar is falling in value. That started in 2002, and it has made great money since that time.

Why Your System Works

When we first started coaching traders in the early 1980s, most of our clients were options and futures traders.[1] A huge major bull market in stocks started in 1982, but very few stock traders came to us for coaching.

By the early 1990s, futures traders were beginning to get nervous because the trends had dried up and the markets were dominated by big commodity trading advisors. At that time, there were great trends in currencies, so many of our clients were trading currencies.

In the late 1990s, futures traders or currency traders seldom attended our workshops. Everyone was an equity (stock market) trader. Many stock day traders came to the workshops seeking advice.

Today, in 2004, the tide is turning again. More traders are now focusing on futures, currencies, and options. There are still some short-term equity traders and people who think the stock market has started a new bull market. This, too, will change again—probably many times.

What is the reason for the dramatic changes in the types of traders who want coaching and training? One basic reason is that markets change as a result of changes in macroeconomic conditions. And as conditions change, so do the strategies that work in those markets. Something that might have worked in one year might not work in another. One year there might be major trends in the futures markets, and many different futures trading systems might work well. Another year the futures markets might turn flat (meaning futures systems stop working) and equity systems might kick in. Stock market day traders might be able to capture an edge in the market one month and the next month find their edge is totally gone.

Just because your system works today doesn't mean it will work five years from now. One of the worst things you can do as a trader or investor is to keep trading or investing with a strategy that doesn't work. In fact, many of the portfolio managers in the world may be doing that right now. They have systems that just buy stocks—systems that were designed for bull markets, but the odds suggest that we may be in a prolonged bear market for equities. What will happen to them if the average return for mutual funds is negative over a prolonged period of time?

As mentioned, there are six major macroeconomic factors influencing today's markets. These are listed in Figure 15.1. At the end of this

---

Figure 15.1 Major Factors Influencing Today's Market

- The stock market is in a primary bear market. It started in 2000 and could last 15 to 20 years (see Chapter 5).
- Immense deflationary pressures are at work, but the Federal Reserve will go all out to fight that (see Chapter 9).
- The government is printing money at a torrid pace, producing huge inflationary pressures and a potential bull market in gold (see Chapter 10).
- The United States has a huge debt that must be corrected (see Chapter 10).
- The dollar is going down in value (see Chapter 10).
- Interest rates are at extreme lows (good for real estate) but could turn suddenly (see Chapters 10 and 11).

section is a list of resources, most of them free, that will keep you up to date on the trends.

Essentially, knowing how these factors operate is all about *market selection*. When some factors are strong, certain markets are great. When other factors are strong, other markets are great. This information changes regularly, so you need to stay on top of the situation. Markets change; you need to be willing to change as well.

Let's look at a couple of examples. When inflation is strong, the stock market and the dollar are usually weak. During the inflationary 1970s through the early 1980s, there were huge trends in the commodity markets and in gold, which is a commodity. Strategies that would work under those conditions would be trading commodities (i.e., especially momentum trading), trading gold stocks, and investing in assets denominated in strong currencies. Inflationary strategies were discussed in Chapter 9.

As inflation decreased (it was called disinflation), the American dollar became strong. And under these conditions, the stock market was booming. This occurred from the mid-1980s through the 1990s, when the biggest stock market rise in history occurred. Obviously, one strategy that worked was trading stocks. In fact, the methods described in Chapters 5 and 8 were excellent during this period.

In the early 1980s, interest rates topped out at the peak of inflation. The result was a huge boom in the bond market. Because bond prices go up as interest rates go down, it was possible during that time to make double-digit returns just by holding bonds. If you buy a bond yielding 10% for $1,000, your bond could go up to $1,200 if interest rates fall to 8% because at $1,200 its yield is now about 8%. Interest rate strategies were discussed in Chapter 10.

The U.S. dollar gained great strength from 1995 until 2001. This made U.S.-dollar goods (real estate, bonds, and stocks) very attractive. The net result was that foreigners bought dollar-denominated goods, which helped fuel the bull market in stocks and bonds. Investing in dollar-denominated products is profitable when the dollar is going up. However, when the dollar is falling, as it is now, you want to buy investments denominated in strong currencies. These strategies were discussed in Chapter 10.

Stay up to Date

To ensure that your strategies are safe, you need to stay on top of the six factors given in Figure 15.1. To do so, read Chapters 5, 9, 10, and 11, and think about the impact that new laws, policies, and regulations will have on the economy, as discussed later in this chapter. You can consult any of the publications listed here, most of which are free, to update yourself on a regular basis. You'll have to see beyond the bias (i.e., psychology and beliefs) of each author, but you'll get a tremendous amount of information about what is going on in the world of economics.

- Read John Mauldin's free weekly e-mail. Mauldin reads about 200 articles, newsletters, and newspapers every week. On Fridays, he sits down for four hours and writes a 5,000-word essay on the state of the market. To get his weekly e-mail, go to frontlinethoughts.com. You can even download some of the articles he is currently reading, plus back issues of his weekly commentary.
- Steve Sjuggerud, one of the authors of this book, writes a free educational e-letter called *Investment U*. It's full of tips on how the markets work and insights into the state of the world. To subscribe, go to investmentuonline.com. You can also get back issues.
- A free daily e-letter that explains what's going on in the market is Bill Bonner's *Daily Reckoning*. To subscribe, go to dailyreckoning .com.
- Van Tharp's International Institute of Trading Mastery has a free weekly e-mail called *Tharp's Thoughts*. It contains tips on risk control, financial freedom comments, and periodic updates on the market. It also has tips to help you become a peak performer. To subscribe, call 919-852-3994 or 800-385-4486 or go to iitm.com.
- Richard Russell's *Dow Theory Letters*, published every three weeks, is not free, but it's worth the cost. Russell is 80 in 2004, and he's been writing his newsletter since 1958. He's seen it all and tells it the way he sees it. Richard writes a daily commentary on the market that you can download for free six days a week as a subscriber. There is no better way to stay on top of the market than by reading his daily commentary. He's not always right in his opinions, but he is always

informative. To subscribe, go to dowtheoryletters.com. Russell is in no way associated with this book.

You might consider taking a few additional steps to keep on top of things.

Keep Track of the Bear Market

Track changes in the S&P 500, the Nasdaq, the Dow, and any foreign stock markets you are interested in, on at least a weekly basis. You might also look at *Barron's* every week to determine the price-to-earnings ratio of the major averages and their dividend yield. Changes to the 1-2-3 model will be in several of the free newsletters we mentioned.

Track Inflation and Deflation

Track the CRB Index (a collective index of commodities), interest rates, and gold on a weekly basis. This information is updated quarterly in IITM's free newsletter.

Keep Track of Debt

Go to the Federal Reserve's website on a quarterly basis to get the latest debt figures and read the suggested free newsletters.

Track the Value of the Dollar

Watch the dollar index on a monthly basis. You can find this information by going to the Federal Reserve website. The Big Mac Index is published several times each year in *The Economist* magazine and online.

Track Real Estate

Watch interest rates on a weekly and monthly basis. When they start heading up, be prepared for potential trouble. Be especially cautious if the Federal Reserve starts to raise interest rates and mortgage rates start

---

ACTION STEPS

➤ Subscribe to the publications mentioned to stay on top of what is happening to the big picture.

➤ Subscribe to IITM's free e-mail newsletter, *Tharp's Thoughts*, to determine when the various strategies given in this book will and will not work.

---

to go up. If you know a real estate broker, check with that person monthly about sales in your area.

You can get most of the information recommended at bullandbear wise.com. Look at the prices over the last week and over the last five weeks. Once you are up to date on this information, sit down each month and ask yourself if any of the major trends have changed. If you believe they have, then determine what the implications might be for the strategies that you've picked in your financial freedom plan.

Understanding the Money Game

There are major inefficiencies in the market, so the market can be neither efficient nor random. These inefficiencies have to do with human psychology; laws, rule changes, and government policies; and the games "big money" is current playing to make money. All these factors influence macroeconomics and how well your strategy will work. And if you understand the money games being played, finding the right strategy becomes easy.[2]

Human Psychology

The first major inefficiency is human psychology. There is now a branch of psychology dealing with how inefficient human beings are at making decisions. And it has developed into a new area of economics called behavioral finance. Here are a few examples of inefficient decision-making in that arena.

People would rather be right than make money. As a result, they hang on to losses so they might be right later, and they close out their gains quickly so they'll be right now. Another version of this says that people make risky decisions when they are losing and fail to take wise gambles when they are ahead.

Human beings jump to conclusions too easily from too little information. Once they've formed such a conclusion, they ignore a lot of contradictory information in order to hang on to their conclusions. As a result, those who have losing portfolios will believe anything that says they'll make their money back soon. At the same time, they'll ignore evidence about how overvalued the stock market is.

Human beings will buy stock as it continues to make new highs with the idea that this trend will continue forever.[3] In addition, when the market is so overvalued that a decision to buy is totally illogical, people start flooding into the market to buy stock and hold it forever. This is human greed at its peak.

Similarly, when market valuations get so low that free money is to be found everywhere, most people will vow never to buy another stock. In fact, that's when most people start to sell. This is the fear factor in the market.

Although much of this book is devoted to helping you become efficient in your decision making, most people will not change. These psychological factors will always operate in the market.

Laws, Rule Changes, and the Government

Other changes and inefficiencies come about when major new laws are enacted. For example, many people believe that the Tax Reform Act of 1986 law precipitated the savings and loan crisis that we faced in the late 1980s. It certainly caused a major ripple in the real estate market as certain activities that were once low-risk ideas for the wealthy suddenly became illegal and unprofitable. In 2003, the Bush administration passed a major tax bill. People who understand the impact of that bill on the markets, especially in terms of the loopholes that might be created or closed, will profit handsomely.

Regulatory agencies make rule changes that can also have a major impact on various trading strategies. For example, when we started writing *Financial Freedom Through Electronic Day Trading*, day-trading of stocks was the hot topic. However, after we submitted the book to the publisher, a major rule change took effect that required stocks to start trading in decimals instead of fractions. This meant that the smallest change in price was now a penny, not ¹⁄₁₆ of a dollar. This rule change had a major impact on one of the strategies described in that book as the bid-ask spread on some stocks narrowed from ¹⁄₁₆ to one penny.

Within a year of the publication of our book, the SEC ruled that day traders could get four-to-one leverage on their money, but they had to have at least $25,000 in their account. Those who made four day trades within a specified period of time would be considered day traders. This even applied to short-term traders who got stopped out of trades the same day they were entered, even though the traders might have held their positions for weeks had they gone in their favor. Since most small trading accounts didn't have $25,000 in them, this rule change had a major impact on short-term trading. Many small account holders got out of the market permanently.

And let's look at policy changes from the executive branch of the government. The Clinton administration gave the country a strong dollar policy, but it also gave the United States a huge balance-of-payment deficit. The Bush administration dropped the strong dollar policy and concentrated on fighting terrorism around the world. This led to increased government spending and huge government deficits, which have weakened the dollar further.

The bottom line is that rule changes could have a major impact upon your strategy. You could save a lot of money by knowing in advance when a strategy would stop working as a result of such changes. And you could make huge amounts of money by knowing which strategies would work in the future as a result of policy changes. However, if you follow the steps outlined in the next section for determining how your strategy will perform in various types of markets, you should be able to escape any serious damage from these sorts of changes.

What Big Money Does

The last area that has a major impact on market strategies is a sudden change in what big money does. Let's look at three examples to illustrate how a sudden change could have a major impact on your investment strategies.

One example of how big money makes changes that affect macroeconomics is the exporting of U.S. jobs overseas. Manufacturing plants are being moved to China, and service industry jobs are being moved to India. This trend is costing America jobs and is a major deflationary force in the market today. This trend affects your strategies.

The second example of what big money does is the way the mutual fund industry convinces many people to buy and hold stocks. As mentioned in Chapter 6, mutual funds get paid just by having your money in their fund. They decided they could do well by getting just 2% of your money every year, and they don't get paid for good performance. They said you'd make good returns if you put your money under the care of a stock market professional and kept it there for the long run. They even convinced you to measure mutual fund performance by how well they'd do with respect to certain stock market indexes every year, rather than how much money they made you. It has been an interesting game.

Most funds were formed during the last great bull market, and their managers have never seen a major bear market. When fear really starts to come into play on the downside, to the point where no one wants to buy stocks ever again, the mutual fund industry could collapse. This would mean a huge drop in the stocks that make up the major indexes as the funds have to bail out of those stocks to meet redemption requests. This will certainly cause a change in what big money does, but it shouldn't have any impact on your investment strategy if you follow the guidelines in this book.

If you make 50 trades in a year, you can draw a marble from the bag for each trade to simulate a year's worth of trading, then replace it after it is drawn. If you do this several hundred times, you'll have a good idea about what to expect in the future. If you do it thousands of times, you can determine actual probabilities of various outcomes. You'll find this exercise very valuable in giving you some idea of what to expect from the market in terms of losing streaks and drawdowns.

Drawing out 50 marbles ten thousand times would take you quite a while, and keeping rack of the data would be tedious. As a result, for those who would like to save time, IITM has developed the simulator Know Your System, introduced in Chapter 14. You can request a report from Know Your System to evaluate various position sizing strategies and tell you what to expect from your system. You can do it yourself or use this shortcut to save time.

Figure 15.3 shows the input screen from Know Your System. Once again, let's look at the data from the marble game described in Chapter 14. You might assume that this represents a trend-following system in a volatile market (so our R-multiple distribution would represent trading in highly volatile markets trending up or trending down). This time assume that you make 10 trades per month. Let's ask Know Your System to simulate 120 trades so that we'll know what to expect from the system each year. Incidentally, the simulation is still based on the R multiples of the 10 marbles given at the outset to represent the system. However, if you make 120 trades each year, you'd probably have at least 50 to 60 different R multiples in your sample. To obtain the most accurate estimate of our system's performance, let's do 10,000 simulations.

Notice in Figure 15.3 that once the R multiples are entered, you automatically get a report showing some initial statistics plus a plot of the R multiples in the graph. You get the expectancy (which is the mean R multiple) and its standard deviation.[5] You know that our system will produce an average gain of $0.8R$ per trade (the mean R multiple) but that there is a large variability in the sample since the R multiples range from $10R$ to $-5R$. You also know that the system wins 20% of the time and that the average gain is 6.67 times as big as the average loss.[6]

The next screen in the simulator, which is not shown, determines how many trades to simulate. This will be 120 trades per year for the

Figure 15.3 Data Entry for Our Simulator

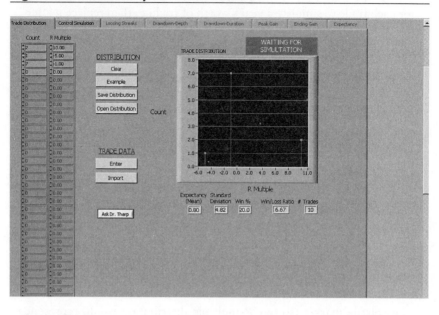

example. It also asks how many trades are made each month, which in this case is 10, and how many simulations to run. It will allow anything from 2,500 simulations (fastest) to 10,000 simulations (most accurate). Our example will do 10,000 simulations.

The first thing you want to know about your system is what you can expect in terms of losing streaks. Most people get upset when they have three or four losses in a row. They think their system is broken when they get 10 losses in a row. But remember that the system (i.e., the marble game) that was plugged into the simulator wins only 20% of the time. Thus, you can expect 8 out of 10 trades to be losers, and you should expect some very long losing streaks.

Figure 15.4 shows the Know Your System report screen on losing streaks in this system each year. Notice that the average streak is 16 losses in a row and that the maximum number of losses is 52. Obviously, if you cannot tolerate long losing streaks, you could not trade this system. The simulator shows you that information right up front.

Figure 15.4 Losing Streaks in Our System

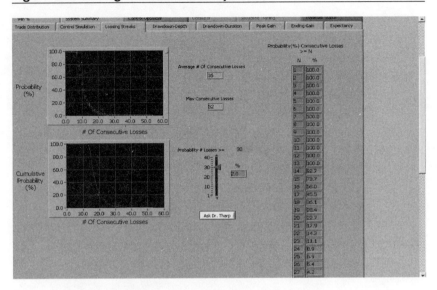

However, look at the top graph and the table in Figure 15.4. They both show that in 120 trades you have a 100% chance of a losing streak of 13 in a row. The table shows cumulative probabilities. Notice that you have a 6.9% chance of a streak as big as 25 straight losses. And, although the table only goes to 28 straight losses, we can see the probability of bigger losses on the bottom chart and using the arrow. The arrow is set at 30 straight losses which has a 2% chance of occurring.

The next thing you might want to look at is the size of drawdowns in our system in terms of R. You learned about this type of analysis in Chapter 14 as a way to determine position size. Simulation is one way to determine how big such drawdowns can get in terms of R.

Figure 15.5 shows the drawdown analysis for our system. The first thing you might notice is that over 120 trades you will get an average drawdown of 29.3R. That's huge and it might be one reason not to trade this sort of system. Now if you were risking only 0.5%, it would translate into about a 15% drawdown. But if you were risking 2%, you might have to endure a drawdown as big as 60%, which very few people can

Figure 15.5 Our System's Drawdowns in Terms of R

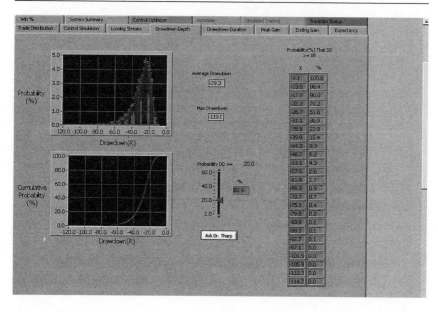

tolerate. Again, the Know Your System report tells you a lot of information about the system that might determine whether or not you are willing to trade it.

The top graph in Figure 15.5 shows a histogram of the various drawdowns in terms of *R*. Notice how they peak at around 25*R*. The bottom graph shows cumulative probabilities. You can see that you have 100% chance of a drawdown as big as 9*R* and even a 40*R* drawdown has about a 10% chance of occurring. The really shocking information from this graph, however, is that in 10,000 simulations of 120 trades, we had one drawdown as big as 119*R*. That means that even risking as little as 1%, it's possible (although unlikely) to get a drawdown that would cause the account to go to nearly zero.[7]

The next question you might ask is how long the drawdowns will last. And since Know Your System knows you make 10 trades per month, it will report how long your drawdowns might last both in terms of number of trades and in terms of time (i.e., months). This information is shown in Figure 15.6.

Figure 15.6 Our System's Drawdown Duration

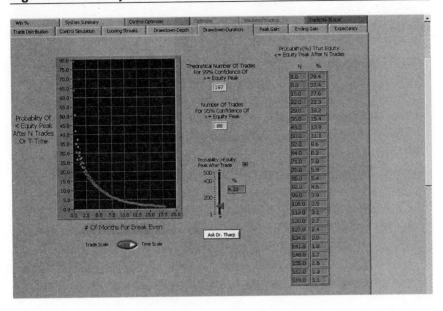

The first number that stands out from the analysis in Figure 15.6 is the number of trades necessary for a 95% chance of getting a new peak equity. This number, shown in the box in the middle of the figure says you'll need 88 trades. In other words, when the system is in a drawdown, it will need 88 trades to be 95% certain of getting a new peak equity. Worse yet, as the top box shows, it will need 197 trades to have a 99% certainty of a new peak equity.

This probably sounds like enough information to convince some of you to throw away the system. However, very few systems can tolerate this kind of analysis. The graph is set to show the number of months to an expected new equity high. And as the graph shows, you might require eight or nine months to have a 95% chance of a new equity high. (The graph actually displays it as less than a 5% chance of being down after that period of time).

Now that you are probably convinced that you could never trade this system, let's see what you can expect from it on the positive side. First, let's do an expectancy analysis. What are the chances of this system

Figure 15.7 The Expectancy of Our System with 120 Trades per Year

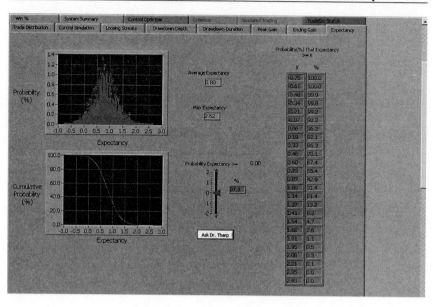

making money in a year? Even though the expectancy (the mean R multiple of the system) is 0.8, what kind of range does it show? What's the probability of getting a negative expectancy after 120 trades? The data is displayed in Figure 15.7.

Our first good news is shown by the arrow in the bottom center of the figure. It asks the question, What is the probability of getting an expectancy that is greater than zero? The answer is 97.3% of the time. Thus, if you make 120 trades in a year and you practice appropriate position sizing designed to minimize risks and keep you playing the game, you can expect to make money almost every year. Now our system doesn't seem so bad, does it?

Next, let's ask what kind of gain you can expect in terms of R at the end of 120 trades. Knowing the expectancy and the number of trades, you should be able to calculate the average gain easily. Since the expectancy is $0.8R$ and there are 120 trades, the average gain should be the product of those two numbers, or $96R$. Let's see if the report from Know Your System produces the same results.

Figure 15.8 Average Gain in Terms of R After 120 Trades

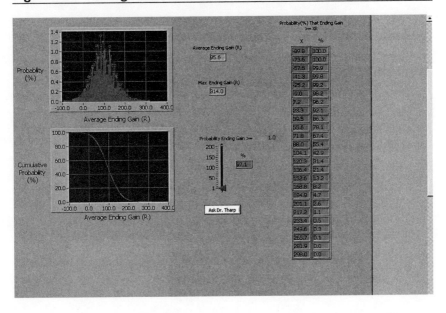

Figure 15.8 shows the average ending equity in terms of R for our 10,000 simulations of 120 trades. And as expected, the average ending gain in terms of R is 95.6R—very close to our expected number. This means that if you risked 0.5% trading this system you could probably expect to be up by nearly 50% each year. Now perhaps the system seems better.

Before you get too excited, let's look at the range of results. The box at the center of the page shows that the maximum ending gain was 314R. Very nice results! However, the table also shows that one simulation got a negative ending equity of −89.8R—a very shocking number. Furthermore, the arrow in Figure 15.8 shows that the system has a 97.1% chance of being up 1R or more after 120 trades. This translates into a 2.9% chance of having a negative R value at the end of 120 trades. Thus, you must again ask yourself if you would be willing to trade this system given its possible downside. Your average gain would be 96R, but could you tolerate the possibility of that 89R drawdown after 120 trades—even though the chances of it occurring are very slim?

Figure 15.9 System Summary Statistics

| Trade Distribution | Control Simulation | Loosing Streaks | Drawdown-Depth | Drawdown-Duration | Peak Gain | Ending Gain | Expectancy |
| Win % | System Summary | | Control Optimizer | Optimizer | Simulated Trading | | TradeSim Status |

System Summary Results

TradeSim Variable	Value	Avg -Sigma	Avg	Avg +Sigma
# Trades	120.00			
Avg # Trades Per Month	10.00			
Win/Loss Ratio	6.67			
Expectancy		0.37	0.80	1.23
Win %		0.3	0.7	1.2
Loosing Streaks			16	
Drawdown(R)		-40.5	-29.3	-18.1
Peak Gain (R)		58.4	105.8	153.3
Ending Gain (R)		43.9	95.6	147.4
# Trades For Break Even (95%)	86			
95% Drawdown Duration (Months)	8.8			
Yearly Gain(R)	96.0			
Avg Yearly Gain/Avg Drawdown	3.3			

System Considerations

CAUTION:
1. All results assume that previous trades statistically represent trading system.
2. The trading system may change performance over time.
3. All results assume correct accounting for commissions & slippage.

PERFORMANCE:
1. Expectancy is good.
2. Drawdown is typical.
3. Expect at least 16 losses in a row.
4. Yearly gain, relative to drawdown, is excellent.

FUTURE CONSIDERATIONS:
1. You must monitor your system carefully to insure performance stays within excepted bounds.
2. This performance analysis should be coupled to money management to control reward & risk.
3. The addition of other uncorrelated systems will likely improve overall performance.

Save To Spreadsheet

Ask Dr. Tharp

If not, then you probably couldn't tolerate many trading systems. If you don't ask yourself this question, you will stop trading the system very early and turn a safe strategy into a dangerous one.

Know Your System will also report on your system's peak equity in terms of R and the range of winning percentages of ten thousand 120-trade simulations. But let's skip those charts because they probably won't change your mind about the desirability of trading this method.

Instead, let's look at the summary report for this system, shown in Figure 15.9. The summary report gives you a total picture of the system. It shows all of the results you just looked at, giving mean and values of plus and minus one standard deviation.[8]

Thus, you know that the expectancy is 0.8R, plus or minus a standard deviation of 0.43R.

You know that the average drawdown is $-29.3R$ plus or minus a standard deviation of $11.2R$. And you know that your average ending equity will be $95.6R$ plus or minus a standard deviation of $51.8R$. You know that it takes 88 trades to have a 95% chance of having a new peak equity once you get into a drawdown. And, of course, the question you must ask yourself is, do I want to trade this system?

You probably should perform this analysis for each type of market in which you plan to trade your system. The results might suggest that you'll trade fewer types of markets than you originally thought.

Before moving on, it's important to understand that simulations will give you an accurate picture of what to expect from your system only if you've entered a fairly accurate R-multiple distribution from your system. *If your sample is not accurate, the results of the simulations will not be accurate either.*

Now, let's learn how to determine if your system is working.

ACTION STEPS

Download a free sample report of Know Your System from IITM's website, iitm.com.

How Do I Know My Strategy Is Working? The Periodic Review

Let's say you've done each of the following action steps.

1. You've reviewed the macroeconomic picture. You feel fairly confident that conditions have not changed enough to affect your strategy.
2. There are no recent changes in laws, regulations, or economic policy that will affect your strategy.
3. You understand the logic of your strategy and you know the kinds of markets in which it will work. You've either designed filters to help you screen out trading in undesirable markets or you simply look over the markets to make sure your system will work.
4. You've collected the R multiples from at least 50 trades for each type of market you expect to trade.
5. You've analyzed the R multiples thoroughly by plugging them into a simulator such as the one available from IITM. You've decided that you can live with the potential downside of that system.

If all these conditions are met, you need to continually evaluate your strategy. If none of the conditions are met, find another strategy that will work for you.

But let's assume that all the conditions are met. Now you must ask yourself how you will know your system is working. And your system could break down in several areas, including the possibility that your sample of R multiples did not accurately represent the system. Perhaps there were some big R multiple losers that you didn't know about. Perhaps it's not as accurate as you thought it was. Or perhaps the big R multiple that you were counting on occurs much less often than you expected. You must use your judgment and common sense. That's why trading and investing are an art form of sorts.

The best way to answer such a question is to do a periodic review of your strategy. Consider doing this after every 100 trades. You might also consider doing one if you run into conditions that the simulator told you had less than a 20% chance of occurring. These might include a long losing streak or a drawdown in terms of *R* that is much bigger than you'd hoped. You might also keep a running total of your expectancy after every trade (by summing the *R* multiples and dividing by the number of trades). If your expectancy gets too low, which should occur only 20% of the time or less, consider doing a periodic review.

Two types of conditions can trigger a periodic review. The first is system performance that is out of the ordinary. A great trader once said that his system was designed to make between 20% and 40% each year and have peak-to-trough drawdowns of less than half of that.[9] You'd think his criteria for doing a periodic review might be when he had a drawdown of 15% to 20%. However, one year he made 50%. That was more than his system was designed to make, so he assumed that he could also have a bigger drawdown than he'd typically expect. Thus, he adjusted his position size so that his strategy would have less volatile performance.

The second condition that should trigger a periodic review is the passage of time or a fixed number of trades. Earlier we suggested 100 trades, but you should do a periodic review every year or every quarter, depending upon how often you think it might be necessary.

When you do your periodic review, ask yourself the following questions.

Is the performance of my strategy worse (or better) than expected? Do I need to adjust something? For example, if you have 12 straight losses and you don't believe that's likely from your system, you might want to do a periodic review.

Does my strategy involve some sort of imbalance in the market that no longer exists? Some of the best strategies involve arbitrage opportunities that arise from an imbalance. For example, one of our clients figured out how he could capitalize on the relationship between the U.S. dollar and the British pound. This was before there were easy ways of doing so directly by trading currencies. He did so by trading sugar in dollars in New York and in pounds in London. He wasn't really trading sugar—he was trading the currency relationships. He said that he was making a million dollars per month doing so and that you could not buy sugar without him opening up one of his spreads. It was a sweet deal while it lasted. However, the regulators soon figured out what he was doing and started quoting London sugar in U.S. dollars as well. While economic fundamentals did not change, the basis for his strategy did. You need to know your strategy well enough to determine if it requires some critical relationship. And if that critical relationship suddenly changes, you need to drop that strategy and find another one.

What kind of market conditions have we had since the last review? Here you are looking for whether the market has been flat and volatile, trending up and quiet, or any of the other possibilities given earlier in this chapter. Next ask yourself what kind of performance you can expect given current market conditions. If your strategy's performance is

---

KEY IDEAS

➤ Familiarity with your strategy allows you to execute your plan with confidence. Be sure you understand the macroeconomic conditions under which your strategy will work and monitor those conditions by keeping up with the suggested readings.

➤ Depth of understanding will be your mental support during tough times and allow you to objectively assess its performance, so be certain to know how your strategy will perform in each of the six types of possible market conditions.

➤ Collect R multiples from at least 50 trades in each market condition and request a report from Know Your System so you can determine how your strategy will perform and if you can tolerate its downside.

➤ Do a periodic review after every 100 trades or when your strategy's performance dictates to determine if you need to switch to another strategy.

➤ During the periodic review, ask yourself what kind of markets we have had and what you can expect from your strategy during those markets. If your results match, your system is not broken and you don't need to change.

ACTION STEPS

➤ Make sure you understand how your system will perform when economic conditions change.

➤ Ensure you know how your system will perform in each of the six market types.

➤ Schedule your first periodic review now.

---

within normal boundaries, fine. If it is outside the boundaries, then you either need to make an adjustment or change to another strategy.

Once you've asked these questions and answered them to your satisfaction, your periodic review is complete. In most cases, you probably won't need to do anything. But if your research suggests that something is wrong, you may need to adopt a different strategy that's more appropriate for today's conditions.

Notes

1. This chapter is written from Van Tharp's experience coaching traders with systems.

2. IITM's Advanced Peak Performance 202 workshop covers games people play, including money games. Also several issues of Van Tharp's newsletter, *Market Mastery*, explored this topic. For more information, call 919-852-3994 or 800-385-4486, or go to iitm.com.

3. You might argue that our efficiency strategy for trading stock follows this bias. However, what it really does is capitalize on the bias. As long as there is a frenzy, you make a profit. But when the stock starts to drop, you have your 25% trailing stop and get out. Furthermore, you never risk more than 1% of your portfolio in any one such stock. This strategy is a far cry from how the average person participates in the stock market.

4. Van K. Tharp, *Trade Your Way to Financial Freedom* (New York: McGraw-Hill, 1999).

5. The standard deviation is a measure of the variability of a distribution around the mean. You can expect two-thirds of a

distribution to fall within plus or minus one standard deviation of the mean.

6. If you normally maintain a portfolio of trades (i.e., 10–20 trades at a time), then you need to know how correlated those trades could be. This topic is beyond the scope of this book.

7. You wouldn't be bankrupt because on each trade you'd risk only 1% of the remaining equity (not 1% of the starting equity). Thus, you'd be risking 1% of a decreasing equity on each trade.

8. With a normal distribution, two-thirds of your data will fall within plus or minus one standard deviation of the mean and approximately 95% will fall within two standard deviations. Thus, you can tell from the mean and standard deviation when you have statistical outliers (which usually indicate that your system is broken).

9. A peak-to-trough drawdown is the loss from an equity high (or peak) to the next low, usually expressed as a percentage. Thus, if your monthly ending equities were 100,000, 110,000, 112,000, 123,000, 118,000, 119,000, 115,000, 114,000, 117,000, 113,000, 115,000, and 117,000, you made $17,000, or 17%. You had a peak-to-trough drawdown from $123,000 to $113,000, or 8.1%. Your peak equity was $123,000; then it went down to $113,000 before it started going up again. However, if it continued down from the current level of $117,000 and dropped below $113,000, then you'd have a new peak-to-trough drawdown.

PART V

THE FUTURE

At this point, you know all of the steps dealing with financial freedom, so if you are not doing it, there is only one thing stopping you—you. Many people consider working on themselves to be a scary topic. We have a simple, logical method to make sure you don't repeat your mistakes. If nothing is stopping you, you can skip this part. But chances are that the people who want to skip this section are the ones who need it the most.

First, Chapter 16 discusses the most important topic in your success: personal accountability. You'll learn how you create the results you get. You'll also learn that if you don't understand how you do this, you are doomed to repeat your mistakes forever. But when you begin to take charge of your life, your experience starts to become a learning experience that allows you to continually move forward.

Next you'll learn how to protect your future by teaching financial freedom to your children and grandchildren. In Chapter 17 Justin Ford presents a saving and investment technique that your children will enjoy, one that can make them financially free soon after college.

Chapter 18 presents a four-step plan to get started now. You'll learn that the only thing stopping you is you. You'll review the symptoms of self-sabotage and discover resources that will help you achieve financial freedom.

CHAPTER 16

FIXING YOUR MISTAKES: THE KEY TO IT ALL

"Was it Linda's fault that she lost money? Absolutely not—for the simple reason that she was deliberately and knowingly misled about the stock's prospects. In other words, the broker lied."

—MARTIN WEISS

The most important trait a winning investor can have is personal accountability. It's the foundation for everything else.[1] Did you lose a significant amount of money in the stock market between 2000 and 2003? If so, ask yourself why. Spend a couple of minutes thinking about it and then write down your top seven reasons.

Before we look at your answers, let's look at what a typical investor did during that time period. Let's look at the case of Joe Smith. Joe worked for a high-tech firm, Cree Research, in Durham, North Carolina. He was fortunate to have gotten options on the company stock at $3 per share. When Cree went to $35 per share, he exercised his options and purchased 500 shares of stock. At the end of the year, he discovered that he owed tax on $16,000, even though he never actually received that money. However, he felt good as Cree stock kept going up and up.

In 1997, Joe also started buying stock in his IRA, which was worth about $100,000. And over the next two years he bought stock in Compaq Computer, JDS Uniphase, Enron, WorldCom, eToys, and Cisco Systems. While those stocks might sound like a prescription for disaster now, they were great choices at the time.

In 1998, Joe was convinced that he understood how the market worked. He took out an equity line account on his house for $150,000 and put all of it into the stock market. He'd bought Qualcomm with his equity line money, and his portfolio now was worth over $1,350,000.

By the end of 1999, Joe thought he was a genius. He'd made exceptional profits—once-in-a lifetime profits—but he wanted more. Had he understood the principles in this book, he would have realized that he could easily have had financial freedom. But Joe wanted more.

So, when the bear market started, Joe held on to everything. His goal was to hit the $2 million mark in the stock market. He had almost reached his goal at the start of the bear market, so he kept everything, hoping for a turnaround. Joe was also reluctant to sell his stocks because of the tax consequences. By the end of May 2000, he thought he'd made a mistake, but after three terrible months he couldn't imagine that the market could decline any more so he held on to his stocks. He didn't want to sell at the bottom. Everyone was telling him that the only way to make money in stocks is to buy and hold, and he believed that. However, at this point, he decided that he would probably sell some of his holdings when his stocks got back to their high levels at the beginning of the year.

Since Joe was a good friend, I gave him some coaching on trading. I said that if he didn't want to sell his stocks, he should at least evaluate each stock. Would he still be willing to buy that stock if he didn't already own it? Would he at least be willing to put a 25% trailing stop on his stocks, as if he'd entered today? And finally, would he be willing to reduce his size enough so that with a 25% drop he still would not be risking more than 2% of his portfolio on each stock?[2]

By April 2000 Joe's Cree stock had declined from $194 per share to $89 per share. However, all he could think about was that he had been required to pay taxes on the conversion of his options.

By the summer of 2002, Joe had sold eToys at about 6 cents per share (he could have sold four days later at 40 cents even though it subsequently collapsed). He had unloaded half of his position in Qualcomm. He'd also unloaded his Enron stock when it collapsed. He'd gotten about 35 cents per share. The rest of his portfolio was still intact, only now it was worth about $220,000 and he still had the $150,000 debt on his house.

At this point, Joe was furious. He had several scapegoats to blame for his huge losses. He was really concerned about the people who had recommended the stocks he had bought. Then he joined a class action suit against Enron executives. He was convinced that they were responsible for his huge losses in that stock. Joe was devastated when World-Com joined his list of disasters. "Why me?" he thought. "The world somehow has my number. The stocks I've bought seem to not only collapse, but they make news in a big way. What's going on?" he wondered. At this point, his total portfolio was worth less than the debt he had on his house.

When asked who was to blame for his losses, Joe listed the following culprits:

1. the corrupt analysts who recommend the failing stocks
2. the IRS, for charging such high taxes on his profits
3. the borrowed money he used to finance his investing
4. the people who advised him to stick with a buy-and-hold strategy
5. the newsletter writer who recommended some of the stocks he bought
6. his broker, for not cautioning him on what he was doing
7. corrupt CEOs who cheat their shareholders

Joe later thought of an eighth reason he'd lost money—me—I was at fault for not insisting that he follow my advice.

How about you? Is your list of reasons for losses similar to Joe's? What you put down is not nearly as important as how you framed your responses. Your answers could fall into three categories. Most people blame things on people or events. All of Joe's answers except number 3 (the fact that he borrowed money) fall into this category. If your answers also fell here, you're not alone. We are trained to find scapegoats to blame for what happens. However, there is a better way.

The second category of responses is undetermined. Joe's third response would fall into this category. He might be admitting a mistake (i.e., that he borrowed money to finance speculation in the market), but he might be blaming that money as well. It is hard to tell.

Joe didn't have any answers that fell into category three, which is personal accountability—recognizing the mistakes he had made. This self-analytical response is critical to investment success or any other kind of success in life. However, most of us are taught to blame external forces and to use the court system to punish those who victimize us. When we do that, we learn absolutely nothing. You only begin to learn from your mistakes when you can acknowledge them. Incidentally, you should be able to list all of Joe's mistakes after reading this book.

So let's look at the bottom line on Joe's situation. He has learned nothing from his experience in the stock market. He has no concept of the mistakes he made, and he would probably repeat them if given more money. After reading this book you should have a much better idea of the mistakes you have made, and when you finish this chapter you should know how to fix them.

The Brutal Truth: People Get What They Want

Ed Seykota said in *Market Wizards* that "people get exactly what they want from the markets."[3] This observation certainly applies to Joe. Let's look at a few of the things he wanted.

- He wanted to believe he was an expert in the market. He got that wish—at least for a while.
- He wanted to avoid paying taxes. In fact, he even got to deduct $3,000 for capital gain losses in each of the last three years.
- He wanted to hang on to his stocks while he hoped they would return to previous high levels. He didn't have to sell, so he also got that wish.
- He wanted to believe that he was right and he did believe it, so he got that wish as well. He always believed his stocks would come back and he still believed that about the stocks he still owned.
- He wanted to believe that he was a victim of what others did to him. And he certainly got to be a victim.

Notice that Joe got everything he wanted, even though he lost a huge amount of money.

Taking Personal Responsibility: The Fastest Way to Reach Your Goals

What Joe lacked was personal accountability. The belief that you create your life is the core belief behind success. You must believe that you are responsible for what happens to you if you are to be a great trader or investor. In fact, you must believe that you are responsible for what happens to you if you are to be great at anything.

This topic really came into my consciousness about 20 years ago, when I was studying *A Course in Miracles*. It states:

> *Projection makes perception. The world you see is what you gave it, nothing more than that. But though it is no more than that, it is not less. Therefore, to you it is important. It is the witness to your state of mind, the outside picture of an inward condition. As a man thinketh, so does he perceive. Therefore, seek not to change the world, but choose to change your mind about the world. Perception is a result, not a cause.[4]*

The implications of this passage were beyond my comprehension at the time. It was stating that I create the world I see—that no matter what I see out there, it came from within me. I was totally responsible for my own reality.

I really didn't believe that I created my own life at the time, but I was willing to assume that it was a useful idea. I had a chance to test that thought one day in 1982, when I was driving my son to preschool. A car made a left turn in front of me, and the result was a head-on collision. My car was totaled. My son's head cracked the windshield, but he wasn't hurt. I hit the steering wheel and received a severe cut on my face. My car sat at the roadside for about six days, was ticketed, and eventually towed away. By every standard of our society, the other person was at fault. I was a victim.

However, based upon the teachings of *A Course in Miracles*, I decided to explore how I might have created that accident. When my thoughts turned in that direction, I came up with a lot of possibilities. For one,

I hated my car. It was a 1975 Buick Skyhawk with about 100,000 miles on it. Buick had made that car for a light rotary engine but then abandoned the idea and placed a large V-6 engine in it. The front end wasn't built for such a heavy engine, so it was always out of alignment. the tires and brakes needed to be replaced every 3,000 miles. My wife and I had purchased a house in Southern California, and we needed every penny to make our mortgage payments. We could not afford a new car. I was stuck with this one. Not a day went by that I didn't think about how much I hated that car. So did I create an atmosphere in which I might be receptive to having that car destroyed? You bet I did. I was shocked when I figured that one out.

That kind of analysis is second nature to me now. And it's very clear how I create my world. Sometimes I'm not happy with what I create, but that's usually because there was some part of me, something inside, that I did not acknowledge. And that part of me is what creates what I don't like or didn't expect.

When I actually started to believe what was being said in *A Course in Miracles*, my life started to change. The most profound change was that I began to actively create my life in a more productive way.

Personal responsibility is the most important characteristic for people who want to transform themselves. If you believe in personal responsibility, you can change. If you don't believe in personal responsibility, then change is hopeless because things always will happen to you. Harry Palmer, the founder of Avatar, has a famous quote on this topic: "You experience what you believe, unless you believe you won't, in which case you don't, which means you did."[5]

In 1992, I launched my first two-week school for professional traders. At the time, a bank was willing to sponsor the school and give trading funds to the graduates.[6] My staff interviewed about 250 traders and invited 25 of them to attend a screening workshop. At that workshop, I was looking for traits that told me these people had the potential to be great traders. One of those traits was personal responsibility.

One of the candidates in the screening seminar was quadriplegic. He'd been in a football accident and was confined to a wheelchair. When I suggested that he might have caused his accident in some way, he became furious. He was a victim, he said, not the creator of his experience.

He didn't make it into the school, but he did start on a self-transforming journey. He started doing the 365 lessons in *A Course in Miracles*; he worked through the Peak Performance home study course; he attended workshops and did personal consulting work with me. At some point during that journey, he came to the conclusion that he was responsible for his football accident. He said it was the most liberating decision of his life because it meant that he was totally in charge of his life. He could now start creating his life, because he was no longer a victim. He got himself a service dog and trained it to do many things to ease his day-to-day life. He even trained it to open the fridge and get him a can of beer.

Honestly Admitting Your Mistakes

Frequently, when I give a talk about the psychology of trading, I'll play a marble game similar to the one described in Chapter 14. People start out with $100,000 and risk that money on 30 random marble draws. They win or lose based upon what they risk and the payoff of the marble that is drawn. If you recall, the game consisted of seven $1R$ losers, one $5R$ loser, and two $10R$ winners. Thus, you win only 20% of the time. And in 30 trades, we can get some long losing streaks.

When I play the game with a group of people who do not understand trading, expectancy, and position sizing, I usually get interesting results. Typically, we'll have 30 marble draws, replacing each marble after it is drawn. Let's say that the net result of 30 marble draws was a positive $20R$, so that someone who risked $500 on every marble draw would have made $10,000. Despite the positive draw, we usually have a third of the room going bankrupt, another third losing money, and the final third making a huge amount of money. That is an interesting result because everyone in the room was responding to the same draw of marbles.

I add another twist to the game by having people in the audience pull out the marbles. When someone pulls out a losing marble, I have the person continue to pull marbles until he pulls out a winner. Inevitably, during a 30-trade game, we'll get a long losing streak of 7 to 13 straight losers that might include the big $5R$ loser. And through this procedure, that streak will be associated with a particular person. At the end of the game, I ask the audience, "How many of you think you lost money because of this person?" I point to the person who pulled the losing streak, and many hands go up in response. They believe they lost money because someone pulled out losers. (The game allows me to observe people getting frustrated and irritable, some even thinking that they could pull out better marbles.)

When people blame someone else for their losses, they have no chance to learn from their mistakes. In this game, they lost money because they risked too much on one or more of the marble draws. In fact, since there is a marble that loses five times what you risk, anyone betting 20% or more at any time is risking bankruptcy. If they don't understand that and blame someone else, they will repeat the mistake. They may not even recognize their mistake because they are so busy blaming.

The same result occurs in the current market scenario. If you play the blame game or the victim game, there will always be someone to blame. There will always be an Enron or a WorldCom. Company executives will always prefer to enrich themselves rather than their shareholders. Analysts will always recommend stocks that their company wants to promote. "Experts" will always tell you that you should buy stocks and hold them for a long time. Brokers will always try to persuade you to do things that are advantageous for their firm. These things will always happen, but you can choose not to play their game.

Those who have lost money between 2000 and 2003 probably made one or more of the eight key mistakes. How many of the factors that you listed at the beginning of this chapter included one or more of these mistakes?

1. You didn't have a plan or rules to guide your behavior.
2. You didn't know your financial freedom number, but were concentrating instead on how much you could accumulate.
3. You didn't have a preplanned exit point when you entered the position (or you didn't follow it).
4. You didn't practice wise position sizing (i.e., you risked too much).

5. You didn't have the discipline to follow these rules.
6. You became very emotional about your trading.
7. You allowed outside sources to distract you from your plan, or you didn't have enough conviction to follow the plan.
8. Most important, you didn't acknowledge personal responsibility for your behavior.

If you included at least three of these mistakes in your list at the beginning of this chapter, you are probably well on your way toward future success in the market. If you ignored all of them, you need to do some major self-analysis. And here is an interesting question: Did you list some of the factors for Joe, but not for yourself? If so, why?

All of these topics have been addressed in this book. If you've taken the time to learn them, you can turn losses into learning experiences. And learning produces success and gives you the promise of financial freedom.

So how do you fix your mistakes? It's not that difficult.

Correcting Mistakes to Get You Back on Track

Everyone with exposure to the market should consider spending five minutes at the end of each day doing a debriefing. The first thing you do is ask yourself, did I make any mistakes today? Here a mistake is defined as not following your rules (assuming, of course, that you have rules).

If you didn't make any mistakes, you are finished. Just pat yourself on the back for doing a good job. However, if you did make a mistake, then start the correction procedure. First, acknowledge that you made a mistake. It is the ultimate statement of self-responsibility. If you blame external factors, you cannot correct mistakes. You are more likely to repeat them.

Once you've acknowledged the mistake, the next step is to determine the circumstances under which you made the mistake. For example, suppose a stock goes through your predetermined stop-loss point and you do not get out of it. That's a mistake because you didn't follow your rules. You need to correct any behavior that keeps you from getting out of the position. It might happen because you tell yourself that it will come back. Or it might happen because it gaps through your stop and you decide that it's gone down too far to get out. You need to rehearse in your mind the act of picking up the phone and getting out as soon as the price drops to your stop point—no matter what the circumstances are. When you mentally rehearse a behavior like that, you put it into your unconscious mind and make the behavior automatic. It's a very powerful process.

Many of our mistakes occur when we are stressed. Stress is an evolutionary response that helped primitive people deal with danger. Primitive humans needed more physical strength when confronted with a danger. Thus, adrenaline is pumped into the body during times of stress. This diverts blood flow away from the brain and into the major muscles of the body. You have more energy and strength, but your ability to process information shrinks down to almost nothing. As a result, you tend to revert to primitive, poorly thought-out behavior in stressful situations.

Mental rehearsal bypasses this primitive mechanism. When you rehearse something enough times, it becomes an automatic response for you. Then it just happens without your having to think about it.

Now let's run through an example, so you can see how it's done. After the market closes is a good time to do your daily debriefing. And all you do is review the trades you made during the day and notice if you made any mistakes. If you have written rules and plans to guide your trading/investing, then mistakes are quite obvious.

Suppose that today you were away from the market. You were busy doing other things and you didn't even check the market. You still do a daily debriefing to determine if you broke any rules. At the end of the day, you check the market and discover that one of your stocks dropped about 40% during the day. Your stop-loss was only 10% from the open, so you incurred a loss that was four times bigger than you should have. Even though you didn't do anything, you still made a mistake by not getting out of the market on this trade. It was an error of omission. As a result, you cannot pat yourself on the back.

Now you must determine what the external circumstances were that contributed to the situation. That's an easy one for you: you were very busy with your job and didn't have time to check the market.

The next step is to devise solutions to the problem. You begin brainstorming and come up with the following possibilities:

First, you can put stop orders in with your broker each day.[7] You've been reluctant to do that because you want more control over them and you're afraid that the broker's firm might lower the stock's price just enough to grab your stock and then take it back up to the original price. Nevertheless, a stop entered with your broker is one solution, especially when you go on a trip.

Second, you could give someone else the responsibility of watching the market for you at times when you are not available. You can think of three people who could do that—your spouse, your son, and your best friend, who has a more flexible work schedule. You would, of course, have to pick people you trust because they will have access to your account.

Third, you could close out positions the night before when you know that you cannot watch them for a while. This really isn't an acceptable alternative because it means that you've suddenly become a much shorter-term trader than you want to be. Also, commissions will consume a much larger percentage of your trading profits because of the increased activity.

The fourth solution you come up with is to force yourself to look at the market at least hourly on such days so that you can deal with any dangerous situation that might arise. You have some real reservations about this solution because you might not have the time, or you might just forget.

Your fifth solution is to find a brokerage company that will sell out your positions when the market drops to your bail-out point, but not actually make them known to the market. You call the customer service department of your brokerage company and ask how they might handle such orders. Your broker says they enter stop-loss orders into their computer system. They do not become part of the market unless the stock hits your exit price. However, if the stock does hit your exit point, then these orders automatically go into the market as a sell-at-the-market order.

Your main reservation with this last solution is that will you find yourself getting stopped out at a loss much more often because the broker may have been lying about your order not being part of the market until your price is hit. You are also concerned about how much more you'll lose when your order is just dumped into the market to sell when the market is in a free fall and you are not even involved in the order. Nevertheless, you decide that this solution is probably the best one. You'll try it for a while and monitor the results.

The next step is to mentally rehearse the solution. You decide that when you know you are going to have a day when you'll be distracted at work, you'll immediately put these stop orders on your broker's website. You rehearse doing the steps in your mind.

You now imagine yourself putting a stop-loss order into your broker's computer as soon as you get any warning that you'll be busy. You see yourself doing this four or five times until it seems natural for you.

That's it—you're finished. You now have a potential solution that will avoid the problem of getting stuck in a position from which you should

---

KEY IDEAS

➤ You create what happens in your life, meaning that you have control of your life.

➤ When you take personal responsibility for creating what you don't like, you can begin to see the mistakes you might have made.

➤ When people blame what happens to them on people or events outside of themselves, then they tend to repeat their mistakes.

➤ You can avoid repeating mistakes by doing a daily debriefing and following the correction procedure given in this chapter.

have exited. You also agree to assess the effectiveness of this solution after you've been stopped out five times to determine if you seem to have more losses or if you are getting terrible executions on your orders (i.e., you want to get out at 20 but you get out at 18.5).

Table 16.1 lists some common mistakes investors make and shows potential solutions, including references to specific chapters in this book.

Table 16.1 Common Investor Mistakes and How to Correct Them

Mistake	Solution	Reference
Become too greedy	Develop a financial freedom plan and make sure you understand the expectancy of what you're trading.	Part 1 and Chapter 13
Don't have an exit point	Develop a low-risk strategy.	Chapter 13
Lose more than 2% in a trade	Develop a position sizing strategy.	Chapter 14
Lose more than 15% in six months	Simulate your system to determine what could happen and base your position sizing on the worst-case drawdown.	Chapters 14 and 15
Become too emotional	Rehearse discipline techniques.	Peak Performance course
Become distracted and don't follow plan	Determine how distraction occurs and rehearse behaviors to avoid.	Chapter 16
Blame something/someone else for what happens	Acknowledge control, determine mistake, and follow correction procedure.	Chapter 16
Cannot execute trades due to fear	Develop plan in which you have confidence; rehearse discipline techniques; consider the possibility of self-sabotage.	Parts 1 and IV and Peak Performance course
Plan stops working	Review your plan and how to improve it. Have conditions changed?	Chapter 15
Life seems out of control and you lose heavily	Look at key events that cause losses and stop trading. Do a thorough self-analysis.	Peak Performance course
Six months pass and financial freedom number is not lower	Do a self-analysis and consider your commitment. Review your financial freedom plan. Consider the possibility of self-sabotage.	Peak Performance course

---

ACTION STEPS

➤ Complete the exercise at the beginning of the chapter on why you've lost money in the market.

➤ Determine if your typical reasons involve blame or personal responsibility. If they involve blame, turn them around by figuring out how you created the situation.

➤ Go through the list of common investor mistakes in Table 16.1 and determine how many of them apply to you. Follow the solutions given.

➤ Make a resolution to do a daily debriefing. This procedure can be used to correct all sorts of mistakes, not just investment mistakes.

Notes

1. This chapter was written from Van Tharp's viewpoint as a coach for traders and investors.

2. I actually wanted him to limit his exposure to 1%, but he wouldn't consider that because he'd be liquidating about 70% of his holding by doing so. And he still didn't want to pay the taxes he'd owe.

3. Jack Schwager, *Market Wizards* (New York: New York Institute of Finance, 1989).

4. *A Course in Miracles* (Tiberon, CA: Foundation for Inner Peace, 1985), 415.

5. Harry Palmer, *ReSurfacing: Techniques for Exploring Consciousness* (Altamonte Springs, Fla.: Star's Edge International, 1994), 104.

6. The bank subsequently pulled out when a senior officer asked, "Who is Van Tharp? How do we know he can get us Harvard graduates, and how do we know they will be qualified to work here?"

7. A stop order is an order to your broker to sell at the market once a particular price is hit.

CHAPTER 17

SECURING YOUR FUTURE: EDUCATING YOUR KIDS AND GRANDKIDS

JUSTIN FORD

"Dripping water can pierce a stone."

—CHINESE PROVERB

I'd like to show you how, starting today, you can get your children to apply a little effort over time in a crucial area of life that is usually neglected when it comes to kids. I'm talking about money and how your kids can become financially free shortly after they finish college.

By beginning a hands-on program today, not only can your kids or grandkids grow wealthier year after year, they can do it without giving up their dreams. They'll have the luxury to choose careers that match their interests, values, and talents rather than simply working for a paycheck.

It doesn't matter if your children are interested in becoming CEOs or not. Even if they have no interest in business—if they're aspiring firefighters, nurses, doctors, teachers, pilots, or social workers—they can achieve significant wealth by the time they begin to raise families of their own.

What's more, they'll have done it themselves—but with your guidance. That's because I'm not talking about setting up a trust fund or raising your children with silver spoons. I'm talking about a natural way to train them to begin practicing good money habits from a very early age. By applying a consistent effort now, they can dramatically increase their chances for success in this practical aspect of life. They will avoid the stress of uncontrolled consumerism and a crushing debt load, and they will grow wealthier as they grow older.

Developing Concrete Habits

Talk to most adults about balance sheets, profit-and-loss statements, cash flow, leverage, or return on equity, and their eyes will glaze over. Talk to most kids about these matters, and you'll lose them even sooner. But building wealth is not about understanding these financial concepts. It's about mastering a few fundamental habits that create wealth over time. After all, there are MBAs and bank presidents who have gone broke. They knew better; they just didn't *do* better. There are accountants and stockbrokers who live from paycheck to paycheck. Their struggles probably aren't caused by a lack of knowledge, but by the fact that they never mastered the personal habits of consistently building wealth instead of debt.

So it is with money. It may not be the most important thing in life, but it is a necessary part of life. And you will be doing your children and grandchildren a great service by helping them to acquire good money habits from an early age and to build wealth consistently, every month and every year from now on. And you'll do it with an emphasis on doing rather than simply "knowing how."

In this way, their knowledge about financial responsibility, money, and investments can grow naturally—in lockstep with their experience and their steadily compounding wealth. As a bonus, in the process of building that wealth they will have to exercise virtues that are very useful in other areas of life as well: discipline, patience, and foresight.

And the rewards will be more than monetary. They'll enjoy a sense of achievement. They'll understand what can be accomplished by consistently applying a little effort over time, and they'll be more confident in all their financial dealings—whether buying their first home or car, negotiating a salary or fee, or not falling for a quick-money pitch.

So let's start planting the seeds of your children's future wealth right now. You can start by asking them a simple question.

How Would You Like an Increase in Your Allowance—Say Between $4,000 and $18,000 a Month?

"Kids, how would you like an increase in your allowance to maybe $4,000 or even $18,000 a month?" Try that statement at the dinner table. The reactions will range from surprise to excitement to humor to skepticism.

When the commotion subsides, let the children know that you're serious. Tell them, "I'm going to show you how you can collect that $4,000 allowance every month. And that's just for starters. From there it could rise to tens of thousands of dollars every month. In fact, I'm going to help you get that allowance starting today. Are you ready?"

Now that you've got your children's attention, explain how the system works: "First, I'm going to give each of you two dollars. It's my gift to you. One of the two dollars you can spend however you please—on candy, toys, or whatever you want. The other dollar you're going to save—permanently. That means you're not going to spend it for any reason whatsoever for at least 30 years, maybe longer.

"With every dollar you receive from now on—whether it be allowance, a birthday present, or money you find in the street—you're also going to save half permanently and spend half. If you keep doing this, and I'll help you, in a few months you should have a hundred or maybe even a few hundred dollars in your permanent savings. At that point, we'll count it out together and I'll invest it for you. By 'invest' I mean I'm going to buy a piece of a company, or companies, for you. You will own small pieces of businesses."

You'll find the best words to use with your children, but this dialogue should give you the general idea. They'll understand how you're going to help them create this wealth when you introduce a simple, yet effective, savings technique I call the two-box system.

The Remarkable Two-Box System™ for Instilling Good Money Habits

The moment you introduce the idea of saving and investing to your children, you're going to make that idea a reality by doing two things. First, you'll give them two dollars so they can make their first allocation among spending money and savings. Second, you'll make sure they have two boxes to put their money in. These can be cardboard boxes decorated by your child, desk safes, or piggy banks. One will be for their spending money (which is the same as "temporary savings"). The other will be for their permanent savings. That's all they need to begin developing good money habits.

To make sure they understand what you mean by permanent savings, try relating the following example.

"Let's say you want to buy a new skateboard, one that costs $80. To do so, you'll have to get the money only from your temporary savings—never from the permanent. The easiest way is to set up a separate box for the skateboard. We'll call it the 'skateboard fund.'

"Now let's say you get $20 from Grandma. You put half, or $10, in the permanent savings. Instead of spending the other half or putting it in the temporary savings box, you put in the skateboard fund.

"A month later, you get $100 over the holidays. You've got to put $50 of that money into permanent savings. The other $50 you can spend, put in your temporary savings, or add to the skateboard fund. You decide to spend $10 on candy and comic books and to add $40 to your skateboard fund. Since you had $10 there already from the money Grandma gave you, you now have $50 saved for your skateboard.

"A few weeks later you get $30 in birthday checks. Again, you have to put $15 of that in permanent savings. You spend $10 of the remainder on the movies and popcorn, and you add $5 to your skateboard fund. You've now got $55 put away toward the skateboard.

"Now you get $60 from selling lemonade, washing cars, and doing chores around the house. Half goes into permanent savings. You spend $5 on cards and add $25 to the skateboard fund. You now have $80 for the skateboard. That should be enough, except that you need $5 more for sales tax.

"You pick up $20 in allowance over the next couple of months. You put $10 in permanent savings, you spend $5 on candy, and $5 goes in the skateboard fund. This gives you a total of $85 in the fund—enough to cover the skateboard and tax.

"Notice that while you were putting the money together for your skateboard you also added $115 to your permanent savings. That money is going to pay you a big allowance every month when you grow up—long after you've retired the skateboard."

The skateboard fund is an example of a special savings box, one that is funded strictly from spending money and does not interfere with permanent savings. Table 17.1 shows how the amounts in your example would be allocated to permanent savings, temporary savings, and the skateboard fund.

Why Half Is Good

In case you think you're asking a lot of your children by having them save half of every dollar they receive, let me ask you, when was the last time you could spend 50% of every dollar *you* made on whatever you want?

For most people, the answer is never. By the time you're done paying the mortgage, food, clothing, income and property taxes, utilities,

Table 17.1 How to Buy a Skateboard and Grow Rich at the Same Time

Income	Source	Add to Permanent Savings	Spend from Temporary Savings	Add to Skateboard Fund	Balance in Skateboard Fund	Balance in Permanent Savings
$20	Grandma	$10	$0	$10	$10	$10
$100	Holiday	$50	$10	$40	$50	$60
$60	Chores	$30	$5	$25	$75	$90
$30	Birthday	$15	$10	$5	$80	$105
$20	Allowance	$10	$5	$5	$85	$115

WHISTLING WHILE SHE WORKS

When I published my *Seeds of Wealth* program a few years ago, I received a flurry of orders one day and called the post office to pick them up. As the mail carrier—a woman in her early forties—tossed the packages into the back of the truck, she asked me what was in them. I gave her my standard reply, emphasizing the purpose and nature of the program.

"It's a parent-directed savings, investment, and financial education program for children," I said. "It doesn't only teach them good money habits. It also gets them to start practicing those habits so that by the time they're young adults they'll have a half-million dollars or more working for them, no matter what they do for a living."

Without missing a beat, she said, "I have a half-million dollars. My dad did this kind of thing for me when I was young. Every dime I got a nickel, dime, or a quarter—from the tooth fairy, you name it—he made me save some and we invested it. He was a real Buffett-type value investor. Today, I have investments worth over a quarter of a million dollars and I own my house outright, also worth over a quarter of a million dollars. To this day, I love my dad for it!"

This woman had an upbeat energy about her. She seemed to be doing exactly what she wanted to do for a living. She wasn't an office type. She loved being outdoors and dealing with people. She didn't have the best job in the world in terms of salary, yet she had accumulated a significant amount of wealth just because her dad got her to start young.

That was nearly four years ago. I recently spoke to this woman again. Her dad died since the last time I saw her, and he left her a considerable amount of money even though he never had a high-paying job either. Her own investments have continued to do well. She drives a brand-new Lexus and now has a net worth in the seven figures. She still works at the post office because she has a lot of good friends there and she likes her job, whistling while she works.

car payments, medical and dental bills, education expenses for the kids, health insurance, homeowners' insurance, gas, auto repairs, and home maintenance—not to mention funding your retirement plan and the kids' college funds—you're lucky if you have more than 10% of your income left to spend as you please.

Children don't have any of these bills. In effect, they have 100% disposable income. They don't have to pay rent or alimony, the government doesn't tax their allowance or household chore money (up to the $11,000 gift tax exclusion), and they can even earn up to $4,700 a year from a job tax-free (since the effective tax rate on the first $4,700 of earned income is zero). If you don't train your children to build wealth now, while they have 100% disposable income, they may learn the opposite lesson as adults: to automatically spend all they earn, or even more than they earn.

Preventive Medicine for the "Gimmes"

From my own experience, I can tell you the two-box system is not a great sacrifice for kids. On the contrary, this simple technique should help your children enjoy what they do have all the more without becoming spoiled or contracting the dreaded "gimme" disease.

My youngest, for instance, just turned nine, but he's known since he was five exactly how much of each dollar he gets he must put into the permanent savings box on his dresser and how much goes into his temporary savings box. He counts out the permanent savings with me twice a year and I invest it for him. He can spend all or part of the temporary savings as he pleases. We've counted out hundreds of dollars from his permanent savings box in the last year alone. That means he's also had a few hundred dollars to spend. He's truly a happy kid. I couldn't imagine he'd be any happier if we decided to let him spend all of his money. In fact, he's developing habits now where he wouldn't *dream* of spending all of his money!

The same goes for my 11-year-old son. When he won $50 and a pen in an essay contest, he immediately divided the money among the two boxes. He splits his allowance and chore money the same way.

My oldest is 14, so he no longer receives an allowance. Yet every two weeks he puts half his yard-work earnings into his permanent savings and spends the other half as he pleases. He does the same with money he receives for Christmas and birthdays, and he'll do the same with the money he earns when he takes his first part-time job.

These habits are now second-nature to all three of my boys. They have better money habits than I did just 10 years ago, and that's the whole point.

Six Super Savings Ratios

The 50% savings rate applies, of course, only to children five and older while they live at home and have no real living expenses. For other stages in their life, I recommend other savings rates. I call them the *Seeds of Wealth* saving ratios because they can assure your children life-long financial success.

- *Tycoon tots: 100%.* Until your children are ready for kindergarten, you're likely to save 100% of every dollar they receive, simply because they're too young to want to spend money.
- *Wonder years: 50%.* Beginning at age five, your children should save half of every dollar they receive.
- *College days: 10%.* When your children are in college, counsel them to save 10%. Money is extremely tight at this time, but by saving at least 10% of whatever they scrape together they learn that there is never an excuse not to save.
- *Single working adult: 15%.* Once your children are on their own in the working world, they should save 15% of their current income. This may seem high to most young adults, who tend to consume all of what they earn, but it shouldn't be a burden for your kids because they acquired the habit of saving at an early age.
- *Just married: 15%.* When your children first marry, it still shouldn't be a burden to save 15%. In fact, it may be even easier because they are likely to have two incomes in the household.
- *Married with children: 10%.* When young adults start to raise a family, money becomes a more pressing concern. With their ingrained

attitudes toward saving, your children will be able to downshift easily to what was for a long time the traditional savings rate of 10%. And by then they will have built up a significant amount of wealth that will compound along with their 10% savings year after year.

Making the Seeds Grow

Now that your children have begun planting the seeds of their future wealth, let's see what happens when you make those seeds grow, as shown in Table 17.2.

Note in the table that if your children average just 10% returns (about the total returns of the broad market during the entire twentieth century, including all bull and bear markets), they would accumulate approximately $500,000 by the age of 36. At that point, 10% returns would generate $50,000 in gains a year, or about $4,167 a month. There's the $4,000 monthly allowance you promised!

If your children use the strategies outlined in this book to realize higher returns, they can achieve that allowance even sooner. At 15% returns, they could amass roughly $350,000 by age 28. From that point, the same 15% returns would generate about $52,500 a year, or more than $4,300 a month. And if you achieve high-watermark returns of 20% over the long term, your child accumulates assets worth $274,000 by the age of 23. From that point, 20% returns generate about $54,800 a year, or $4,500 a month.

That's quite a monthly allowance!

Of course, your child could always give himself a bigger "allowance" if he allows his nest egg to grow a little longer before tapping it. Let's say he's using the strategies in this book to achieve 15% returns and he decides to wait until the ripe old age of 30 to begin paying himself an allowance. In that case, he would pay himself 15% of roughly $487,000 (the amount accumulated at 30). That's equivalent to about $73,000 a year, or more than $6,000 a month. And if he's pulling down 20% returns, he can pay himself 20% of $1.1 million at age 30, equivalent to about $223,000 a year, or $18,000 a month.

Either way, if your children decide to take on a new life challenge in their twenties or thirties, whether it be starting a family, going back to school, or writing the great American novel, they will be in a good position to do so.

The income assumptions in Table 17.2 are modest. The table assumes average income in the form of gifts, allowance, and household chore money of just $2 a day through the preteen years. Young teenagers may earn $25 a week mowing lawns or baby-sitting in the neighborhood. The table further assumes that high school teens may take

Table 17.2 From Tots to Tycoons

Age	Income	Savings in %	Savings in $	Compounded Annual Returns		
				10% Wealth Accumulated	15% Wealth Accumulated	20% Wealth Accumulated
1	$730	100%	$730	$803	$840	$876
2	$730	100%	$730	$1,686	$1,805	$1,927
3	$730	100%	$730	$2,658	$2,915	$3,189
4	$730	100%	$730	$3,727	$4,192	$4,702
5	$730	50%	$365	$4,501	$5,240	$6,081
6	$730	50%	$365	$5,352	$6,446	$7,735
7	$730	50%	$365	$6,289	$7,833	$9,720
8	$730	50%	$365	$7,320	$9,428	$12,102
9	$730	50%	$365	$8,453	$11,262	$14,960
10	$730	50%	$365	$9,700	$13,371	$18,391
11	$730	50%	$365	$11,071	$15,796	$22,507
12	$730	50%	$365	$12,580	$18,585	$27,446
13	$1,300	50%	$650	$14,553	$22,120	$33,715
14	$1,300	50%	$650	$16,723	$26,186	$41,238
15	$5,200	50%	$2,600	$21,256	$33,104	$52,606
16	$5,200	50%	$2,600	$26,241	$41,059	$66,247
17	$5,200	50%	$2,600	$31,725	$50,208	$82,616
18	$7,800	10%	$780	$35,756	$58,636	$100,076
19	$7,800	10%	$780	$40,190	$68,329	$121,027
20	$7,800	10%	$780	$45,067	$79,475	$146,168
21	$7,800	10%	$780	$50,431	$92,294	$176,338
22	$50,838	15%	$7,626	$63,863	$114,907	$220,756
23	$50,838	15%	$7,626	$78,637	$140,913	$274,058
24	$50,838	15%	$7,626	$94,889	$170,819	$338,020
25	$59,510	15%	$8,926	$114,197	$206,707	$416,336
26	$59,510	15%	$8,926	$135,436	$247,979	$510,315

Age	Income	Savings in %	Savings in $	Compounded Annual Returns		
				10% Wealth Accumulated	15% Wealth Accumulated	20% Wealth Accumulated
27	$59,510	15%	$8,926	$158,798	$295,441	$623,090
28	$59,510	15%	$8,926	$184,497	$350,023	$758,420
29	$59,510	15%	$8,926	$212,766	$412,792	$920,815
30	$71,620	15%	$10,743	$245,860	$487,065	$1,117,870
31	$71,620	10%	$7,162	$278,325	$568,361	$1,350,038
32	$71,620	10%	$7,162	$314,035	$661,852	$1,628,640
33	$71,620	10%	$7,162	$353,317	$769,366	$1,962,963
34	$71,620	10%	$7,162	$396,527	$893,007	$2,364,150
35	$87,480	10%	$8,748	$445,802	$1,037,018	$2,847,477
36	$87,480	10%	$8,748	$500,005	$1,202,631	$3,427,470
37	$87,480	10%	$8,748	$559,628	$1,393,085	$4,123,462
38	$87,480	10%	$8,748	$625,214	$1,612,108	$4,958,652
39	$87,480	10%	$8,748	$697,358	$1,863,985	$5,960,879
40	$89,900	10%	$8,990	$776,983	$2,153,921	$7,163,843

after-school or weekend jobs that pay just $100 a week. That part-time income assumption rises to $150 per week for the college years.

These are all modest assumptions when you consider that most high school and college students made more than that 20 years ago. We might reasonably expect future earnings to increase in coming years.

For the earnings assumptions for adults, we used the average income for college graduates per age group, according to the latest U.S. census. In 2001, those figures were as follows:

Age Group	*Average Income*
18–24	$37,828
25–29	$44,281
30–34	$53,292
35–39	$65,093
40–44	$66,894

To make this a more useful gauge of incomes for the college grads of tomorrow and 20 years from now, these figures compound these numbers at 3% for 10 years.

> ### KEY IDEAS
>
> ➤ If you educate your kids early, they can be financially free shortly after they finish college or perhaps even earlier.
> ➤ Use the two-box system and the key ratios to help them put away money for their future.
> ➤ Every six months or so, take the money out of the permanent savings box and invest it using some of the strategies recommended in this book.

Conclusion

Visit iitm.com to receive a free copy of my e-book, which explains how to:

- teach your children to avoid debt
- put your children's money in a tax-free account
- invest their money so they'll be financially free shortly after they finish college.
- get their college education paid for easily

As the author of *Seeds of Wealth*, I teach parents and grandparents specific techniques for helping kids develop lifelong wealth-building

> ### ACTION STEPS
>
> ➤ Discuss money and finances with your children from an early age.
> ➤ Start using the two-box system today.
> ➤ Go to seedsofwealth.com/van for more information on Justin Ford's 300-page *Seeds of Wealth* program.
> ➤ Get a free e-book on securing your future from iitm.com.

habits. Every once in a while a parent will ask, "What happens when my children come of legal age and gain control over their investment accounts? What's to prevent them from squandering the wealth they've accumulated?"

The answer to that question is that the program outlined here is about helping your children not only to build wealth, but to develop responsible financial habits. They'll have created that wealth themselves through their own discipline. They'll know wealth is not an easy-come proposition and are less likely to have an easy-go attitude about it.

To find out more about my complete program for teaching wealth habits to your children, go to seedsofwealth.com/van. You'll learn how your children can become financially responsible and save money while they are doing it.

CHAPTER **18**

GETTING STARTED NOW

"Vision is not enough; it must be combined with venture. It is not enough to stare up the steps; we must step up the stairs."
—VACLAV HAVEL

You've completed a journey through some of the best thinking available on the subject of financial freedom. You might already be financially free or you might be just six months away. However, the only way to determine where you are is to begin the journey. So ask yourself, what are you going to do now? Are you going to say that it sounds interesting but seems like too much work? Or perhaps you believe it cannot be done or that *you* cannot do it. Well, it can be done and many people have done it. You can too, but you must begin now.

"The definition of insanity," according to Benjamin Franklin, "is doing the same thing over and over and expecting different results." As we've stressed throughout this book, the choice is yours. If you are determined to upgrade your level of financial freedom, this chapter lays out ways for you to take action. And if you're really committed to transforming your financial experience, we suggest that at the end of this chapter you stop and write down one thing you will do within one hour to get your momentum headed in the direction of your goals.

To help you get the optimum benefit from the time you invest in this book, our final chapter summarizes and integrates the concepts presented, calls you to action, and provides resources to help you take action immediately. So dig into this chapter and commit yourself to act-ing now on the transforming steps you want to take to upgrade your financial journey.

Step 1: Develop Your Financial Freedom Plan

Start your trip toward financial freedom with your final objective clearly in mind. Review the Preface and all of Part I of this book. When you've completed that and have a clear understanding of the concept of financial freedom, calculate your own financial freedom number and develop a plan for lowering your number down to zero. The steps were laid out for you in Part I, so all you have to do is complete the exercises in that section to begin your journey. Once you've done that, you'll have a good sense of your starting point and a map to begin your journey. Make sure you apply each step so that you can take the quickest path to achieving financial freedom.

ACTION STEPS

➤ Calculate your financial freedom number as described in Chapter 1.

➤ From Chapter 2, write down your commitment to pay yourself first and to give regularly to charity.

➤ Revisit Chapter 3 and write down your plan to cut expenses and reduce your debt.

➤ Make a plan to redeploy your assets so that they feed you instead of eating you (see Chapter 4).

➤ Attend an Infinite Wealth Workshop through IITM to change the way you think about money. We'll guide you through the steps to financial freedom and provide you with strategies to help you on your journey, including expert tax advice and passive income-producing strategies.

➤ Attend IITM's Infinite Wealth course in the comfort of your home or car with the Infinite Wealth Audio Program.

Step 2: Learn the Key Factors Influencing Today's Market

You've learned about the six major factors influencing today's market.

- We're in a primary bear market (see Chapter 5).
- You must know where we stand with respect to the inflation versus deflation game (see Chapter 9). The world is under intense deflationary pressures.
- The U.S. government has vowed to fight deflation at any cost, making inflation quite likely (see Chapter 9).
- Understand what is happening to the dollar with respect to other currencies (see Chapter 10). As of this writing, the dollar is becoming a weak currency.
- Understand what is happening to debt and to interest rates in the United States and around the world (see Chapter 10).
- Know the primary factors that are impinging upon the real estate market. What will happen to real estate given what's going on in today's market? (See Chapter 11.)

Once you understand the factors influencing the market, you can determine what strategies for reducing your financial freedom number will work best for you in today's market. Select at least three of these strategies for further evaluation and possible implementation. Have at least two primary strategies and at least one backup.

We reviewed a lot of promising strategies in Parts II and III. Here are the choices we suggested:

- Using Ken Long's weekly mutual fund switching strategy for your retirement plan. The strategy had to be modified due to changes in the way funds operate, so the full details were not included in this book. Please request a free updated report from iitm.com.
- Implementing the bear market mutual fund strategy in Chapter 7.
- Shorting overvalued stocks during red light mode.
- Following a trusted newsletter recommendation such as Steve Sjuggerud's *True Wealth* or D. R. Barton, Jr.'s *Ten-Minute Trader*.

- Trading efficient stocks when we are in yellow light or green light mode with the stock market.
- Finding highly undervalued stocks that sell at less that 0.6 times Graham's number.
- Finding a good professional hedge fund manager to do it for you if you are a qualified investor.
- Investing in gold, gold stocks, real estate, or other hard assets when there is strong evidence that we are in an inflationary mode.
- Staying in cash (or perhaps gold) when deflationary forces dominate the scene.
- Using the max yield strategy when the dollar is in a downtrend.
- Investing in the Rydex Juno fund when interest rates start in a consistent uptrend.
- Investing in one or more of the real estate strategies recommended by John Burley in Chapter 12. These include the buy-and-hold, quick cash, and cash flow strategies. Each is geared to a different investment objective and market climate.

You have a huge selection of strategies here. Pick three or four that seem right for your assessment of the market climate. Two will be your main strategies and one will be a major backup. And if your strategy involves doing business with someone else, be sure to do thorough due diligence before you begin.

You can't be a concert pianist without knowing your scales; you can't play pro basketball if you can't dribble, pass, or shoot; and you can't achieve financial freedom if you don't know the factors that are influencing the strategies that you might use for your investing. A good way to keep abreast of the macroeconomic factors influencing today's markets is to subscribe to the materials recommended in Chapter 15.

Step 3: Understand and Implement Risk Control

Now that you've selected several strategies you feel comfortable with, become a specialist in them. Concentrate on whatever is working the best for you, keeping your backup strategies in mind.

ACTION STEPS

➤ Review all of the key macroeconomic factors influencing the market and be sure you understand how they could affect various investment strategies. Keep your worksheets up to date.

➤ Select at least three of the strategies mentioned in this book that you might use to decrease your financial freedom number. These should be strategies that you would expect to be strong in the current macroeconomic environment.

➤ Keep yourself aware of the big picture and how it might change the effectiveness of your strategies.

To become a specialist in any strategy, you must be able to implement the risk control techniques given in Part IV of this book. Be sure you understand the six fundamentals that were presented in Chapter 13 and the information on position sizing in Chapter 14.

With that information you should be able to calculate:

- your worst-case exit point (i.e., $1R$ loss) for any strategy
- your potential risk-reward ratio (i.e., R multiple) for any trade
- the expectancy of the strategy

If you have a full R multiple profile, you can have your system run though IITM's trading simulator, Know Your System, as shown in Chapter 15. Learn what you can expect from a particular trading strategy. Is the upside adequate? Can you tolerate the worst-case downside?

Generally, the key to risk control is to be able to estimate the R-multiple distribution for the strategy you are going to implement. You can do this by trading the strategy on a small scale or gathering historical data and testing it through paper trading. However, it is very important to not begin any strategy until you thoroughly understand its risk-reward profile and its expectancy.

Once you have at least 50 *R*-multiple distributions for your strategy, you can develop a position sizing strategy for your techniques. Hopefully, we've impressed upon you the importance of position sizing to meet your objectives. If your position sizing is too big, you can lose a lot of money even if you have a great strategy. Instead, your position sizing strategy should be designed to keep you in the game through the worst possible scenario in the short run so that you get to enjoy the long-term expectancy of the system. This is one of the keys to making money with your strategy.

For advice on implementing effective risk control and position sizing techniques, consult the following resources by Van Tharp, available through iitm.com:

- *Trade Your Way to Financial Freedom*
- *How to Develop a Winning Trading System to Fit You* (audiotape workshop)
- *Money Management Report*
- *Position Sizing: Secrets of the Masters Trading Game*

ACTION STEPS

➤ Study the different investment strategies from Parts II and III of this book and see which fit your objectives and your personality.

➤ If you plan to use more than one strategy, write down your plan for how you will implement each strategy. Give yourself enough time to climb the learning curve on one investment type before tackling another.

➤ Identify the resources that will help you become proficient with your selected strategies.

➤ Implement the appropriate risk control techniques to make your strategy safe and profitable.

Step 4: Work with Yourself and the Next Generation

There comes a point in everyone's investing career when you need to upgrade your own performance in order to improve your investments' performance. These are the times when you need to work on yourself and correct the mistakes you have made in your investing life.

Chapter 16 outlines one of the pivotal steps in this process—taking responsibility for your actions. This is much tougher than it sounds because you have to give up the blame game, the victim game, and the many other games we play so that we don't have to take responsibility for our actions. Only when you can take full responsibility for what happens to you and your investments will you be able to correct your mistakes. At this point, you can deliberately create your life.

In Chapter 17, Justin Ford outlines a solid plan for educating children so that they grow up with a high level of financial intelligence and build wealth with your help. The chapter gives great advice on how to encourage saving from an early age.

Although it is not a topic of this book, I'd also recommend that you work on yourself. Many of you will end up sabotaging your own efforts to achieve financial freedom. For example, see if any of the following fit you:

- You go through this book, but you cannot develop even a simple plan to gain financial freedom. It all seems too hard.
- You keep buying things instead of cutting expenses, even though those things have nothing to do with maintaining your lifestyle.
- You develop a plan and adopt several workable strategies, but you cannot follow them.
- You cannot seem to control one particular emotion that repeats over and over again. Most people, of course, are never aware of doing this, because they just think that things are happening to them that cause the emotion. Nevertheless, those things (and that emotion) just come up over and over again. In other words, if you have a persistent, noncontrollable problem with a negative emotion, then it's probably self-sabotage.

- You repeat the same mistake over and over again.
- You persist in doing things that you know are not in your best interest.
- You feel numb to your feelings and believe that you never get emotional.
- You don't do the preparation that you need to trade well even though you know that it is important.
- You read through this book, but you keep procrastinating on the action steps.
- You want financial freedom, but you don't seem committed to it.
- You have very little joy in your life.
- You feel depressed.
- You feel glued to the negative news on television.
- You watch television for three hours or more each day.
- You feel insecure. You worry that everything will crash around you, especially after reading about the factors affecting the market.
- You experience internal conflict. Part of you knows what you should do, but another part of you pulls in another direction.
- You develop a plan for financial freedom that you know will work, but six months later you still have not lowered your number.
- You want financial freedom, but you can't remember your number the day after calculating it.
- You don't feel worthwhile.
- You believe that if you could just develop financial freedom, you'd feel better about yourself.
- You've always had a ceiling to your wealth, and no matter how hard you try you cannot get beyond it.
- You are a perfectionist, but you never seem to get things right.
- You have to be right all the time.
- You hate one or both of your parents (a major symptom of self-sabotage).

If one of these symptoms describes you, then you probably have a major problem with self-sabotage that you need to overcome before you can achieve financial freedom. There are a number of things you can do to help yourself here, and we'll suggest a few, beginning with the least expensive.

- Consider doing the 365 lessons contained in *A Course in Miracles*. This course costs about $20 and requires about 10 minutes per day of your time. The lessons tend to have a heavy religious overtone that might turn off some people, but you don't have to believe any of it. Just do the exercises and you'll be surprised at some of the major changes that occur in your life within the first 90 days. The program is available in bookstores or through iitm.com.
- Take the *Peak Performance Course for Investors and Traders*. This home study course, designed to help you understand yourself better, contains a number of exercises that deal with self-sabotage. You'll require two to three hours a day for several months to complete the course, and if you dig deeply, you'll see dramatic changes in your life. Learn more about it at iitm.com.

ACTION STEPS

➤ Review Chapter 16 and ask yourself if you accept full responsibility for all your investing decisions and results. Are you ready to live deliberately?

➤ Set up a regular time to review your investment performance. This should be based on your investment frequency but should be at least once per quarter. Use this time to correct mistakes. Make the assumption that you create any problems that occur and look within yourself to fix those problems, using the resources suggested.

➤ Teach your children the core tenets of financial intelligence as outlined in Chapter 17. For more information on helping your children achieve financial freedom, consider Justin Ford's *Seeds of Wealth*. It is available through his website, seedsof wealth.com/van.

- Consult a therapist/coach to get at the root cause of your self-sabotage. Find one who can help you solve the problem in 10 to 15 hours of work; otherwise there are probably less expensive alternatives.
- The International Institute of Trading Mastery, Inc., has a number of workshops that help with self-sabotage. Learn to apply cutting-edge tools that will allow you to break through to your highest levels of performance. More information is available at iitm.com
- Try an encounter workshop such as Landmark, Lifespring (Legacy in North Carolina), The Forum, or Avatar. Most are one-time events that will help you now but are difficult to repeat with the same impact, although they will give you useful tools. One exception is Avatar, which can be repeated. We have no connection with any of these organizations.

We set out to share with you a road map for your journey toward financial freedom. Our hope is that you will not just read and learn but that you will "go and do." We'd like to close this book with a challenge to help you get started now on your path toward financial freedom.

Check the clock right now. Our challenge to you is to write down three items in the next hour:

1. One thing that you will do *today* to start or continue your journey toward financial freedom
2. A definite date to finish all of the exercises in Part I of this book
3. A definite date that you will send an e-mail to us at safestrategies@iitm.com with an update on your journey; this date should be at least six months—but no more than one year—from now

This will serve two purposes: it will help you to be accountable for carrying out your plan, and it will help us enjoy the story of your progress.

All the best to you as you head toward financial freedom.

If you have any questions or comments about this book, would like further information about any of the authors, or would like any of the free supplements or reports mentioned in the text, please contact us at:

International Institute of Trading Mastery
519 Keisler Drive, Suite 204
Cary, NC 27511
Phone: 919-852-3994 or 800-852-IITM (4486)
Fax: 919-852-3942
E-mail: info@iitm.com
Website: iitm.com

INDEX